STUDIES IN EXTENDED
METAPSYCHOLOGY

STUDIES IN EXTENDED METAPSYCHOLOGY
Clinical Applications of Bion's Ideas

Donald Meltzer

with

Mariella Albergamo
Eve Cohen
Alba Greco
Martha Harris
Susanna Maiello
Giuliana Milana
Diomira Petrelli
Maria Rhode
Anna Sabatini Scolmati
Francesco Scotti

Published for
The Harris Meltzer Trust by

KARNAC

© The Roland Harris Educational Trust
First published 1986

This edition published in 2009 by
Karnac Books Ltd
118 Finchley Road, London NW3 5HT

Copyright © 2009 by The Harris Meltzer Trust
www.harris-meltzer-trust.org.uk

British Library Cataloguing in Publication Data

A C.I.P. for this book is available from the British Library

ISBN-13: 978-1-85575-649-6

www.karnacbooks.com

Contents

Acknowledgements

Although the work of genius is solitary, for its ultimate realisation it must feed the hunger for knowledge (K) of many lesser workers whose combined efforts produce a 'school'. The non-political sense of this troublesome term is illustrated in this volume to which many people of different countries have contributed, in seminars, personal discussions, supervisions and by presenting in public the clinical experiences to which they have applied the ideas of genius. Of these many it is only possible to acknowledge, on the title page, some of the latter category to whose courage I pay respect and to whose generosity I am indebted.

Many of my vague notions have been given greater precision by Martha Harris, while my misuses of the English language have been corrected by Catherine Mack Smith, and Francesca Bion who also read the proofs. It was not thought worthwhile to include either a bibliography or index in a volume which is meant to be a report on continuing work.

Morning approach't, Eve relates to Adam her troublesome dream; he likes it not, yet comforts her:–

> Best Image of my self and dearer half,
> The trouble of thy thoughts this night in sleep
> Affects me equally; nor can I like
> This uncouth dream, of evil sprung I fear;
> Yet evil whence? In thee can harbour none,
> Created pure. But know that in the Soule
> Are many lesser Faculties that serve
> Reason as chief; among these Fansie next
> Her office holds; of all external things,
> Which the five watchful Senses represent,
> She forms Imaginations, Airie shapes,
> Which Reason joyning or disjoyning, frames
> All what we affirm or what deny, and call
> Our knowledge or opinion; then retires
> Into her private Cell when Nature rests.
> Oft in her absence mimic Fansie wakes
> To imitate her; but misjoyning shapes,
> Wilde work produces oft, and most in dreams,
> Ill matching words and deeds long past or late.

Milton: *Paradise Lost,* Book V

Introduction

Perhaps in imposing yet another book it is necessary not so much to apologise as to issue a warning. In the early days of writing, persecutory anxieties are predominant. The fear of producing rubbish, of misconstruing and misrepresenting the precious ideas of others, of misusing the English language, of bringing shame to one's friends – all these preoccupations make writing a torment. But ambition, counterphobic attitudes, defiance of one's internal persecutors – and hope – push one on.

It is now 'later' – Act III, as it were, and whether it is comedy or tragedy is not yet clear, but the drama of one's life has taken shape. Internally each time one is promised by an inner voice, "This is the last payment for all you have received." The persecution has gone, one's limitations are clear. It now becomes an unburdening – of "accretions of stimuli"? Hopefully not. But while the passing on of one's own perception of the vision of genius may look like a legacy it is in fact a Deed of Trust that is being foisted on the unwary. For the visions of genius have 'fishhooks' that fasten in one's heart through their piercing beauty of conception and one's view of the world is changed thereby. Catastrophic change lurks in the pages, and the lament, "I'll never be the same", plays softly in the background.

The problem with one's own Deed of Trust is to avoid being apostolic and instead to seek only to assist and to enable others to read the text of genius, to eschew replacing it with Gospel. I have tried to avoid this pitfall in Book III of *The Kleinian Development* by making clear what I think of as the Wittgensteinian Position – "I am in a muddle." In this present volume I try another method, namely "This is how it has come into my consulting room."

The structure is accordingly rather rambling; like an Alpine village each structure is positioned according to the rocks beneath. Each paper or chapter has been forced by thrilling clinical experiences, and each, therefore, has its own preamble of reference to Bion's vision of the mind as an apparatus for creating thoughts to represent emotional experiences and for using these thoughts for thinking about these experiences. I have arranged them in an order that has a certain internal logic but they remain only loosely, and in a sense jaggedly, interconnected.

It will of course be noticed from the title page that many of the most illuminating experiences have been in teaching situations, hearing the clinical material of younger workers. I have, with permission, relayed their material virtually unchanged. One of the advantages of having such material for exposition is this: in our field of psycho-analysis there is always the question of evocation by the analyst, and of compliance by the patient – what Freud once called "dreams that follow on." It is useful to be able to demonstrate that the Bionic "level", or the possibility of viewing psycho-analytical transactions from the Bionic "vertex", is there in every consulting room. Indeed why limit it thus? It is present in every personal interaction.

But the Bionic "level" or "vertex" is not the same as the language with which we seek to describe it. The spoken language, with its song-and-dance accompaniment, conveys and evokes. The written word, in unpoetic hands, has no score – only a libretto. The vision of genius is spatial, tactile, musical, extending both forwards and backwards in time, delicious, pungent. Was it Bion's joke to call it "common sense"? What we cannot convey in the flatness of printed prose must be accepted as a limitation, but we can try to avoid creating new and redundant linguistic muddles or superfluous complications.

The most important of these muddles derives from a long history of philosophical struggle about meaning and intention to which, I believe, Bion's division of mental life into proto-mental (non-symbolic, nominative, externally factual, quantitative) and mental (emotional, symbolic, internally orientated, qualitative, aesthetic), has brought a great clarification. At the boundary between proto-mental and mental he has placed a hypothetical, "empty" concept, alpha-function, the mysterious, perhaps essentially mysterious, process of symbol formation. If we are faithful in our language to this differentiation we would need to reserve the word 'meaning' for the representation of emotional states by the symbols created by alpha-function for use in the construction of dream-thoughts. Words used to name the facts of the external world, the conventional signs for communication, would be said, accordingly, to 'signify', to have 'significance'. The grammatical constructions obey the laws of logic and have their base in the external world of causality, a finite world where quantity is discernible, or where at least quantification is useful. It may seem a pity to yield up such a lovely word as 'significance' to this less poetic function, but its containment of 'sign' as its root requires it. What shall we then use to express the ramification of 'meaning'? I would suggest 'import' or 'importance', for it carries the implication of something introduced by an act of imagination. It is, after all, for the wide sphere of imagination that we are trying to construct a precise vocabulary. This leaves the ambiguous word 'feeling' to be placed. In so far as it signifies an emotion it would seem to have a different reference from when it signifies an intuition. But I think that in fact the two are extremely closely linked. When we say, "I have a feeling that . . .", do we not mean something like, "I have an emotion that I cannot name but can only define in terms of a phantasy of the 'as if' variety"? Bion has called this a "premonition" in the sense not merely of an anticipation of a fact, but anticipation of an emotion not yet formed. The background of these linguistic distinctions will be found in the Chapter II – What is an Emotional Experience?

It seems likely, from clinical data, that the process of alpha-function is always attempting to find representations for our emotional experiences, if we can tolerate them. But the structure of the personality, with its heavy armouring of conventional modes of response, often intervenes to prevent this from occurring. The observations are not made available but are quickly wrapped up in conventional descriptions, as a newspaper does. I have traced this process in Chapter VIII – Facts and Fictions. Bion's emphasis on the primary role of observation of the facts, both of the external objects and events, and of the internal response, contains, by implication, a warning against premature transformations using language, whether in the consulting room or elsewhere.

But the question of tolerance of mental processes and of their attendant pain also enters into the operation of alpha-function. Its incipient products can be cannibalised by a "reversal of alpha-function" to produce what Bion calls "beta-elements with traces of ego and superego". This process is examined in detail in the corresponding chapter reprinted here from Book III of *The Kleinian Development*. It is these *beta-elements with traces of ego and superego* (which I hope to be forgiven for abbreviating as 'betes') which are the stuff of hallucinations and delusion formation, in Bion's formulation, as described in the chapter on hallucinosis (see p. 105).

By following his own division of the mind into proto-mental and mental organisations, Bion draws the distinction between an apparatus which needs to "unburden itself of accretions of stimuli" and one which needs to handle the "pressure of thoughts". The proto-mental apparatus needs to instigate actions, either in the outside world (social, in conformity with the Basic Assumption Group) or within the physiological organism (psychosomatic states) or, by reversing the function of the sense organs (hallucinosis). In contrast, the mental apparatus needs to restrain itself from actions in order to contain the processes by which the teeming thoughts are organised and developed in thinking. Action is, as it were, only finally resorted to when communication and thought have reached their limit. The distinction between the Kleinian concept of projective identification as a mechanism of defence and the Bionic idea of container-contained as part of the apparatus of thought is developed in Chapter V.

How early this interplay between mental and proto-mental takes shape to compete, as it were, for the soul of the child, is illustrated in Chapter XIII – A One-Year-Old Goes to the Day Nursery. This little drama serves to highlight the central problem of truth function, where truth is taken to mean "The true meaning of my emotional experience", with all its solipsistic limitations. By developing his differentiation between plus and minus emotions (L, H, K, and −L, −H, −K), Bion laid the groundwork for a new approach to truth and understanding as against un-truth and mis-understanding. These issues are developed in Chapter VI – The Concept of Vertices – Shifting versus Multiplication; Chapter VII – The Limits of Language; and Chapter IX – An Enquiry into Lies, distinguishing un-truths from the 'fictions' described in Chapter VIII.

It was Bion's ultimate step, taken in Book III of *A Memoir of the Future*, to show how the structure of the personality mirrors and is mirrored by the social structures in which we live. The Caesura of Birth, as he called it, with its attendant liability to leave split-off and incommunicado parts or all of the pre-natal organisation of the mind-body (the "soma-psychotic" part of the personality) prevents our observation of incipient emotionality. This goes on at a somatic level when it has not, as yet, found mental representation (Freud's 'Id' as the mental representation of bodily tensions). This unavailability of potential emotional facts places great limitations on our ability to think, as can be seen in children whose mental development has been seriously arrested. Development of our understanding of the plight of these children and the potentialities for therapy is outlined in Chapter XII, while its general application to pedagogical problems, both in schools and in the family, is developed in Chapter XIV.

In Bion's work the viewpoint eventually emerges that development *is* happiness. The fictitious balance of payments of pleasure and pain have little to do with it, for every step in development requires a "learning from experience" and the traversing of a "catastrophic change". This latter is touched upon in Chapter XVI – On Turbulence. Chapter XV – On the Perception of One's Own Attributes and its Relation to Language Development – explores the limits of self observation and the power of introspection to penetrate into the unconscious processes of the mind. Chapter XVII is perhaps an inexcusable self-indulgence and is best read as comic relief.

I

Field or Phase – A Debate on Psycho-Analytical Modes of Thought

The rationale for shifting from theorising to model making has been pleaded at some length in *The Kleinian Development* and I will not repeat these arguments. In brief it seems clear that psycho-analysis, as a method for studying the workings of the human mind, is essentially a descriptive science and its field of study is phenomenologically infinite by its very nature. That is, the range of phenomena which this method is peculiarly suited to study by means of the transference is that embraced by the capacity of the mind to form symbols for the purpose of representing the meaning of emotional experiences so that they may be stored as memory (rather than held as recall), used for thinking (rather than merely being manipulated by computation and logical operations), and transformed into a variety of symbolic forms for communication of ideas (rather than being transmitted as bits of information). If this symbolic area be taken as the essence of mind as differentiated from brain its extensive development would appear to be the crucial function which marks off man from other animals. That it is a capacity not uniquely possessed by the human animal is evidenced by its indubitable, though limited, development in animals who live in close domestic relationship to man. Whether any computer yet developed can exhibit it I do not know, but see no reason why it should not be a potentiality of such machines.

Correspondingly there is little doubt that much of the management of our daily lives lies outside the symbolic area in habitual acts, social adjustments, contractual relationships and bodily functions. While the psycho-analytical method may enable us to detect the incursion of non-symbolic mindlessness into areas of activity and relationship that require emotion, symbol formation, thought, judgment, memory and decision as the background to action, the therapeutic method essentially stands helpless before such types of pathology. Experiences with groups, with autistic children and with schizophrenics demonstrate this essential impotence. As therapists we must wait patiently for the inception of symbolic functions in order to contribute to the patient's mentality in a way that can facilitate growth and development. It seems likely that in most psychotic areas of the mind incipient thought is stifled and produces a debris of proto-phenomena (Bion's alpha-function in reverse, the genesis of hallucination and delusions, psycho-somatic phenomena, and Basic Assumption Group Mentality). Where this debris of nascent thought is evidenced it may at times be possible for the therapist to gather up the fragments and reconstruct the thought that would have developed had it not been stillborn.

Taking this panoramic view of personality functioning the question must arise, pertaining to the model of personality development, whether we are to follow the tradition in psycho-analysis and speak of phases (primary narcissism, symbiotic phase, autistic phase, etc.) or elect a field theory as our preferred mode of thought. Such a debate cannot aim at establishing the question of 'correctness' since we are not dealing with an area in which causality is seen to operate, the field being infinite and essentially creative. We must content ourselves with a more heuristic view and this I will argue.

But before that can be undertaken it is necessary to clarify the meaning and implications of 'field' for our science since it is a term that has been used elsewhere from physics to sociology. The argument for thinking in terms of phases is not a deductive one but has entered into psycho-analysis from Freud onwards as a preconception or assumption based on the analogy between mental and physical development. The evolutionary framework of reference, with its facile slogan about ontogeny and phylogeny, has damped our capacity to think about the evidence of our consulting rooms where even our youngest patients, say those of two years of age, already exhibit the full range of neurophysiological capabilities. Recent evidence concerning the early months of post-natal life and the latter months of pre-natal existence would appear to liberate us from this enthralment with the evolutionary mode of thought, the quasi-biological concept of phases of development. Not that we need to throw away this useful form of book-keeping, but we are liberated from taking its import too concretely and rigidly.

Once we clear ourselves of the automatic tendency to think of development in terms of phases, whether we view them as discrete or overlapping, rigidly biological in their origins or reinforced by environmental factors, we are confronted with an alternative that lacks the neatness and simplicity which makes the phase model so comfortable a tool of thought. Thinking in terms of field requires an effort of imagination which is at quite a different level. First of all, like the philosopher's river that you cannot cross twice (perhaps not even once) the field must be seen to be in constant flux, offering the mind of the subject an infinite range of choice. Of course in practice the field of choice, that is choice in meaning and significance as the background to judgment, decision and action, is limited by the subject's imagination of the possibility of meanings containable within the data at his disposal.

Second, the data available must be considered to be as extensive as the range of the topics, internal and external, of which our sense organs can be cognizent. These first two aspects of the field (of mental experience, awake or asleep, in whatever state of organisation, perhaps short of coma) imply the possibility of the personality being overwhelmed by the sheer bombardment of raw sense data. The impact of torture on personality organisation would be an example of this bombardment. But similarly deprivation of external data, as in solitary confinement and isolation experiments, reveal the opposite stress, namely the difficulty of holding together the field of experience under deprivation of sensa.

A third consideration in defining the nature of the field of personality experience would be the correspondingly infinite variety of organisation which could be imposed by the brain apparatus on this plethora of raw data. This is the area with which Gestalt psychology has made such extensive progress and which tests like the Rorschach utilise so cleverly. It is the area which ethology has so hugely exploited for studying animal behaviour and, by implication, the non-symbolic range of human personality functioning as well. The close bond between this area and neurophysiological functions is well illustrated by the concepts of imprinting, on the one hand, and facilitation, on the other. It is therefore a level of functioning which must be taken into account in the framing of any comprehensive learning theory based on field concepts.

The fourth aspect of the field which grows out of this third one is quantitative: excitations and complexities are the stuff of which emotions are made which stimulate symbolic functioning. By this we would mean that the imprinting process lends to selected gestalten variable degrees of excitation at the one-dimensional or tropism level, based partly on inherent patterns (Bion's innate preconceptions) and partly on the facilitating effect of prior experience. This quantitative aspect of attraction and repulsion, with its immediate thrust to action, either of approach or withdrawal (the linear or one-dimensional consequence), introduces a rheostatic function into the one system which must have direct links to the vegetative nervous system, and, in a long-range way, to the hormonal system as well.

At this point of excitation in the development of the momentary experience of the field, a stage is set for the emergence of two-dimensional functioning, that is mimicry of the superficial qualities of appearance and behaviour of other creatures. Group behaviour, the 'adhesive identifications' of post-autistic children, the political behaviour impelled by slogans and propaganda which paralyse thought – all of these illustrate impressively this level of functioning.

But the stage is also set for the initiation of symbolic functioning which can introduce meaning into the situation when excitation is transformed into emotion. This is the three-, and later four-dimensional level which Freud recognised as "introducing thought between impulse and action." If we tentatively accept this description of the subject's mind and the field of experience to which he is momentarily exposed (again it must be stressed awake or asleep, etc.), we can recognise immediately that such a model sets a huge task for the descriptive scientist as compared with a phase model for development. Part of the charm of the phase model consists in exactly this implied simplification of the field that views the range of choice at all levels as severely limited by biological readiness. A field theory must move this hierarchic structure of biological readiness to a very sophisticated level of conceptual possibility imposed by the internal logic of concept formation. This aspect of the problem has been set forth succinctly and brilliantly by Roger Money-Kyrle in his paper 'Cognitive Development'.[1]

Granted that a field model multiplies the descriptive task, we may feel undaunted when we consider both its implications for our view of human experience and the scientific advantages which attach to this. The implications are not difficult to draw forth; they mainly concern the equipment of the individual child, extending back to some period still in utero, *vis-à-vis* the equipment of the individuals in the world about it. We shall no longer be able to view the foetus as isolated in the womb any more than we can consider that a man's home is his castle, as if its situation were both impregnable and internally simple. The field of the foetus may not be as wide as the field of an adult but its boundaries still include a vastly complex source of sensory data from the mother's body and beyond. Light, sound, vibration, changes of gravitational orientation, temperature and acceleration all impinge upon it. Its aqueous medium is more like the forests of the sea than a fishpond in the garden.

Furthermore, as regards its equipment, for lack of convincing evidence to the contrary we must consider the foetus fully equipped, though as yet inept at utilising its apparatus and devoid of a teacher. Even here we cannot be absolute for in a very cogent sense the nature of the equipment teaches its own use. The very fact that the foetus can get its thumb into its mouth places it in a position to explore both sides of the relationship, of thumb exploring mouth as well as mouth investigating the uses of the thumb. The heart of narcissistic organisation is thus available to be juxtaposed to the wealth of object relations. Observations and imagination become necessary, limited by the fact that one can never with certainty know what the other, the object, feels, experiences, thinks, wants, hopes or fears.

[1] *Collected Papers of Roger Money-Kyrle*, Clunie Press, 1978.

Following this line of supposition, lacking, as we do, convincing evidence for or against it, we must draw the conclusion that by the time the foetus emerges from this underwater world its experiences have been far more conducive to thought and judgment in the narcissistic area, in which body and personality are as yet indistinguishable, than the object-related one. Enclosure prevents any extensive consensual validation of its discernment of the qualities of its objects. But we will not assume that it has had a happy time, that narcissism means self-love, that all has been secure, free of dread or nightmare, of deprivation and tension. Hamlet's misgivings about death ("Who knows what dreams . . ." etc.) must be taken as equally applicable to the pre-natal experience, even though the dreams must lack the definition and plasticity that the visual mode lends them.

How then shall we imagine the experience of the world outside the womb bursting upon the newborn? Not as something totally new in its data, although these would be intensified and more defined. The anoxia of the first moments is almost certainly not a new experience since this is the central item in so-called 'foetal distress'. Drying up would, certainly, be a new sensation, as would the visual definition of objects, and probably its own body parts. Also certain companions of its incarceration would be missing, particularly the sounds of the mother's body and the souffle of its great companion, the placenta. If we are to take a field viewpoint we would have to imagine the delicate balance between the impact of catastrophic change and evocation of a brave new world, a balance which would not only be affected by the events of birth but would be set against the backdrop of the intra-uterine way of life. Bion's understatement of it as a "caesura" helps us to correct our bias towards a catastrophic view.

And here perhaps lies the crux of the field view which experience of analysis of adults and children, evidences from infant observation and growing awareness of the category of primary failures of personality development all seem strongly to suggest. Does the world outside the mother's body arouse both intense aesthetic response and immediate nostalgia as the primal emotional experiences stimulating the symbolic realm? Does the beauty of the mother as a whole object and of her breast as a part object immediately begin a fugue relation to the experience of the absence of these objects? Can the baby in that state of limited experience imagine that this exquisite object is elsewhere, or can it only perceive the space where it used to be as a persecutory thing? Is the oscillation between part and whole object relations and between paranoid-schizoid and depressive positions already in operation at birth? From the field point of view it is thinkable and, perhaps, even essential for consistent application of this mode of thought.

With this clarification of the field view and its implications in action we may now turn to the question of its scientific advantages, having already acknowledged its arduousness as a principal drawback.

The first advantage is this, that unlike the phase viewpoint a field theory has no inbuilt theory of causality to beg the question of choice based on judgment. By acknowledging that many of the personality's operations lie in the non-symbolic area and that this more primitive mode always is at hand as an alternative to emotional experience, meaning, judgment and the other burdens of individuality, we may still construct a model of mental development of the personality free of determinism. This liberates our own imaginations from severe strictures and limiting preconceptions so that we can be free to observe without having an ideological axe to grind.

Second, the field viewpoint liberates us from the language which these limiting preconceptions impose upon us. We are likely to be more able, in that circumstance, to tease apart the vocabulary of observations from that of interpretation. The aspiration of 'objectivity' can be replaced by our experience in using the countertransference in the analytical work. The problem is one of dissecting levels of abstraction in the vocabulary of description, our language naturally being very poorly designed for this particular purpose. This is the nemesis of translators and the great pitfall even of reading Freud in English rather than in German.

A corollary to this refinement of the language of description of mental functioning is that the lessening of jargon greatly increases the possibility of liaison among schools within the field of psycho-analysis and with other disciplines, particularly sociology, anthropology, history, pedagogy, aesthetics, linguistics and law. Whether one thinks this is purely an advantage or also a step having its dangers, depends somewhat on one's view of the need for exclusiveness in order that standards may be maintained. That in turn depends on whether one is concerned with psycho-analysis as a medical sub-speciality or as a field of scientific research with various practical applications, of which therapy is the most prominent.

Having briefly outlined the arguments for a field model of personality development over the traditional phase theory, both from a scientific and practical point of view, I would like to turn to the philosophical problem, where, of course, I am far less qualified to speak. Modern physics, with its attack on the concept of time as absolute, and modern philosophy, with its scepticism about either-or alternatives and excluded middles, both find themselves confronted with alternative models for describing the world which seem incompatible. But this has always been so, in the history of thought, from Plato and Aristotle onwards. Schismatic eruptions, at every level, scientific, political, artistic, theological, have proclaimed this tendency and illustrate the vehemence and the violence of the forces of social and individual action which they liberate.

Much of this schismatic tendency can be ascribed to the unconscious assumptions about the world and our lives in-the-world which
would be listed under Bion's category of Basic Assumptions of Group
Mentality. The chief of these assumptions would seem to be of *beginning*, *middle* and *end*, a story, a plot in each individual's life, and, by
extension, in the history of the group, sect, state, continent, world.
Psycho-analytic work is in many ways devoted to helping the individual to free himself from the story-of-his-life that he has been
generating, and believing, from the earliest days. Freud's dictum that
"neurotics suffer from recollections" is no more true than that they
suffer from predictions which are the extrapolations of these recollections. They suffer not merely in the form of view-of-the-world, in
mood, and in tendencies to construe their experiences in a particular
way, they are also driven to realise their predictions in action. This
aspect of "repetition compulsion" functions in fact as a great barrier
to the apprehension of new experiences and damps the mentality to
the impact of new ideas.

Of course it is true that a certain biological 'story' limits the field of
our experience. Each of us was conceived and will surely die, each has
followed the anatomical and physiological programme of his genes.
But his mental life has a very different 'programme' which is in no
sense internal to his organic unity. It is the programme of logical
necessity, of the hierarchy of conceptual possibilities, of the inescap-
able step-by-step progress from disorder to order in the world of
meaning.

And it is here, to my way of thinking, that field stakes its foremost
claim to superiority over phase. One cannot deny that progress in this
imposition of order on the chaos of our sensa of the outer and inner
worlds is step-wise, but it is also different from the ontogenetic
progression of embryology, for nothing is left behind as *anlage*,
nothing is readapted to new purposes as with the gill-arches, nothing
presses for anachronistic representation. On the contrary each step in
personality development transforms an idea into a structure in a way
far more akin to the theological 'incarnation' than to the anatomical
'metamorphosis'.

Because the mental apparatus, or at least that aspect of it that lies
within the symbolic area and is devoted to creating the meaning of
our experiences and construing their significance – because this
apparatus is always in a state of becoming – has no past other than
what has become structure. And it has no future because all is
absolutely, unequivocally un-predictable. This inheres in the infinity
of possibility of elaboration of meaning and the variety of symbols and
symbolic forms by which it may be represented in the mind. Hence
the internal objects of the mind have only a tenuous, formal connection with the parental figures of one's childhood; hence one's

memories of past events are fictions having more or less reference to highly selected facts; hence even one's physical image of oneself is in constant flux, changing with states of fatigue, in different relationships, in varying social contexts. If time and its biological counterpart are the river on which we are relentlessly swept from the watershed to the sea, our minds develop in so far as we breast the current. The entirety of our uniquely human personality comes from this struggle against the atavism of our bodies. It is the task in which we try to aid our children by sharing with them the modes of thought by which, from our interest and attention, we construe meaning in their seemingly primitive behaviour. We seek to counteract the lies by which floating with the current can so easily be idealised. We try to guard them against being caught in the side eddies of perversity where struggling-against-the-biological-current can be effortlessly simulated.

This picture of development, which gives substance to the everyday experience of the uniqueness of the individual can only be sustained in our investigations through the arduousness of a field model and the abandonment of the fictions of *beginnings*, *middles*, and *ends*.

II

What is an Emotional Experience?[1]

It is always a great relief to be forced to undertake a task that one has been ingeniously evading for years. The present one, of clarifying my thoughts about the origins of personality structures is highly personal. However, in committing these to print there is also the hope that the ideas have not become so eccentric or strayed so far from their anchorage in the tradition in which one grew, as to be of little or no interest to others. My own tradition has been medicine, child psychiatry, American and British psycho-analysis, and finally that particular line of development associated with Melanie Klein and Wilfred Bion. When one's teachers have gone there is only their internalised representation to keep one within the bounds of a living tradition, but narcissism being as subtly invasive as it is, one can never be quite sure.

The problem in hand is at the phenomenological level and is, I believe, of great clinical importance. If it is stated in terms we know best, the consulting room, it would go something like this: how is one to distinguish those items of behaviour which are meaningful manifestations of the thinking personality from those which are instinctual or learned social adaptive manoeuvres? Is that too vague and general? Let me try again: how is one to distinguish phenomena in our patients and ourselves which are the consequences of emotional experiences which have been subjected to symbol formation, thought, judgment, decision, and possibly transformation into language, from others which are habitual, automatic, unintentional? Of course this is no clearer but it does expand the vocabulary and allow for a wider investigation of the meaning I am pursuing. For convenience I arrange them in two families, thus:

1. thinking, personality, emotional experience, symbol formation, judgment, decision, transformation, language;
2. behaviour, instinct, learned social response, habit, automatic response, unintentional behaviour.

Let us leave the problem aside for the time being and talk about the history of the line of thought that I am trying to pursue. It was not

[1]Read to the 7th Annual Self-psychology Conference – Toronto, October, 1984.

until *Mourning and Melancholia* and *Group Psychology and the Analysis of the Ego* that Freud's clinical experiences began to force him to revise the theoretical constructions which he had brought into psycho-analysis from the *Project for a Scientific Psychology*. That neurophysiological model, which had done adequate service in providing a means of describing hysteria and repression in a topographical context, quickly became threadbare as the field of study widened, especially when it began to extend beyond symptoms to character structures.

The shift to a structural model took Freud, in one leap, from an explanatory science concerned with causes to a descriptive science concerned with meaning. But even so he was caught in the as yet unbroken philosophical tradition in which reason was bound to language and thought was synonymous with logic. For Freud the system unconscious remained a morass of primitive confusion while thought began at the preconscious where thing-representations were replaced by word-representations. The implication for a theory of child development – that thinking began with language acquisition – was unmistakeable.

Storms of misunderstanding naturally resulted when Melanie Klein, perhaps from a certain philosophical naïveté, pushed this boundary back into the early days of post-natal life through the concept of unconscious phantasy (which Susan Isaacs spelled out brilliantly). But it was not in the nature of her preoccupations to be concerned with the 'how' of this evolution. It was to be taken as in the nature of the human animal, part of its life-history. Similarly when she described the concreteness with which the internal world of objects was apprehended she could be content to say that they came into existence through the interaction of projection and introjection without being bothered by conceptual questions such as, "How does the concept of an internal space arise in the mind?" It remained for Roger Money-Kyrle, trained earlier as a philosopher, to tackle the problem of cognitive development raised by Melanie Klein's vision of the mental apparatus.

But it was not until Wilfred Bion, building on his pre-psychoanalytical *Experiences in Groups*, began to notice the evidences of disorders of thought and incapacity for thought in some of his patients that the tacit assumption which took thinking as part of the natural history of human beings was finally challenged. "Autistic thinking" (Bleuler), "concrete thinking" (Vigotsky), "symbolic equation" (Segal) and many other evidences of psychopathology of thought had been recorded, but I think it is correct to say that Bion was the first to call attention to the problem of the genesis of thought. In the extraordinary (and infuriatingly difficult) books from *Learning from Experience* onwards, he spelled out an integrated theory of thinking, including a theory of its ontogenesis and phylogenesis. It is a great conjectural structure, what he called an "imaginative conjecture", whose clinical usefulness it remains for others to validate.

Central to Bion's Theory of Thinking is the idea that an emotional experience occurs, and if it is not processed into symbolic representations that can be used for dreams, thoughts, memory, thinking, judgment, decision and action, then the "accretions of stimuli" (to use Freud's terminology, which is particularly applicable here) must be evacuated from the mind in some way. He has spelled out the major routes of evacuation: hallucination, psycho-somatic disorder, meaningless talk or actions (beta-screen), group behaviour. By placing "emotional experience" as the first step in thinking processes, Bion has, for the first time in psycho-analytical formulation at least, placed emotion at the heart of the matter. Freud treated it as a primitive mode of communication, after Darwin. Melanie Klein treated it from the viewpoint of its value, pleasure or pain. Only Bion, I think, has seen emotion as the very core of meaning in human mentality, distinguishing it therefore from the quantitative variants of excitement in the neurophysiological apparatus.

Thus ends our historical prelude, returning us to the problem and the core of this chapter: what is an emotional experience and how do we know that it is going on, in ourselves, in another person? Taken from the Bionic point of view we would be trying to define the distinction between human and subhuman mental activity, or, if this seems to be paradoxical, between brain activity and mind activity. While this seems at first glance to be a resurrection of the pre-Freudian idealisation of man's place in the cosmos, closer examination reveals that it is quite the opposite. Extending Freud's revelation of how little man knows himself Bion brings home to us how much of our lives is lived mindlessly, that is outside the area in which emotional experiences are accepted, observed and thought about through symbolisation of the meaning of the emotions aroused. Of course one could rightly say that survival would be impossible if we did not respond with mindless automatic obedience to cultural requirements. We would simply be killing ourselves and one another inadvertently all the time. And in fact people who are mindlessly, automatically disobedient do just that.

No, we are not concerned with the area of mindless social adjustment but with the flight from emotional experiences into one or another type of mindlessness. Bion has given us a basic format for describing the breakdown of incipient thought in what he has called "alpha-function in reverse producing beta-elements with traces of ego and super-ego" (see Chapter XI). This means something like, "Symbol formation commences but meets with such mental pain that it cannibalises what has begun to form and the debris of this has shreds of meaning clinging to its fragments."

If we grant then, for the sake of our argument, that we are intelligent herd animals trained from birth onwards through our aptitude for primitive identification processes (imprinting, adhesive identifications, mimicry, etc.), and are thus creatures encased in a social armour of great conservatism, what else remains that we would wish to call the 'personality' in order to eschew the cynicism of the behaviourists? Bion's answer seems to be that there is another process which he calls "learning from experience" (which stands in contrast to all other types of learning which I will not enumerate here – see Chapter XIV) that starts with the "observation of emotional experiences" and may begin even before birth.

In order to examine this concept in a way that may help to distinguish 'emotional experience' from 'states of excitation' or 'bombardment by stimuli' or similar formulations, I would like to describe a dream of a patient which I have already examined to some extent in a chapter of *Dream-Life*[1]. An intelligent and sensitive woman in her forties, some three years in analysis, and at a time when she was studying Bion's work in connection with her research interests, brought the following dream:

It seemed that there was a gathering and a meal was in preparation. I was asked to set the table which seemed a simple task. But as I proceeded to lay out the usual cutlery for the expected number of guests I became aware that there was a far greater variety of cutlery and more guests than expected. I decided to do it first by collation, separating all the cutlery by type and passing them out, one type at a time. But then it became clear that there was a continual escalation, both of types of utensils, including tools, artist's implements, etc., and even an escalation in the number of guests. Perhaps there was even an acceleration of the escalations. It was clearly a hopeless task for my conscious capacities and would necessarily require some highly complex apparatus.

The patient herself though that this dream was an attempt to grasp something about the meaning of Bion's concept, alpha-function, and I agreed. I thought it also had something to do with her growing awareness that she needed an analyst to do her thinking in an area in which she was not yet able to cope for herself.

I think that this dream represents a major effort of creative thought and may reward us for careful scrutiny. What it seems to touch upon is the general phenomenon of the transition from quantity to quality and reminds one of mechanical ideas like 'escape velocity' or 'stalling speed', or the difference between the phenomena studied by Gestalt psychology and those of imagination (Wittgenstein's "seeing as"), or the difference between 'memory' and 'recall'. Let us imagine that there is a critical quantity of bombardment by sensa at which point the central nervous system must either rebel by 'clearing the machine'

[1]The Clunie Press, 1984.

in some way or 'take over', 'escape' from the 'gravitational pull' of causality into the 'infinite' of imagination. Let us further suppose that this critical state is registered as emotion, potentially infinite in variety and nuance.

It is of interest that my patient's dream suggests not only that an escalation is necessary to reach this critical point of breakdown in mechanistic, causal thinking, but perhaps that this releases into an area of acceleration of escalation, a realm of second derivatives, one might say the world of Cleopatra's "infinite variety".

As a lover of animals on the one hand, and, on the other, as the result of hearing reports about infant observation for the last ten years, it seems to me that babies are incredibly intelligent animals. A baby of a few months will grasp the meaning of a mirror which I believe no dog, or even monkey, can ever grasp. But this extraordinary intelligence is alive, perhaps even before birth, to the quality, and not merely to the quantitative level, of sensual experience. I claim, with some insistence, that this is the aesthetic sense; certainly the human baby is alive to the beauty of the world, and to its inevitable fragility. I have seen a baby two hours after birth turn with a look of recognition towards its mother's voice in a room containing several chatting guests. And I want to say, "nonsense", when a baby's first smiles are written off as "wind", or its first cries are dubbed a physiological reflex for expanding the alveolar structure of the lungs. I claim also that *The Tempest* is the great celebration of this conception, as Harold Pinter's *The Birthday Party* is the great tragedy of its perversion.

We are now in possession of a language which may enable us to push on in our investigation. What I have just said contains a classification of emotions: those celebrating the perception of the beauty of the world, those grieving for its fragility, and those aroused by the tragedy of its perversion. It is greatly to Melanie Klein's credit that she reminded us – I will not say "discovered", for the poets at least as long ago as the Song of Solomon have been telling us so – that the world is the mother, and for babies the mother's body is literally their 'world'. What she did discover was that the beauty of the mother's exterior and the mystery of her interior arouse the baby's thirst for knowledge as well as for milk. And Bion's addendum emphasised that it is not only the beauty of the body and its mystery, but of the mind as well that has this impact. For he recognised, as Melanie Klein had begun to do, that this object of wonder was a combined one, maternal and paternal, breast and nipple, container and contained, which he designated by the ancient symbols for female and male, $♀ ♂$.

But if this beauty and mystery arouse the intelligence of the baby to know – that is the important thing, to *know* the mother, in its great biblical sense – Melanie Klein saw clearly that it also arouses the stupidity of envy, or what Bion would eventually call the negative emotions, the desire to *mis*-understand. His conceptual move, to oppose negative to positive emotions as the links in human mental relationships (love (L), hate (H) and knowledge (K)) swept away the traditional confusing apposition of love and hate. His schema contrasts L, H and K as the links of relatedness, to minus L, minus H and minus K as the envious anti-linkage, anti-emotions, anti-knowledge and anti-life. I think it is a classification which places our theory of affects on firm ground for the first time. It is deeply foreign to the Western tradition in philosophy and theology, but not to the Eastern one into which Bion's Indian childhood had dipped him, like Achilles, at the hands of his ayah.

Let us see if we are now in a position to offer a definition of 'emotional experience' in order to explore its significance for a theory of personality development:

An emotional experience is an encounter with the beauty and mystery of the world which arouses conflict between L, H and K, and minus L, H and K. While the immediate meaning is experienced as emotion, maybe as diverse as the objects of immediate arousal, its significance is always ultimately concerned with intimate human relationships.

I have slipped in some new words, 'significance' and 'intimate', which must be justified. It has already been fairly clearly indicated that I am taking 'meaning' to imply a complexity of perceptual experience that is beyond the scope of explanation by causal modes and must be explored by imagination using symbolisation as its first move; that having departed from the finite world of causality 'meaning' sets sail on the infinite sea of the universe of discourse where nothing can be proved, nothing is correct or incorrect. The only parameter of differentiation must be highly individual: either it interests you or it does not. "Yes, that point of view is interesting but this one I find more so!" It is a realm where belief is a capitulation, 'so far and no further' on this sea of discourse and exploration: where the claim of being 'right' betrays the slip into minus K.

Talking of 'meaning' thus, with emotion as its primary manifestation, 'significance'[1] must be seen as its elaboration within the general picture of the world that imagination builds. Whenever an emotion gives birth to a new 'idea', a "catastrophic change" heralded by "catastrophic anxiety" (in Bion's language) is set in train, for the whole cognitive picture-of-the-world (Money-Kyrle) must be re-ordered to take the new idea into account. This gives some lead for

[1] I have left the terminology here unchanged from its original form, but as indicated in the Introduction I would now suggest 'import' or 'importance' leaving the word 'significance' to rejoin its mate 'sign' in the non-symbolic area.

understanding what factors set alpha-function into reverse, namely that a new idea's incipiency is suspected from the first whiff of catastrophic anxiety.

The term 'intimate' human relationships, on the other hand, is the realm I wish to reserve for the emotional experiences that set thought in motion. For convenience I might contrast them with areas of interaction that are so casual as to involve no emotion, or so contractual as to preclude spontaneous emotional response. I will not pause to haggle over 'spontaneous' since it is implicit in the definition of emotional experience. But instead I wish to push on to a conception of 'personality' and its development.

I have already briefly described the exterior armouring of social character acquired mindlessly by primitive modes of identification, training, mimicry, conditioning, etc. All intelligent animals train their young, some, like the timber wolf, very extensively. It is still necessary to survival, but stands in competition with the processes of emotional experience and learning from them through thought from which the picture-of-the-world is constructed by imagination. Bion has spelled out in detail the central role of the thinking mother in enabling the baby to begin this function of thinking and eventually to become autonomous in it through internalisation of a thinking object. Melanie Klein's explorations of psychic reality and her point of view about its concreteness brings psycho-analytical thought into its natural continuity with philosophical (especially Platonic) thought, with theology in general, and mythology in particular. But in order to grasp the grandeur of this conception it is necessary to reduce language to a more humble place than is suggested by, "In the beginning was the Word and the Word was with God and the Word was God."[1] While we may agree that it is "man's finest performance" (Whorf), we must see it as only one of the many "symbolic forms" (Cassirer) by which thought is implemented. Language can be viewed as a progressive sophistication of "song and dance" (Langer) and we must not be surprised if this form of symbolisation is even available in a primitive way to the foetus in the latter months of gestation. There is much in the history of primitive religion to suggest its truth, for chant and dance seem to be the original expression of religious ecstasy at the beauty and mystery of the world. It is surely a mistake to assume that the gods were originally persecutory father figures, invented by cannibalistic warriors. Generous fertility goddesses seem far more likely for the nomadic food gatherers of the pre-ice-ages.

This is where the original paper ended, but it was only a week later, at the University of Naples where we were giving seminars to Professor Anna Maria Galdo's Department of Child Psychiatry, that we heard a presentation by Doctor Mariella Albergamo which so per-

[1] The Gospel according to St John – probably a bad translation of "logos".

27

fectly fitted the paper that I feel it necessary to assure the reader that what follows is a translation of her report unaltered.

The case of Marco

Marco is a young boy, thirteen years old, whom I first met in October and whom I see twice a week. He is tall and thin, his features are still somewhat childish, his expression is intelligent and lively but at times becomes absorbed and melancholy. Although the initial request for therapy had come from his father it is Marco who has taken all the decisions, expressing a great need for help in understanding his "strange way of thinking". His parents parted five years ago and are on very bad terms with one another, his father living in a different town. He keeps in contact with Marco by telephone and is eager for his son to live with him when he reaches the age of fourteen. At present Marco lives with his maternal grandparents while his mother is very irregularly present, being usually away on travels or undergoing medical treatment. When at home she spends whole days in bed. Apparently there is no adult who takes consistent responsibility for Marco and his brother aged nine. Rather it is Marco who seems to make any necessary decisions regarding himself or his brother in this somewhat disordered household. Marco seldom speaks about the guilt he feels for wishing to live with his father as if this meant abandoning the sick mother whom he desires to help and protect.

From the very first sessions Marco communicated accurately 'the state of his thoughts' and he is often more concerned about the way he thinks than about the content of his thoughts. He uses an articulate and subtle language, rich in evocative representations and pictorial images, a language which seems at times to carry him into deep self-contemplation, while at other times he becomes 'scattered' in search of unattainable exactness. But he is clearly charmed by the productiveness of his own mind and wishes me to be enchanted as well. For instance, in the fourth session Marco concentrated on describing to me the colours by which he classifies his thoughts. These colours are meant to convey some sense of emotion but they also represent a classification of time units, hours, days, weeks, months, years, centuries – even geological eras.

Marco expressed the wish that I could look at his thoughts as they unfold so that I might establish connections that would help him to "find his bearings", since the tagging by colours to fix their duration and position in space does not seem to prevent his thoughts from "going away through the door" and getting lost. In a similar way he tries to obtain reassurance during his journey through town en route to the sessions by remembering, with photographic exactness, details of the streets or buses, imagining he knows people he meets and their thoughts. By minute description of these processes he holds my attention evoking my concern as well as admiration for his originality. At times, when he feels obliged to control every thought and movement he compares his mind to a computer which, at any moment, is supposed to give him precise information about the state of affairs. But this continuous self-observation evokes anxiety about "being caught without end in a black swirl in which everything disappears". To offset this he keeps up his spirits by continual humming or telling himself stories "chosen at random".

In the therapy sessions his protection against anxiety is transformed into an intellectual communication which gives the impression that his emotions are disconnected from his ideas. He uses his words to express opinions, philosophical thoughts and abstract concepts about people and emotions but these lack emotional resonance. At certain moments Marco experiences a flood of thought which makes it impossible for him to think consistently about himself and scatters his thoughts into an infinite universe. It is at such critical points that he feels the need to be sure that I understand him. I, on the other hand, feel that it is very difficult to maintain any sense of two-way communication. To give an example taken from a session in the third month:

"When I think of something, I know that it can be unreal because thought and reality are two different things. My thinking never stops and I can never stop to consider what I see – for instance that painting is placed in that position but it could be shifted .01 degrees or .02 or .03 and so on. One has to consider every possibility. But in this way one never stops thinking. My thoughts run one after another, they become billions and I can do nothing . . . only die."

"To avoid thinking of all the possibilities I keep thinking: 'Nothing is perfect'. But even saying 'Nothing is perfect' is ridiculous because if it is true that nothing is perfect then not even the statement 'Nothing is perfect' is perfect because if the statement 'Nothing is perfect' is perfect you can no longer say nothing is perfect. But even all that I'm saying has no sense because there is a great difference between what happens to me and what I can say, and then it becomes something else: what I say is only a symbol, what I feel are sensations, not words."

While this hyper-productiveness of thoughts seems to lead Marco to the same absence of bounds and of consistency that he feels in moments of unthinking, to the "black swirl" of anxiety, it is noticeable that the tone of that long speech was serene, objective, perhaps a little euphoric, and displayed pride in his own intelligence. The emotional effect on me, however, was to create anxiety which I felt as a risk of colluding with the charming display of his intelligence, of dwelling on his grown-up philosophic productions, losing sight of his vulnerability and suffering.

In later sessions Marco expresses in a more childish and more direct way his need to free himself from his anxious feeling of emptiness by creating many reference points with the things in the room, the colours of the walls, the pattern of the wood of the desk, particularly when he finds patterns resembling objects and feels that they are known only to him; this seems to reassure him that he occupies an exclusive place in my mind. More recently there has appeared a method of limiting his thought productions expressed by the image of the "Archer of No". This is an imaginary figure, full of charm, in shining armour (white or black) which appears on the battlements of a great castle and shoots arrows towards his thoughts. When an arrow strikes a thought it has the effect of annihilating that thought and stops further production.

At times Marco feels freed by the archer's intervention because it stops the bewildering movement of thought hyperproductivity; at other times, on the contrary, he feels robbed of his thoughts.

This figure of the archer has replaced the ineffectual use of the word 'No' which was meant to perform this same function before the therapy. It seems therefore that one could say that this first period of therapy has replaced an ineffectual mechanical function with an object which performs that function adequately. This dazzling and idealised image shows also the intense anxiety felt by Marco in regard to an object which exerts a strong attraction and influence. It is felt to have an absolute power which he vaguely connects with me.

As the Easter holiday approached, and his fourteenth birthday as well, Marco produced a session which seemed to mark a major turning point in the transference. This was the first session of the week and the thirty-first session of the therapy.

Marco speaks to me about the Easter holiday which he will spend abroad with his father. He is worried that his days of vacation may not coincide with my own. He will be back on such and such a day – shall I be back also? He thinks a little, then he asks me what we talked about the last time: "If I'm not able to remember I can't think about anything".

I tell him that he needs to find his thoughts and needs me to remember in order not to feel the fear of losing me, for if he goes away with his father for a vacation he might not find me again if he could not remember me nor I him.

"Right now I remember what we spoke about: about the idea that I could be suffering from cancer, and then about my not having told my mother that I was coming to you for therapy." He remains silent for a while then says, "It's been a long time since the Archer came! He came right now." (This is the first time that this has happened during a session.) "But he's been very mild, not violent. In fact I remember the things he has erased, I can see them as if they were wrapped in a very thin veil: they were all the things I was doing before I started coming here to you."

I suggest that the Archer-me perhaps does not want him to think about anything else but the therapy when he's here and so she removes all the other unrelated thoughts and feelings, even feelings that make him feel lonely and worried.

He says that it was a friendly Archer, indeed he left a white vacuum and it is a good thing that he isn't forced to think about home problems that he can't do anything about. "If I think about those home difficulties I can't think about things to say to you and if I were unwilling to be set free from home problems I couldn't come to you." Then he self-interprets: "It's just like with Mummy and Daddy: if I stay with the one I am supposed not even to think about the other or he gets angry." (Clearly here referring mainly to his father.)

He remains thoughtful for a while, with an abstracted look, then he exclaims, "How strange! Sometimes I'm very preoccupied with the idea of some particular goal. I think about it for a long time, I imagine it in a thousand ways and then it ends and I don't care any more, or it's as if it got lost. For instance, last month I had to decide which high school to enter. Father called me on the 'phone to tell me I ought to enter X school – and I worried that the whole term was already over. I imagined X school, and I saw it shining, set high on the summit; it seemed to me the most beautiful of them all and the most important too and I was very glad. But now that I know that I can go there it has become less important and I see it as nearer, not so high up and it is only a little more shining than Y." (The school that he goes to now.) "It has lost all its beauty."

I wonder if what happens with the school is similar to what happens with me – if I am nearer to him I lose my beauty because I make him feel the fear that if he is with me he has to renounce everything else while if he is not with me he feels sad because he fears to lose me. If only he could find the right distance that would enable him to think that I was beautiful and that what we do together is important without its excluding everything else.

He quickly tells me, as if to reassure me, "When I go away from here I feel happier and lighter, even if I came here feeling sad." And after a while he says, "The therapy resembles the revision of science subjects. When we had to revise since the programme was so wide, I felt sure that I would not remember anything. But then as it turned out I had only to recall one theorem for all the rest to come back, little by little. And so it is with you: at times it seems to me that I have

31

forgotten everything, then I recall one thing, then another and so on. But who knows how it happens that one can remember: it happens to me and that's all."

He remains silent, little by little his eyelids become heavier. He exclaims with some surprise, "I am sleepy! Do you know? I'm not thinking about anything. Now and then I see images and hear some background music, from the Beatles. Recently I have been very sleepy – I even fell asleep reading a book . . ." Silence. "Sometimes I like things that happen to other boys but never happened to me. Ordinary things, or even things other people look on as bad, like illness for instance. I am never ill. I would like to be ill, to take medicine and then feel well as a result."

I speak to him about his need of being cured by me, through sleep.

He stays silent a little longer, slumbering and letting his fancy ride: then he shows me some figures he can trace with his finger following the grain of the wood of the desk, and also that my face is reflected on the surface.

The session is at an end and I suggest that this is a way of leaving *his* mark on *my* desk and *my* face in his mind at the moment of parting.

Commentary

Clearly Marco is a highly intelligent and introspective child who has grown up in an atmosphere of hostility between his parents eventuating in separation and a struggle for his loyalty. This conflict, as well as the natural jealousy of his younger brother, he has dealt with by a premature independence and a sense of responsibility for his chaotic household. A careful balancing act using obsessional mechanisms may have sufficed in latency, as it often does, but the thrust of puberty with its desire for freedom has now resulted in his being pulled three ways instead of two. The consequent attempt to meet the crisis by escalating his obsessional mechanisms will not keep pace with the acceleration of his capacity for observation, desire and emotion. A vision of beauty becomes confused with idealisation, and the dazzle of elitism, for instance about the school, collapses when it becomes available instead of unobtainable. Similarly his idealisation of his own capacity for calculation and recall as a method for orienting himself to the world spins away into meaningless repetitions and minute fragmentation of ideas.

But he notices that the sessions somehow bring relief and he is surprised by the extent of his anxiety about the impending holiday. One cannot but admire the grace with which Marco surrenders to the infantile dependence on the therapist to keep him and his mental events in mind, to perform a function for him. At that moment he can realise that the same surrender to something internal also results in the function being performed. The pleasure of infantile dependence, like being ill and being cured quite enthrals him as he rehearses, with the grain of the desk's wood and the reflection of the therapist's face, the prospect of remembering her in separation, perhaps in the course of some dreamy masturbatory activity.

III

A Klein–Bion Model for
Evaluating Psychosomatic States[1]

The outlines of a model for construing the significance of disturbances in somatic functioning lie distributed throughout the writings of Wilfred Bion from *Experiences in Groups* to the last volume of *A Memoir of the Future: The Dawn of Oblivion*. (Clunie Press, 1979). The steps in its development cannot be well understood without some reference to the model of the mind as an apparatus of thought that he constructed during those thirty years. The total excursion of his creative flight of imagination has a strikingly circular orbit which started with the discovery of the mindlessness of the participation in Basic Assumption Groups, and ended with the suggestion that pre-natal parts of the personality tend to become split off at the "caesura of birth" and to remain in a state of primitive social organisation without the means of mental representation (the "soma-psychotic level" of mental life, equivalent to the earlier formulation of "proto-mental apparatus" as the substratum of Basic Assumption mental-ity).

In this condensed paper I will try to trace the steps by which this wide circle of imaginative conjecture was traversed, but it must be realised that this effort of abstraction, and, as it were, paraphrase, may seem to gain in clarity while its loss in evocative richness is less obvious. There is also the possibility of misrepresentation of Bion's thought in this my personal reading of him. Perhaps I should add, "in 1985", or perhaps even, "in April, 1985". For the sake of subsequent discussion and reference I will describe Bion's progress in steps despite the artificiality of such a method.

Step I *Experiences in Groups* – 1961[2]

Man brings from his animal and prehistoric past the tendency to herd, group, to create a tribe or clan organisation in which the individual members participate in a manner more primitive than that characterised by symbol-formation, thought, judgment and decision. The mode of operation is in a sense purely logical, deriving all

[1]Previously published in 'Soma, Psyche, Sema' – IES Mercury Editoria, Rome, 1984.
[2]Originally published in *Human Relations*, Vols. I–IV, 1948–1951.

decisions by logical operations from a basic assumption regardless of evidence. This logic, being primitive, is subject to what would appear to be fallacies to sophisticated thought. This Basic Assumption Group Mentality has its origins in a deeply unconscious level, the "protomental apparatus" whose operations correspond closely to Freud's description of Primary Process and the prescription that "in the first instance the ego is a body-ego". This seems to mean that at this primitive level the ego does not make mental representations of emotional experiences but both construes them *as* bodily states and reacts to them *with* bodily states and actions.

Step II   *Learning from Experience* – 1962

When an emotional experience impinges on the mind its disparate elements of sense data, internal and external, exist in a state of beta-elements which must be worked upon by alpha-function to produce alpha-elements from which symbols may be formed and organised into the narrative of dream-thoughts as the first step in thinking. To whatever extent this transformation fails, the residue of beta-elements must be dealt with as "accretions of stimuli", which can neither be used nor stored as memory. The means of their evacuation are several, one of which is the "beta-screen" of pseudo-communication of non-sense (which probably corresponds to Esther Bick's delineation of the "gift of the gab" method of "second-skin" formation).

Step III   *Elements of Psycho-analysis* – 1963

But other means of evacuation of beta-elements may also be discovered amongst which the recourse to the protomental apparatus is in evidence, *namely through regression to group-mentality and its near ally, somatic innervations.* In either instance the central issue is the loss of mental function at the level of symbol formation and the creation of meaning and significance for the emotional experience.

Step IV   *Transformations* – 1965

But the clinical problem is not only one of loss of meaning and significance but also the creation of meaninglessness in the form of *hallucination, hallucinosis* as a mode of perception, or *delusion formation* as a system of pseudo-thought. In these three methods for evacuation of beta-elements, the sense data of the emotional experiences are dealt with as if the meaning and significance were already inherent in the data and need not be created by the laborious, conflictual and anxiety-laden processes of thought (alpha-function; Ps↔D; container-contained; L, H and K links; catastrophic anxiety). The attendant sense of certainty is evidenced by the poverty of imagination which cannot conceive of errors in perception or thought, nor of alternative hypotheses for construing significance.

Step V *Attention and Interpretation* – 1970

Development of the personality may then be construed as proceeding by a series of leaps forward under the thrust of the "new idea" which generates "catastrophic anxiety" by virtue of its requirement that all previous experience must be reviewed and reorganised in the new light, or at least from an additional "vertex" or point of view. While this process of development may be retarded by the processes of thought which psycho-analysis is accustomed to study under the rubric of "mechanisms of defence" which modify the anxiety, whole areas of the personality may be excluded from integration in development by the processes which "evade" anxiety (lies, delusions). Still other areas may remain totally outside the sphere of symbol-formation and thought by virtue of thought disorder (beta-screen, group mentality, hallucinosis or psycho-somatic innervations).

Step VI *The Dawn of Oblivion* – 1979

These latter processes, which lie outside the bounds of dream-thought and rationality, have their seat in those parts of the personality formed during the *latter period of gestation, the pre-natal parts* which form the *soma-psychotic portion of the personality* (originally called the *"proto-mental apparatus"*). In order to introduce meaning into these processes and thereby assist in their elevation into the sphere of symbol formation, thought, judgment and decision, it is necessary that the *therapist perform the alpha-function* of which the patient is incapable in this particular area of experience. And in order to do this the therapist must be capable of an *excursion of imaginative thought, or dream-thought, that embraces the intra-uterine experience as a 'world' quite different from the 'world' of projective identification*. It is this 'world' that Bion has attempted to transform into a language of dialogue between the "pre-natals" and the "post-natals" in certain sections of this astonishing book.

Discussion

Bion's model deserves perhaps a word or two to stress problems of differentiation of phenomena met in the clinical situation. First of all, by stressing the origin of psycho-somatic phenomena in processes outside the sphere of symbol formation and thought, he implies an important distinction from other phenomena which involve either body sensations or somatic innervations such as conversion, hypochondria and somatic delusions. This latter category is perhaps more uncertain in its clinical delineation and may be seen to straddle the two areas being within the symbolic sphere in obsessional patients and outside it in psychotics.

But the main indications of the theory are technical. It implies that we cannot expect to deal with psycho-somatic phenomena by interpretation of content whether they present as disease entities or as transient events in the course of analysis. We must set ourselves an entirely different task, namely that of *discovering the emotional experience which the patient is unable to dream about* and to do his dreaming for him. One implication is quite clear, that we cannot perform this function intellectually; it requires an unusual degree of identification with the patient, an unusual depth of reverie in the session, and an unusual degree of tolerance of feeling mad oneself. This also implies at this point of the discussion that we must entertain the hypothesis that it may be a mad theory which finds its appeal within a psychotic part of our own personalities.

One source of inspiration for the imagination of these pre-natal states comes from observational and therapeutic work with infants and very young children. The technique of infant observation developed at the Tavistock Clinic by Esther Bick and now used so extensively in the training of child psychotherapists, has emerged as a surprisingly powerful research tool, making it possible to press the limits of therapeutic technique into the first year of life where primary arrest of development is in evidence.

IV

The Protomental Apparatus
and Soma-psychotic Phenomena

When Wilfred Bion's life-work in psycho-analysis made its full amazing circle towards his last years, this was nowhere more strikingly illustrated than in his return to the early interest in group phenomena. By applying what he had then discovered about groups to what he later learned about the structure of the mind of the individual, he was able to formulate, in the fictional presentation of *A Memoir of the Future*, a conception of group life within the individual person as a distinct level of mental functioning allied to narcissistic organisation but not identical to it.

This idea had perhaps been implied in his earlier formulations on Basic Assumption Groups. There, in *Experiences in Groups*, he had suggested that of the three BA Groups only one may be active at a particular moment while the others are confined to the "protomental" level with its intimate relation to bodily processes. This constituted his indication of direction for research into psycho-somatic phenomena. It was not stated explicitly but in retrospect one can discern a hint of internal BA group life. This evocation of primitive, perhaps tribal, life in the depths of the mind which can surface as group behaviour or, conversely, express itself through bodily processes, has a frightening, even haunting, impact. Bion seems to suggest that we must think of the stages of bodily development, even the embryonic stages, and certainly the pre-natal months or weeks, as having distinct representation in the structure of the self.

But in this schema, this "imaginative conjecture" of his, the mentality of these primitive parts of the self differ very much from those processes which psycho-analysis has been designed to study. Just as the functioning in the BA Group sweeps away the most important attributes of individual mentality, such as observation, thought, judgment, these primitive parts of the personality do their thinking with the body and obey laws that are closer to neurophysiology than to psychology. Correspondingly the members of the BA Group obey the dictates of the dominant Basic Assumption. Thought in its creative aspect, using all the varied apparatus which Bion attempted to describe through the Grid, container-contained, Ps↔D, and tranformations, finds no place in the mentality of the BA member who needs only the equipment characteristic of the computer to design the actions for which the Basic Assumption has programmed him. Consequently it is a world characterised by degrees or quantities or excitation rather than the infinite variety of emotional nuances. It is a world of rules and measurements rather than of principles and qualities. Learning is instilled by reward and punishment and virtue *is* obedience. The great terror is expulsion from the group and the great reward is a place in the establishment of authority, perhaps eventually the top post. This top post of "leader" stands in contrast to the ultimate development in the thinking mind of a "mystic" part of the personality, as described by Bion in *Attention and Interpretation*.

Like so many of Bion's ideas this one is too strange at first glance to excite more than confusion. Eventually, however, as it hovers in the background of the mind it begins to shed a new light on the clinical phenomena of one's consulting room. This paper will now attempt to illustrate, or at least to evoke, what may be an illustration of these notions in a clinical setting. Here is an imaginative conjecture based on Bion's extraordinary one: suppose that the primitive BA level of the mind, organised as an 'establishment', if strong enough, may have direct access to those complex humoral, haematological and healing processes which ordinarily protect our bodies from the various noxious events which threaten them. Suppose further that this 'establishment' treats these processes to which it holds, or claims to hold, direct access and the monopoly, as a 'privilege' which it dispenses with an open hand to the 'obedient' self. Suppose further that in order to survive in the internal and external worlds it is necessary for the thinking parts of the personality to acquiesce in the rules of the two 'establishments', internal and external, and to make for itself, quietly as it were, elbow-room in which to carry out the passionate interests and relationships that are the heart of the life-in-the-mind. If at some point an enlargement of this elbow-room were to take place which ran counter to the requirements of the internal 'establishment', might the individual find himself in a kind of legal-political trouble exactly analogous to that pursuant to a 'breach-of-the-peace' or 'anti-State activity' in the outside world? Might the thinking parts of the personality find that the privilege of immunological products had been cancelled and that everyday processes of defence against bodily enemies, external ones like bacteria, for instance, or internal enemies like primitive cell mutations, no longer operated. It would be similar to one's water or electricity being cut off. The house would soon become uninhabitable unless archaic modes of coping could be revived. But where would one find a well or an unpolluted river? Whose wood could one scavenge by hook or by crook?

Here then is a clinical account to which this imaginative conjecture lends a frightening aura of reality and mystery.

An intelligent and attractive unmarried woman in her thirties found that the experience of watching the development of her younger sister's baby over a period of several years aroused a slumbering interest in her that was very different from her feelings about her profession in which she was an outstanding success. Not only did the yearning for marriage and motherhood receive a new vitality but a keen interest in psychology, especially the type of psychology directly connected to infant and child development, began to arise. It was true that her original interest in economics had been of a psychological or sociological sort but rapid promotion in the civil service had soon taken her, with her outstanding orderliness of mind and great organisational ability, into the realms of the top people in government and thus away from research in the field, that is 'in the field' of her field.

Being by nature a kind and enabling person (in no sense a typical bureaucrat) her relationships with colleagues were uniformly pleasant on the surface. She had many friends, both men and women, she enjoyed the good income she earned, living well with only herself to support. Her family relations were cordial and satisfying, for she loved both her parents, the efficient and capable mother and the upright father who so adored his wife and the three fine children they had reared. But into this happy and eminently well-adjusted life a canker of discontent had entered. She found herself wanting to get back to the "field", to more direct work with people, investigating life rather than participating in its management. She had heard of analysis of course; now she read some of the literature with interest and thought of being analysed but could find no reason for taking up an analyst's time when there were so many suffering people who clearly were in urgent need of help.

Into this restive situation a new factor entered quite unexpectedly. A routine examination revealed a small mass in the breast, its removal was recommended and on surgical investigation it was found to be malignant. But there was no evidence of metastasis and the prognosis was deemed to be very good. However, the emotional impact was tremendous though this did not take the form of anxiety or even of depression. Instead her response was more one of guilt and regret for having allowed herself to be swept along by success and carried away from the genuine paths of her passionate interests, both professional and personal. At this point she resolved to have an analysis, feeling it was now justified.

It is with the first year of this woman's analysis that I wish to concern myself here, for the purpose is merely to illustrate the "imaginative conjecture" put forward as a substantial statement of Bion's extraordinary insight into mental organisation. Miss E was, from the beginning, a stunningly cooperative analysand, quickly coming to enjoy the sessions, bringing rich material with a high degree of openness, courageous when the process caused her mental pain and ready to put her trust in the ethics and sincerity of the analyst. But it also became clear that this represented both her excellent social character and a highly complex psychopathological organisation. Without competitiveness, but rather with the sincere helpfulness that was illustrated in a dream of *helping an old man to cross the road safely*, she managed to be my patient and my guide, sparing me embarrassment or demands. But she limited the number of sessions to three per week on the grounds of finance and would not consider a lower fee per session.

The emergence of this acting-in-the-transference as character structure could be traced to her third year as the means of coping with the birth of her younger sister. But it had apparently started to disintegrate in puberty. Inability to join in the sexual games of the village children, to which her siblings took as ducks to water, threw her into a period of isolation, preoccupation and inability to work at school from which disgrace she was rescued. This rescue took the form of individual tuition and promotion to prefect which led smoothly on to head-girl and the commencement of her career, for her character and intelligence, kindness and patience, efficiency and sound judgment formed a rare combination indeed.

Miss E bore the shock of investigation into the transference boldly and the material moved rapidly in two directions. One of these was a minute scrutiny of life-in-the-establishment; the other was an incursion into her sexual disappointment, that is disappointment over her inability to yield herself to a passionate relationship. In the areas of money, comfort, security, status she had discovered a pattern of conservatism that invaded and dominated her undoubtedly passionate nature. Fires began to break out in her dreams, then babies and prams caught fire mysteriously and finally, to her horror, she found herself in a role reminiscent of Mrs Gandhi and her sterilisation programme, ordering the destruction of whole litters of kittens on the grounds of hardship to the mother cats.

Clearly two separate problems had been catapulted forward by the experience of the cancer and the threat continuing to hang over her and over both of us in the analytic situation. (That it was a serious countertransference problem became clear when, on returning from a holiday break in which she was to undergo her first bone-scan for secondaries, she took an unconscious revenge that gave me a few grim minutes: for she entered the consulting room looking grey and lifeless, beat about the bush for some ten minutes before mentioning *en passant* that her mother's sister had suddenly died, after which her demeanour changed completely. Oh yes, the bone-scan? That was all right.) The first problem was one of heart's desire versus social usefulness. How could she justify abandoning a career in which she performed so well for one in which she had good reason to doubt her characterological suitability? Would not all her training as a professional economist and her wide experience as an administrator be jettisoned for selfish ends? But the second problem only compounded the first: if this career had, as indeed she was convinced it did have, the unconscious structure and meaning of a group-organised sexual perversion could she be sure that she was indeed doing good in the world rather than harm? Had the moving experience of watching the development of her little niece brought in its wake not only this flux in her desires and interests but perhaps the cancer as well?

Oddly enough, a peculiar little episode, involving questionable technique on the analyst's part, seemed to have the effect of Miss E's abandoning herself to dependence on the analysis to resolve this quandary. One day she entered the session with a six-inch split in the seam of her trouser seat and she indicated, in passing, that she was bound for an important conference. I was dismayed but held my tongue until, at one point, she suddenly developed an excruciating cramp in her leg and seemed not to know how to relieve it. I decided to instruct her about pressing and stretching the tendons and then, when the cramp relaxed I also told her of the defect in her slacks, interpreting both items as a cry from her body and her mind for evidence of sympathy for her predicament. She subsequently asked for a fourth session after a penny-wise type of dream.

The material of the analysis now took a leap forward, persecutory in nature, referable historically to a six-month's period of evacuation to an aunt's home at a very early age. Figures of a bad-big-sister sort began to appear in dreams in the form of colleagues whose hostile and aggressive characters she feared and distrusted. Reverberations of very early toilet training, conducted on the Truby King pattern, also appeared in dreams of her mother being demanding and impatient (which she is not in fact) and also in the transference. Coming without dreams was felt as failing to meet the requirements although also regretted because of the bright illumination they shed. In this context an episode of 'Holocaust' on television struck Miss E most forcibly and she dreamed that *she was helping to load children on to flatcars*. The following week of analysis brought a series of dreams which had a great impact on both of us and I wish to examine them in some detail. I would like to do this by laying out their manifest content in sequence and then weaving together the associations and interpretative work.

Friday   *A headmistress was meeting her staff and began by indicating that she was putting a man teacher in for an OBE. But then it seemed that discussion resulted in a decision that he should be retrained, which took the form of his having motorcycle training with a squadron. They were all lined up and at a signal shot off through an open gate, all except our re-trainee who next, probably as a disciplinary measure, seemed to be an inmate of a concentration camp. He was seated in a chair and was being systematically beaten in the face and head until his skull was deformed and his brains protruded. Miss E, who witnessed this relatively unmoved was however overcome with horror when the man's moustache was then cut off and she said to his tormentor, "Haven't you done enough?"*

Tuesday
    a) *There was a pool of alligators and she was meant to swim in it like the other children but felt afraid.*
    b) *A woolly baby elephant with an undeveloped trunk, but he was nonetheless strong enough to "stand down".*

Wednesday
    Her sweet-jar was cracked through the middle.

Thursday
    (The third dream from the Tuesday session which she had been unable to recall at the time.)
    She was to catch a train at Euston or St Pancras or King's Cross. At the first station, the train ran through without ever opening its doors; at the second, she entered the train but it never moved; at the third it was necessary to cross the tracks to board it by negotiating the fare with the conductor.

Friday
    "Norma Dixon" was coming towards her down a train platform and at first seemed to have no teeth but when she came closer did have teeth.

During this period the patient had been involved at work in reviewing the proceedings of a government committee which was investigating the methods by which universities evaluated candidates. She had been more and more impressed by the language of the establishment and its statistical modes of thought which seemed totally to disregard the existence of feeling individuals. But she was equally struck by her own distortion of values in this setting where concern for the trappings of status (like the moustache) seemed to exceed that for any forms of mental suffering other than humiliation. The alligators in the pool seemed to be the "allegations" by the children (students) against the adults, but Miss E realised how frightened she would have been, and for that matter still was, of opposing authority in her own interest. In defence of the interests of others, the underdogs, she could be intrepid. This woolly baby elephant, probably protesting about the failure of his trunk to develop, could only "stand down" i.e. from giving evidence, while the patient had meant to say "stand up" i.e. for his rights. The three different "train(ing) stations" represented her view of the systematic harassment and frustrations that the establishment, as the "enemy of promise" imposed upon the younger generation to reduce them to obedience to the will of the group, the "Truby King" method, as it were.

To the Wednesday session, that of the cracked sweet-jar dream, Miss E came in a very emotional state. She had been reading Sylvia Plath's 'Bell-jar' and had also seen a programme about Stevie Smith and the 'Drowning, not waving' poem. As I listened to her talking about these two poets in the apparently unrelated context of the dream I kept having a silly idea which only gained strength when she turned back to the dream to explain about the glass sweet-jar she gets from the neighbourhood shop for kitchen staples, such as sugar and rice, and the plastic ones in which she keeps fertilisers for her garden. I kept hearing in my mind a parody of the childish riddle, 'When is a door not a door? Answer: when it's a jar.' But I heard, 'When is a jar not a jar? Answer: when it's adored.' Finally feeling that it had enough link to the lives of these two poets, to Miss E's description of her father's adoration of her mother and the differentiation between the glass and plastic jars and their uses, I cautiously mentioned it to the patient and she began to weep. There followed a lengthy description of how she had always felt that she could never bear a marriage like her parents' although it seemed to her to be one of the happiest she had ever come across. And then the first shy and tentative criticisms of her mother's character appeared. She is a splendid woman, handsome and capable, efficient and kind, controlling everyone with velvet-gloved hands and voice to match. It was unfair to speak of her so. Had she ever felt the mailed fist? Never! We agreed that some projection, perhaps traceable to her toilet training, seemed suggested.

When the patient appeared on Friday obviously upset and promptly told her "Norma Dixon" dream we were both perplexed as to its possible connections. Clearly it had some link to the three train stations, but all I could add at the moment was that someone without teeth saying "normal diction" might certainly pronounce it like "Norma Dixon". She had never known anyone of that name; perhaps a girl at school? However, "normal diction" reminded her of an event the previous day which had quite bowled her over by its cold-bloodedness. While discussing with a man and a woman colleague the possibility of her agreeing to join a committee they were setting up, Miss E mentioned that the emotional upheaval of her cancer had made it difficult to decide on future plans. The woman had replied, "Well, yes, it's early days yet, I suppose", and proceeded to back away from the invitation.

Clearly, Norma Dixon's dream-teeth were false teeth that could 'smile and smile and be a villain'. Normal diction of the establishment was of this sort so that the object of it could not tell from the tone whether he was to be put in for the OBE or retrained in a concentration camp. Was it 'showing the teeth' as in snarling or smiling? Were you to be treated as waving when in fact you were drowning?

Now Miss E herself has a lovely voice, smooth and musical, modulated with eloquent but unpretentious diction. This area of ambiguity in speech seemed to be equivalent to the general ambiguity of her life-style where status and security seemed incongruously blended with kindness and generosity, where egalitarian principles fused mysteriously with benevolent elitism. This central conflict in her life had first declared itself in what had become a landmark of the analysis, the 'sten-gun dream'. In that dream *she had been invited by the chairman of the committee to take a sten-gun and go up onto the roof to fight with the other committee members. But once she had climbed up the ladder she saw that the members gathered with their guns on an adjacent roof were her friends. She refused to fight and climbed down. But at the bottom of the ladder there was now a mob, confusion.*

This dichotomy between order and chaos, between the mob and the establishment seemed not to have any middle ground to form a spectrum of social organisational possibilities. It seemed to be a choice between the OBE and having your brains bashed out, to say nothing of the humiliation of moustache-cutting. Where was the world of privacy, intimacy, individuality? It was true that her family, parents originally, and now all three children, were actively involved in national and local politics, but the picture of family life sounded close, tender. Yes, there was perhaps a certain sense of aristocracy in the family, partly based on her mother's beauty and character, partly on her father's high position, partly on their social superiority to the other families of the small village of her childhood. But it had not really been snobbery. She could remember that it did always upset her, even from puberty, when political debates broke out at the dinner table. No one else seemed upset, but she always had to act as a moderator.

At this time in the analysis, a friendship of many years' standing with a divorced man, B, seemed to be breaking up as his love for his children was drawing him back to his ex-wife. This was having a somewhat disorganising effect on Miss E and when she came to the Wednesday session, which had been changed to the evening at the analyst's request, she reported that it turned out to be a fortunate change because she had completely forgotten a meeting she had had to attend which would have conflicted with the usual session time. She had also slept through her alarm – unheard of! Her dreams were scrappy:

1. *Centred round an object something like a blown fuse, black with carbon* (bearing some resemblance to her kettle which had fused because of a loose wire).

2.   *There was some sort of chase or escape, very anxiety-laden.*
3.   *She and a former chairman of the committee had to make speeches but she had
forgotten her notes and had had to talk off-the-cuff. It was very banal. But
the peculiarity of the dream was that she and A were not addressing an
audience but a canal or river – no, a canal.*

Miss E and B had walked for a long time by the river the previous
night and he had wept as he told her that he could no longer bear the
growing estrangement from his children due to living away from
home. She had felt hurt despite her sympathy for him when he had left
early. She would not want to be in the position of a mistress and was
reminded of another chairman, C, who had died in a plane-crash
when on a business trip with his mistress. (A, B and C are all men in
high positions in government with whom she has had strong friend-
ships but only towards B has she felt any sexual attraction.)

The session was a disappointing one for her as I was unable to do
much more than listen. The one tentative suggestion that I made, that
perhaps 'canal' meant 'canaille', did not evoke any response. I had in
mind that B was of French descent and I was also thinking of the mob
at the base of the 'sten-gun' ladder. Certainly some fuse had blown
and some loss of organisation was afoot. To the next session she
brought a vivid dream with which, for some reason, she seemed very
pleased. In the dream *she seemed to be in a crowded kitchen, or perhaps it was
in the street. A large woman, carrying a bundle of knives in her arms, passed
behind Miss E and with a long boning knife dug her in the back. She flared
inwardly with rage but, outwardly calm and polite, turned to the woman and
suggested that she might wrap up the knives for her so that they could be carried
without endangering anyone. The woman replied that she did not really want the
knives and offered some to Miss E. But when these were handed over they now
appeared to be several cheese boards in polished wood with cheese or bread knives
let into the side. Just the kind she likes, so she took them with pleasure. There was
also something in the dream about wood, or woods,* which associated
immediately with a joke among the children from puberty days. It
went like this: (deep voice) To the woods. (high voice) Not the woods!
(deep voice) To the woods. (high voice) Not the woods! (deep voice)
To the woods! (high voice) I'll tell the Vicar! (deep and sinister voice)
I *am* the Vicar!

Now whether my suggestion that 'canal' meant 'canaille' was
correct or not, some image of the Reign of Terror was abroad. The big
woman with the knives certainly sounded a bit like the tricoteuse,
Madame Defarge, who had to be handled with velvet gloves to keep
her in her Queen-Mummy benevolent and generous mood. When I
suggested this formulation Miss E recalled an event that had become
a family legend because it so completely fractured the family's image
of itself. While at dinner one day, during her distracted period of

puberty, her mother reached across to take from Miss E's plate a piece of meat that she thought was going uneaten. To everyone's astonishment, especially her own, Miss E dug her fork into her mother's hand.

The joke about the sinister Vicar also had a family background which emerged for the first time. Her father's great correctness had one blemish – he is in the habit of telling not very funny off-colour jokes. So a Janus-faced picture of family life began to emerge which makes sense of the importance of "normal diction", the iron-fisted voice in the velvet glove. On one side is a picture of the Queen-Mummy, beautiful and generous, with her adoring Consort-Daddy, feeding the children splendidly, but if the political peace is not kept by the moderator the picture can quickly change to the tricoteuse-Mummy who takes your food away, digs you in the back with suppositories, supposedly on orders from (Truby) King and may, at any moment, throw you to the 'canaille'. This smooth and polished cheese-board voice with its cutting edge carefully hidden has clearly been inherited from her "big woman" to protect her from the lewd Vicar (fuck-her) Daddy, whose mistress she would not like to be.

But of course it would be ridiculous to think that this picture of family life which emerges from the patient's infantile unconscious is the whole story. It is greatly at variance with the manifest truth about the family and Miss E's conscious picture. Also the parents' unity as a couple, the way in which the three children have thrived, the professional success of all three and the marital happiness of the other two with their respective children – all these factors tell another story. But after all we are here concerned with the depths of the unconscious and its influence on character, mental health and physical states. It is also important to remember that this is not a research paper but an hypothesis bodied out from suggestive clinical material, aimed at giving clinical substance to Bion's brilliant "imaginative conjecture" concerning the protomental apparatus, or what he later called the "soma-psychotic" level of mental life and its relation to group mentality.

Let us retrace our steps, then, and make a tentative reconstruction of Miss E's development. This baby, who had a passionate attachment to the breast (the meat on her plate) was not given enough time by her efficient mummy to suck at her own pace, thus arousing violent feelings (digging the fork). But the premature institution of toilet training (the boning knife in the back) intimidated her for she felt that the big woman could turn very nasty and throw her to her persecutors if not handled very carefully. Furthermore this Queen-Mummy's adoring consort was not to be trusted as an ally since he was always picking her up and exciting her erotically only to leave her (like B) to go back to his wife's bed. But once she learned to talk like Mummy and could moderate the family atmosphere she felt secure and even enjoyed the sense of superiority that invested the home. This premature type of latency carried her well until it was threatened by the renewed stirrings of sexuality at her menarche when disorganisation and anxiety began to break out causing her to lose her velvet voice and speak off-the-cuff. For a time in her loneliness her only friend was her horse (masturbation) until she was brought back into the fold by special tuition, promotion to prefect and the commencement of her unbroken climb to the top of the establishment ladder. Only vague longings troubled her happy life until her younger sister had a baby and this revived both her sexual and maternal longings as well as infantile violence towards new babies (the children to be loaded on the flatcars). Fuses began to blow and finally a cancer appeared to inform her that she was in serious difficulty and needed help.

This, of course, is only a story based on one year of analysis, not yet given any substance by the evolution of the transference-countertransference process. But this is also the reason that it can so well serve our purpose here, of conjecture, hypothesis. Our hypothesis, to restate it succinctly in less imaginative terms is as follows: there is a primitive level of mental life, the protomental or soma-psychotic, which follows the principles of tribal social organisation of the pre-(?) and post-natal parts of the personality where the primal splitting-and-idealisation of self and objects tend to be at their most severe. If this severity is not modulated by sufficiently good experiences (intra- and extra-uterine?) this level tends to become very split off from the more thinking and socialised personality structures which evolve with mastery of language. From its split-off position this protomental level exercises a strong influence over social character because of excesses of persecutory anxiety of a group-mentality type, with its characteristic catastrophic anxiety, fear of chaos, the mob, the Reign of Terror. So long as a successful integration in group-life can be maintained, which involves a continual placation of the leader of the Basic Assumption Group in force at the moment through automatic obedience, a sense of security and pleasure is achieved and the price being paid is hardly noticed. This price involves a sacrifice of individuality, relinquishment of the pursuit of those interests and desires belonging to the unique thinking parts of the personality which cannot find expression in a manner that lends itself to integration in the group. But if recognition of the pride brings rebellion, the vengeance of the group-leader is swift and can be deadly for it involves the revoking of certain physiological privileges to which the group-leader claims, and may have, exclusive access. When, in contrast, this early splitting and idealisation has been softened by good experiences, parental objects are more clearly distinguished from the group-leader, which is, fundamentally, a part of the self. Then these parental objects are in a position to struggle with this leader for access to these physiological capabilities. These physiological capabilities may perhaps best be described in terms of entropy, the preservation of the body and the mind from having their orderliness invaded by chaos.

V

The Conceptual Distinction between Projective Identification (Klein) and Container-Contained (Bion)[1]

with
Giuliana Milana (Rome), Susanna Maiello (Rome)
and Diomira Petrelli (Naples)

Introduction

During seminars in Rome in the spring of 1982 students of the Rome Course in Child Psychotherapy (related to the Tavistock Clinic, London) presented several cases which Mrs Harris and I had periodically monitored over the previous three years. Two of them, Mario (G.M.) and Francesco (D.P.) were clearly approaching the termination of therapy while the third, Antonio (S.M.), a child who had had many autistic features, seemed to be in crisis regarding depressive anxieties and the capacity for thought. Not only were the three boys of similar age (nine years plus or minus a few months) but the form of the material was also strikingly similar. Resentment of dependence upon a thinking object, hatred of being small and weak, envy of the mother's richness and fertility, and jealousy of prospective siblings were all gloriously displayed in the sessions presented to the seminar. But the strategic significance of the material was quite different in the three children and offered a background for the investigation of this important conceptual problem concerning which there was much confusion: *how do these two concepts, projective identification and container-contained relate to one another? What are the clinical indicators, and how may the distinction be utilised in the clinical situation?*

Before describing the clinical material, a brief theoretical preamble may help to focus the problem. In her 1946 paper on schizoid mechanisms Melanie Klein described the operation of an omnipotent phantasy of intrusion inside the body and mind of another (external) person, producing a form of narcissistic identification and a corresponding alienation from one's true identity. Work by her followers in subsequent years traced a wide range of pathological phenomena to this mechanism, including claustrophobia, agoraphobia, hypochondria, manic-depressive states, disturbances of thought and judgment,

[1]Previously published in *The Journal of Child Psychotherapy*, Vol. 8, 1982, and *La Revue Francaise de Psychanalyse* 2, 1984.

certain psychotic confusional states; as well as demonstrating that the mechanism also operated with internal objects and had a specific connection with certain types of masturbation, anal in particular. Disturbances in character development variously known as pseudo-maturity and false-self also seemed to be a consequence of its wide employment.

Since Melanie Klein's original description closely linked projective identification to splitting processes (schizoid mechanisms), it seemed clear that the phenomena she was seeking to account for by describing this mechanism (phantasy) involved the splitting off and projecting of infantile parts of the personality. The cognitive units, parts of the 'self', were seen to be viable independently of the remainder of the personality and to take up a life of their own within the 'host' personality, producing, in passing, a tenacious linkage manifest in a deep sense of connection and responsibility towards the host personality.

Bion, on the other hand, in designing his model of the mind as an apparatus for generating thoughts which could be used for thinking, utilised the mechanism in relation to mental functions, not merely cognitive parts of the personality. Furthermore he suggested a developmental aspect of projective identification which was in no sense normative (i.e. comparative), as previous attempts to distinguish 'normal' from 'excessive' projective identification have been. Instead he attributed a specific and essential function in primitive communication between the mother and baby to this operation, thus also laying the basis for a new approach to understanding the non-lexical aspects of verbal communication in particular and non-verbal communication in general.

This then was Bion's contribution to description of the phenomenology of projective identification. But in addition he introduced the general model of container-contained into his hypothetical model of the mental apparatus. Although he never stated this very specifically the model employs a language and mode of description which clearly reveals its analogical relation to the field of chemistry. Terms such as "elements", the arrangement of the "Grid" like the periodic table, and the idea of "transformations" rather than, say, transpositions, all imply a chemical model for the apparatus, or crucible, or retort, of nascent thought. The latter addition of "catastrophic change" served to emphasise the violence of the forces of thought requiring containment, and the particular need for a container which was neither too rigid nor too flexible, so that the new idea could develop and yet not destroy its container by its expansive thrust. It will become clear in the clinical material how germane to the experience of children is the Bionic description or model.

One thing, then, is clear from the conceptual point of view: these two concepts, projective identification and container-contained, relate to very different levels of scientific thought. Projective identification, in terms of the Grid, belongs to Row C, Dream-Thoughts and Myths. Container-contained belongs to Row F, Concept (see *Elements of Psycho-analysis*, 1963). One is at the level of symbol-formation, the other at the level of abstraction. It will be clearer if we leave the question of their relatedness to one another and connected clinical problems until the children's material has been described and discussed.

Mario (aged 9, in therapy for about two years).

This account describes the progress of the therapy from December 1981 to March 1982. The chief new development in this interval has been the movement from communication prevalently by means of play, drawings and representations, to verbal communication in which Mario enters into a dialogue with the therapist and talks explicitly about his problems and the work of analysis.

Analysis is referred to as "this situation of ours", an expression which embodies an allusion to the idea of a shared space for thinking. Mario also expresses the same concept in drawings: of two wheels of a train in motion, driven by a single piston; of coal-fired locomotives with two smokestacks and a single boiler for energy; of a house with two roofs joined together.

In a February session, after mentioning his serious worry about his arrested physical growth, he starts drawing but first urges me to "keep on thinking" while he "takes a little rest". A few minutes later, when I make a comment, he tells me that while he is drawing I have to think and only talk afterwards. "You have to pay very careful attention now . . . because now there's hope for me . . . because I . . . you have to . . . me . . ." Using mime and gestures he indicates something tiresome and entangled in his head. I ask if he isn't perhaps telling me that I have to pay close attention in order to help him to understand how his mind works. With a sigh of relief he answers that that is exactly right.

While he speaks of these matters he usually has his back three-quarters turned towards me, spontaneously taking the analytical position, it seems to me, and he puts his head between the two cushions or else between the back of the armchair and a cushion, forming a little space for himself enclosed on three sides. When I ask him why he assumed that position he replies, "– to think". The sense of an inner space emerges in a curious manner in his drawings – they are still entirely flat, without perspective, but alongside the part of the object depicted he draws the sides or the top or bottom, as if the three dimensional volume of the object, perceived in some manner, is broken down into planes again in the act of communication.

Together with the image of an inner space there also appears, forcefully, the anxiety-ridden phantasy of a small being imprisoned in a closed space, cut off from the rest of the world: the child who died in a well at Vermicino[1], the baby chick that cannot hatch and dies suffocated inside the eggshell.

In a design for a house for his dog there is an elevator to carry the puppy up and down, open at the sides. I interpret this as a phantasy of being held in a comfortable space that does not suffocate him and that allows him to look out, to be in communication with the outside world.

During this same period some references crop up that indicate that the child is seeking to connect the present session with past ones. The effort which the patient has begun to make to relate what goes on in his own mind with what goes on in the therapist's mind is continually interrupted by very powerful impulses to understand, causing him, as it were, to tear the interpretations apart so as to make them entirely his own possession.

One Monday morning a month later the doorbell rings twice. When I open the door Mario is not waiting on the threshhold but appears a moment later ostentatiously chewing a wad of gum. As he has done for the past several sessions he begins by pulling up a small wicker armchair to the little table, arranging the cushions with great care to make sure that I am comfortable. He seats himself in the armchair that I generally use and pulls the desk over next to the armchair and the table thus placing himself in a space enclosed on three sides. He takes the two drawing blocks, the old and the new, and leafs through them meditatively. Finally he says, "Today I'm going to talk about filmstrips." (The use of the personal pronoun is a new development). Then he announces that he will use the old drawing block and maintains in silence his wandering, but not distracted, gaze. He is just about to start drawing in the new block when he realises his mistake and quickly takes the old one. Leafing through it he remarks once again that there are still a lot of blank pages and asks if I added them myself (I tell him that he is trying to link up this session with those of the past but that he has not found the way – that in thinking back to past sessions he has realised that there are things there to be used and that these are not to be thrown out and simply forgotten).

On the same page where last time he drew a machine to make animated cartoons, he draws a filmstrip with a series of images representing a boy bending down to touch the ground. He says that this is a boy who did not want to do his exercises but who then does them. ("Is that boy you by any chance?") He smiles and keeps on

---

[1] The reference here is to a tragic accident which received world-wide publicity at the time.

drawing. He adds a little cloud attached to the boy's bottom, a cloud that gets bigger and bigger in the subsequent frames. In the last three frames he writes the words 'The End'. The writing is almost submerged by the ever expanding cloud. He explains that the cloud is the boy's fart. (I try to show him what this drawing might mean in our work but he prevents me by drowning my voice with his every time I start to speak.) Then seeing that I am determined to provide an interpretation he forestalls me with his own interpretation: "This is a labour of patience that keeps going ahead and then at the end, Boom!. No more sessions and no more me coming to visit you." (In this filmstrip we see two aspects of Mario represented. In one there is Mario working, acting, doing things he did not do before; in the other there is Mario who with his bottom sets off a gigantic explosion that settles everything in an instant so that he no longer needs his mother or Dr Milana whom he has blown away with his tremendous fart.) Next to this he draws another filmstrip filling all the frames with lighter and darker shades of grey. "This", he says, "is a classic film", adding that it is a film that you see from far away. (I say that now he does not dare to let me see what is going on inside his head close up, that he shows me his phantasies only from a distance so that I can no longer distinguish the two aspects of Mario, of Mario working and of Mario making his earthquake fart.) He makes a third column of frames which he leaves blank to be drawn in only during the subsequent session. He is rapt in thought, his expression typical of those he has latterly assumed, of someone who is looking for something that he cannot find.

At this point he pulls an incredibly long strand of gum out of his mouth and then puts it back in, repeating this sequence several times. (This strand of gum that goes into his mouth and comes out again I say represents his phantasy of putting into his mouth and eating the things that come out of his body, that he makes himself like the giant fart that will make him grow and Dr Milana disappear.)

He starts talking about the machine for making animated cartoons: he moans with longing at the thought of having one. He suggests that I ask his mother for it, "Because my mother is the type that does not want me to spend money: you've got to tell her, 'This will resolve the boy's difficulties', and then Mummy will buy it for me." (Here we have Lazybones Mario who, rather than get help from Dr Milana to make his mind work, the mind that puts images together and forms thoughts, wants instead to possess a machine that will do the job for him and he wants Dr Milana to help him with this undertaking.) He then comments that he was only joking.

Then he starts asking me if it would disgust me to touch the gum that he is chewing, or his vomit, or shit, or peepee, or an old man's saliva, or his saliva. I try to turn the question back to him by asking why he wants to know but he is insistent, he absolutely wants to know if it would disgust me. With my back to the wall I finally say that peepee *is* disgusting to me, to which he promptly replies that he does not find it disgusting and that, after all, it is nothing but the water that we drink. He persists, asking me whether I would drink my own peepee and he phantasises someone who can put a tube in his bottom and the other end in his mouth so that he can suck out his faeces – or else suck his peepee if he attaches the other end of the tube to his penis. (I interpret this form him as a phantasy of being able to nourish himself by himself with no need for a Mummy-Milana, as he phantasised earlier with his giant fart and also his playing with the chewing gum.)

He sniffs the white paste with great voluptuousness asking if you can eat it and saying that he loves the smell. He looks at it and notes that it has dried up and wonders aloud if someone has touched it, maybe one of his little sisters. (I say that in his phantasy he was trying to confuse the faeces that his bottom makes with the good, lovely smelling milk that comes from his mother's breast. But that now he was seized with anxiety that maybe the two things have become mixed up in reality and that the good milk has gone bad – but that as soon as he thinks this he tries to shift the blame on to the girls that may come into the room when he is not there.) He covers his hands with the paste then goes into the bathroom where he washes his hands very thoroughly.

Commentary

This little boy has clearly been able to find a means of relating in a close and collaborative way to his therapist and to use their "situation" as a foundation for his rapidly developing capacity to think by means of elaboration of symbolic representations of his emotional states and conflicts. But he is also absorbed by the desire to understand how his own mind operates in order to establish his eventual independence of this therapist without an explosion (the "fart" ending for the little boy who reluctantly did his exercises). The analogy to the chick who needs to break out of his protective shell, the tragedy of the child trapped in the well at Vermicino, and the plan for the dog-house all belong to this problem – how to leave the container once its usefulness has been outgrown, neither to be trapped within nor to destroy it.

The solution that Mario evolves is represented in the dog-house with its mysterious lift that can take the puppy to any of the many rooms of the house. But its mystery is also represented in the machine which makes animated cartoons, such as the three he draws himself. Clearly that mechanism already exists and his sense of his possession of it is tied up with the ending of the therapy when "the situation will be resolved". The theme shown by the puppy contained in his house is also represented by Mario's way of appropriating the therapist's chair (while providing for her comfort elsewhere) and enclosing his head in the cushions within the enclosed space of desk and table. The difficulty, however, of letting go of this sustaining alliance finds its mode of expression with the chewing gum which is stretched to breaking point. This stretching of the nipple, testing the strength of the link with the breast, also has its other aspect at a whole object level, the mother-therapist's tolerance of his destructive and perverse aspects with his excreta and secrets. The session following was largely given over to direct expression of his jealousy of the baby-patients who would follow when his own therapy ended.

Francesco (aged 8 years and 10 months, in therapy for over two years – summary by D.P.)

During the period preceding the last Christmas holidays to the beginning of April, Francesco's therapy passed through some difficult periods both for internal and external reasons. The first external cause was the change of venue necessitated by the introduction, following the earthquake, of a traffic-free zone in the town which led to changing the days of the sessions in January and to their reduction from thrice to only twice weekly. This coincided with frequent and repeated illness of the child who for about two months continued to have a few degrees of fever and possibly bronchitis.

In the sessions following those events Francesco appeared disconcerted and irritated, confused and elusive. Often he spent the whole hour in the bathroom playing with his faeces, refusing to come out before the end of the session. After a while I no longer followed him into the bathroom but remained in the room and only interpreted his behaviour when he came back. This gave rise to joking and outbursts of anger on his part which in some sessions culminated in his contemptuously defying me, standing naked in the doorway and demanding that I should "kiss his feet and eat his shit" which, according to him, I should consider "very good and delicious". During an interview that I had at that time with his parents I was astonished to learn that Francesco, although often ill, was more integrated when with his family: he was on good terms with his brothers and socialised well with various friends. I appealed to his parents, who seemed satisfied with his therapy, that we should all three work together at least to restore the number of sessions and by mid-February this was arranged. Although he was frequently ill, losing many sessions, it did become possible for him to spend a longer time in the consulting room and not so long in the bathroom. Finally in the last sessions in February he spoke to me openly of his anger and of his envy of "women" – his mother and me: "They have everything, they have children in their bellies while males cannot have them", and of his intention, when he was grown up, "not to give my little seed to my bride because then she would have everything and I would have nothing; she already has children and would then have too much." So he wished to give her only shit.

The interpretation of these phantasies, in transference terms, as attempts to attack and destroy the therapy and to prevent me from being creative, made it possible to go deeply into some of the themes that had emerged earlier, such as his intolerance of the differences between the sexes and the phantasy about the hermaphrodite who, copulating with another hermaphrodite gave birth to two children, "one in the man's belly and the other in that of the woman". But from time to time Francesco still had to spend some entire sessions in the bathroom. During the preceding three weeks, after having declared himself to be convinced that I "was hiding some family secret", he began to question me about God and about "what there is on the other side of the universe", and why "space is endless". These "ugly thoughts" as he calls them, occupy his mind and make him "suffer". He can think of nothing else and he feels tormented by them, he does not know why. "When these thoughts come to me – I should go to a lovely festival and enjoy myself – you must not let me think about these things." He is afraid of "falling out of the earth, out of the world" and of remaining inside infinity "with nothing to eat". He passed the last session lying in my arms speaking to me and playing the game of the "little horse". For the first time he noticed that I had some white hairs and repeatedly tried to pull them out. The idea that I can become old and die pains him and he wished that "God had ordained it that we die when we are young without becoming old". We then speak about Peter Pan who always remained a young boy and who could fly, and he reminisced about his first year of therapy.

For the first time for many sessions one Monday, late in March, Francesco arrived on time. He entered the room with a satisfied air and came at once to sit in my arms in the usual position, kneeling in my lap. He then very ostentatiously grunted like a pig (I tell him that perhaps he is reminding me and confessing to some "dirty part" of himself which likes to play with dirt and to make clean things dirty, as he did on the last occasion when he picked up some dust and tried to smear the walls of the corridor which had recently been whitewashed.) He admits this and says that he is a Francesco-pig and that the most piggish behaviour is to play with shit. While talking he puts his hand on his bottom. He quickly leaves the room and goes into the bathroom. As usual I do not follow him and remain in the consulting room waiting for him. Before he left, while he was at the door, I had begun to say something about his going away again but he had interrupted me bluntly with, "What do you want, then, that I should shit here?" From the bathroom I hear him making various noises while he behaves in the usual way with the bidet. Now and then he calls me. I hear him speaking loudly in an incomprehensible manner. I am curious to hear what he is saying but I resist the temptation of going to listen. He remains in the bathroom for about fifteen minutes. When he returns he is naked from the waist down; he says he wants to dry himself on the couch. (I say to him that perhaps today he would like to talk about the "piggish" subject in this room also.) He says to me, provocatively, that he has not cleaned the bathroom and that he is not going to do so. "You must do it. Perhaps my shit disgusts you, perhaps you think that it is something loathsome?" (I remind him of our agreement – that he finds the bathroom clean and he must leave it clean. I add that maybe he wants to provoke me, to challenge me and maintain the supposed superiority of his shit.) Actually I discovered later that he *had* cleaned the bathroom. He grumbles something while he lies on the couch; he touches his genitals for a long time. (I say to him that perhaps there are things he wants to tell me but that at the same time he does not wish to do so. He speaks, but in such a way that I cannot understand him. Also beforehand in the bathroom he had said something outloud as if wanting me to hear.) He says that "he was repeating to himself the difference between angels and devils". I ask him what this is. He says, "Angels have wings instead of horns, and devils have horns instead of wings. Angels have goodness instead of evil. Angels have God, who is the Father, devils have slaves and fire.' I ask him who the slaves are. "They are other devils who obey their orders in the fire.' (I say to him, "The Devil is envious and jealous of God, the Father, of his greatness and of his sons. Therefore he tries to acquire slaves and to command them. They must make him strong and powerful as it seems to him that God is with all his angels.") He listens attentively. "It is true", he says, "He was envious of his sons." (I say that according to me all this has something to do with us. He too is sometimes envious of his father's and mother's opportunities of having children and he thinks that I also may have some and that they remain while he has to go away and that this makes him jealous. To dispel this feeling he claims that his shit is a delicious food, produced by himself, and he tries to see me as one of his slaves.) After having listened to me in silence he says, "The Devil ought to have understood that he had to wait until he was grown up and found himself a she-devil with whom to procreate children. But the Devil did not want to wait, he did not believe that he would grow up and therefore he wanted slaves instead of children." (I say that such things do not exist outside ourselves, they are within each of us. In each of us there is a devil-part and an angel-part. He is now trying to separate them and to distinguish between them.) He says that it is true that they are always with us. "The Angel is on the heart's side, on the left, and the Devil is on the opposite side because he has no heart." (I suggest to him that he is telling me that the devil-part can only be merciless and heartless but this is because the devil feels weak and helpless and cannot bear this. He has neither trust nor hope.)

I see that he has begun to touch his penis again and that he is having an erection. (I tell him that the things that we are saying even now cause him to experience these feelings and that therefore he touches himself to be reassured that his penis has not been damaged and that it can grow as large as Papa's.) He says that he wants to make sure that it is growing, it must grow and every day he wants to see if it has grown a little. Meanwhile his mother has knocked. He tolerates being dressed. Before leaving the room he says, "I too when I am angry become wicked."

Commentary

While Mario's fear of a fart-explosion ending of his therapy was purely an internal event, Francesco's approach to termination was confused by the earthquake in Naples and its generally disruptive effect on his life situation and the therapeutic setting. His response was partly somatic and partly a defiant idealisation of his own earthquake equipment, his rectum. While similar in quality to Mario's brief excursion, Francesco's need to test the therapist's tolerance was protracted for there remained, as a basis for mistrust in the maternal transference, a very difficult problem springing from envy of women in general. Once this had been broached this child, with his unusual gift for language, became deeply absorbed with the problem of life and death, good and evil, finite and infinite. Unlike the more scientifically minded Mario whose interest lay in the mechanics of thought, Francesco's artistic bent sought more to explore the emotional dimension of the meaning elaborated by the "ugly thoughts which made him suffer" so much.

It is interesting to note that the position of kneeling on the therapist's lap is reserved for the "piggish" material which, on reaching its full concreteness, must change its venue to the bathroom. On the other hand Francesco takes to the couch for his introspective excursions which he somewhat reluctantly shares with the therapist. He shares, in fact, what he has already worked out for himself, just as he had, in fact, cleaned the bathroom. It seems fairly certain that the therapist's refusal to follow him into the bathroom or to be seduced into eavesdropping on Francesco's bathroom monologue succeeded in drawing him back to the couch and sharing his deepest thoughts.

Much more than Mario, this little boy's capacity for cynicism and distortion of the truth finds a valuable container-representation in the bathroom, for clearly the decision to use or misuse this container is crucial for his finding his way back to the couch-breast of honest thought. As with Mario the bringing together of these two containers, toilet-breast and feeding-breast, is crucial to the establishment of trust in the maternal object. "Perhaps my shit disgusts you."

Antonio (Report by S.M.)

After the Christmas holidays Antonio makes a drawing in which he seems to represent the intense projective identification mechanisms that are at work: all the emotion seems to exhaust itself in the act of projection; there is no operator, no audience and no image on the screen. The drawings that follow show fire, electricity, aggression – particularly a big zeppelin that shoots and throws bombs at a little spacecraft. There is a third element: either the fireman's hose that squirts water to extinguish the fire or a child who throws bombs back at the zeppelin. Antonio seems so frightened of his sadistic attacks that at times he does not want to enter the therapy room. He is very preoccupied about being "big" or being "small". Being small exposes him to being squeezed or crushed, or torn sadistically to pieces (as he does in reality with a little spider). To escape these dangers he becomes the big zeppelin (he makes his penis grow big by masturbating) and shoots by spitting or urinating. The only alternatives seem to be either a small Antonio who will be squeezed or pulled to death by a big Susanna, or a big Antonio who destroys his object. He also clearly expresses phantasies about sexual penetration and his wish to possess the mother and chase away the father. (The parents tell me that he literally tried to take over his father's place in the parents' bed and that his relationship with his father is very ambivalent. I hear about this during one of the monthly interviews with the parents to which, for the first time in four years, the father does not come. I think that his absence might also be connected with the presence in the family one afternoon a week of a young male social worker whose task it is to help Antonio to enter more into contact with other children and to help the mother. Antonio has developed a strong affection for this young man whose Christian name is the same as the father's.)

February is characterised by activities in which Antonio tries to bring about intense sensations and excitement: he masturbates, puts his feet into cold water; I feel that he is seeking excessive heat or cold on the surface of his body perhaps to avoid the burning sensations felt inside himself previously which were too strong to bear. He also undresses completely.

When I understand that he does not really want to communicate anything through these activities in themselves (except the need to avoid something else) I begin to be more active and do not allow him to undress any more or to wash his feet in cold water, and so on, and interpret only what it is that I think he wants to obtain and to avoid through these activities. Many sessions are occupied almost entirely by my physically restraining him and by his violent rebellion against the limitations I impose. He alternates violent aggression against my room (rarely against me) and attempts at erotic seduction; at times he seems to fall back into autism, but more often his attitude towards me is one of sadistic contempt. He communicates images of violent and contemptuous intercourse, that is when he bites the centre of his half rubber sole until he makes a hole in it which he penetrates with a pair of broken scissors. At other times he unexpectedly makes representations which have a much more elaborate symbolic character: the little horse has a fight with the big horse, the big horse is thrown away by the little one, the crocodile comes and bites the little horse's sticking out parts of the body – the legs, tail, ears, eyes.

In March a new theme emerges: on the doorstep he chatters with his mother and says that he wants to become a workman, one of those who change the lamps. I often notice, by the way, that Antonio arrives in intense dialogue with his mother and regresses only in the therapy room. He starts making drawings in which he almost exclusively uses yellow: sun, stars, mountains filled with yellow, a yellow tunnel with lights inside, a ladder and a workman-child. If he does not succeed in his drawing he gets angry, crumples or tears up the paper, wants to undress, attacks the room and masturbates. He tries to take over my chair when I have to get up for any reason: "I want the big chair." He cannot bear to be smaller than me and to need my help.

In a session towards the end of March, Antonio sits down at the little table, takes a sheet of paper from the drawer and the light green felt tip pen. He draws a tunnel with lights inside and a round shape (the head of the workman-child?). He would like to tear the paper up and says, "one can't see". (I prevent this and say that he fears not to be able to show me, as he would like to, what he is feeling inside himself. He wants to throw the drawing away as if he thought that I should not try to see together with him the things that "one can't see well". I say that the tunnel has to do with dark and light, with the things that are not yet understood but which we can try to understand – this is what I am helping him to do.)

He gets up to take the darker green pen. He draws many equal shapes which seem to be entrances and exits of tunnels. I ask him and he confirms this. He draws a little child next to the first tunnel, erases it and draws a larger one who is walking. Then comes a double tunnel and he says it is dark, it is the Underground; inside the tunnels there are rails and a platform. He says "Barberini" (the name of the

Underground station at which he gets off when he comes to the session). Then he draws the same itinerary many times, starting where the child walks, and he says, "pavement".

(I say that he is telling me how he comes each time to see me. Many tunnels – he has been coming many times, and he shows me his journey in the dark tunnel in the Underground and then the way he walks to come here. And here we are together, talking about where it is dark and where there is light. (He looks up at the ceiling where the light is on.) Here in our room there is a lamp that makes things light and when there is a light then one can see and understand. I refer to his drawing and the fear that one cannot see. He knows that the light in here is also our talking together, our thinking to understand better, and that this feels like making more light inside himself where at times he feels it is like a dark tunnel. When he says that he wants to become a workman who changes the lights it means that he wants to be able to make more light inside himself with his thoughts. For the time being he comes here for me to help him to make more light.)

While I talk he draws indeterminate scribbles over the road from the Underground to my place, like an aimless trip, and then he lets himself slide down to the floor. He says, touching his shoe-laces, "Big people don't take off their shoes." And then adds something about babies not taking off their shoes either. He touches his penis. (I show him the last scribbles and say that all of a sudden he had been feeling small, weak and confused, maybe when I told him that he is not yet big enough to make light himself, and that he needs me. Now he would like right away to be big enough, to be big like big people; to make his penis grow big quickly, and he wants his foot to be naked, instead of the penis, to produce strong sensations inside himself, and so to escape from the difficulty of producing thoughts, and of feeling and understanding that he needs his therapist.)

He sits at the table again and draws the lift and then something else that I don't understand but that looks similar to the lift. Under both of them he draws a sign which clearly looks like a penis. Then again there are indeterminate scribbles underneath.

(I say that he drew and named the lift which is outside the session and which represents the last part of his journey to come to me. Here he has made a penis. Maybe when he comes up in the lift he feels himself to be a big lift-penis that wants to penetrate into my flat and body. But when he wants to penetrate into me that way, with the whole of himself, he feels confused, as in the drawing, and it becomes difficult to think and talk with me because he feels himself to be confused with me inside me.)

He says, "I want Mummy." He is lying on the floor again and touches his penis; I feel that he is concentrating to try to urinate. A dark stain appears and gradually enlarges on his trousers. He utters some "broken" word and laughs triumphantly. He tries to climb up the doors.

(I say that I believe he wants his mummy because now she is not near him and he can feel her to be distinct from him. I am near him and he can see me and this makes it easier for him to feel confused and inside me. He would like to be separate and understand but he is also very frightened of this; he is attacking and dirtying my room with his urine because I remind him that it is not true that he is inside me and that he is not big and strong enough to be able to do everything himself, the workman-child. He wants his mummy because it is difficult to bear that he and I are not one and the same thing and that therefore he fears to feel like a fallen-down child when the session ends.)

At the session two days later Antonio comes with his father. Passing through the corridor he stops to peep through the keyhole of the closed waiting-room door. In our room he does the same with the door that, according to him, prevents him from entering the "Signora's" room.

He wants to take off his shoes and says, "Big people don't take off their shoes, babies don't take off their shoes." (He often says to himself, like an admonition, the contrary of what his desire would induce him to do.) One shoe wasn't tight enough and he manages to strip it off. He is lying on his mattress and I am near him to prevent him from taking his sock off. His tongue moves quickly in and out of his mouth. (A snake? Antonio is fascinated by snakes and looks in encyclopaedias to find out all about them.) He is isolated.

(I say that today he came in and cast his eyes over the other rooms as if he wanted to stay there, everywhere. He would either like to be as big as his daddy or as tiny as a baby, and not like the boy he actually is. He would also like to undress so as to get merged with me and produce in himself sensations which he could set up as a barrier against his acknowledging that he is with me, near me. He would like to be confused with me inside me and to control me from inside like when he spies on the Signora's room, or else to be a tiny baby as he was once, so tiny that he could manage to remain confused with his mummy.)

He tries for a long time to take off his sock and makes attempts either to be cleverer or quicker than me. He repeats the sentence about the big people who take off, or who don't take off, their socks; he says "broken" words, bites his nails. Then he says "Daddy – at two and a quarter", the time for the end of the session.

(I say that today, too, it is easier to think of daddy who is outside and whom he does not see; it is more difficult to communicate with me. In fact I am very near him to prevent the sock being taken off.)

He tears off little bits of rubber from the sole of his shoe and bits of wool from the carpet selvedge which he eats.

(I comment that he is producing out of the sole and the carpet many little bits of sole and carpet which are of no use any more by themselves and that he is trying to confuse and mix up the bits outside and inside.)

He touches his penis repeatedly and squeezes it. His eyes are vacant and his face is pale.

(I say that in order not to feel his feelings or how his thoughts move inside him he moves his penis instead. It seems as if he was feeling all inside his penis which is growing big and this makes him feel lonely, far away or lost inside S through his penis.)

He wishes to urinate and I feel that there is some urgency and that he wants to do it in the bathroom. The urine goes into the toilet, only the last jet is directed aggressively against the toilet paper; then he wants to play about with the water. I prevent him from doing this and show that I am determined to go back to the therapy room. He struggles but verbalises the memory he has of a past comment of mine – one does not think in the bathroom.

(I tell him that he came to the bathroom to urinate into the right place, the toilet, but then he did other things, urinated outside, played with water, which means that he wants to soil, flood and drown our thinking and confuse things again. When he came here I think he wanted to urinate in order to discharge the bits of sole and carpet about which we had been talking and which he felt to be all in a mess inside him and which prevented him from thinking.) I say this while preventing him from making a mess with the water and trying to guide him towards the therapy room but without using too much physical force. He replies "yes" to my interpretation in a completely normal tone of voice and he goes back to our room by himself. He takes a sheet of paper and chooses the black pen. He sits down and draws a tunnel with a street leading into it. He says "curve" as he draws a curve. He isn't satisfied and would like to tear it up (I don't let him and say that we can try to understand together why this tunnel is not right. I add that, anyway, what he has shown to me is the exit of a tunnel, black and dark; maybe he has been feeling throughout the session up to now that this was where he was inside a dark, black tunnel.) He draws a double tunnel, with rails, still black. (I say that this time it seems to me to be the tunnels of the Underground: an entrance and an exit, it is himself who comes into the session and then goes out again, at the beginning and at the end; and the tunnels represent what he has been feeling like today; he has entered into a kind of dark tunnel inside himself, or inside where he cannot see or understand anything, and then he has been able to come out of it and to think about it and to draw and tell me how he has been feeling before.)

Commentary

In this little boy, with his more serious defects in personality structure, more serious than either Mario or Francesco, we nonetheless see a very similar process of testing the durability of the container. But in Antonio's case the testing is not in the interests either of being able to liberate himself from dependence (as with Mario) or to resolve the deep split in the maternal objects imposed by his envy (as with Francesco). His testing has a more primary purpose, namely to establish the fundamental goodness of the container. Clearly its goodness has two distinct dimensions, its resistance to evil, either of attack or seduction, and its containing goodness, enlightenment, truth. The "new theme" which appears in March is therefore a shift from the Oedipal competition with the daddy's horse-penis to identification with the workman-penis that "changes the lamps" which illuminate the tunnel of the containing mother.

But Antonio's capacity for thought based on symbolic representation is far less developed than either Mario's graphic or Francesco's verbal capacities. He struggles to imagine the things that "one can't see" in the face of tempestuous impulses to negate and destroy both his own efforts and the assistance of his therapist. He has succeeded in finding a representation in the Underground system for his experience of union and separation from the mother and for the place inside her where illumination by the truth can take place (also represented by the playroom and its lamp which he inadvertently looks towards).

He has also found a representation for the process of divesting himself of this thought-enabling relationship through taking off his shoes and immersing his feet in cold water. But unlike Mario's puppy-lift internal mechanism of thought, Antonio's lift represents his dependence on the mother to lift him to the breast in the face of his genital incapacity to penetrate her tunnel of light as the workman-penis. In the following session he discovers that his eye, and therefore his imagination, can affect this penetration of the breast were it not that his eye-tongue can also be the snake which bites holes and fills itself only with rubbish.

Faced with this destructive capacity of eye-tongue-penis Antonio is impressed by the therapist's insistence that "one does not think in the bathroom". So he returns to the chamber of maiden thought (Keats) to approach once more this difficult problem of finding a representation for his despair. And now it is clear: he wants to represent the tracks going in and out of the tunnels, but they always seem to hit the ceiling at the entry instead of penetrating to the interior. He is trying to invent perspective with no Uccello or Piero to help him.

Discussion

We cannot assume that Bion's creative thought which has given us the concept of container-contained has also done all the work of exploring the meaning with which its relative "emptiness" in its original form can be filled. The task here is to use the splendid clinical material evoked by the analytic method, and its painstaking pursuit by therapists and children alike, to explore the meaning of "container" by relating it to the claustrum revealed by the study of the pathological consequences of projective identification.

We have learned that the consequent states of mind set in motion by projective identification fall into two great categories, as the name suggests: the projective phenomena and the identificatory ones. In this instance we are concerned only with the projective phenomena and what they reveal of the structure and the implications of the claustrum. The contents of the claustrum were ably described as early as Melanie Klein's explorations of the pre-genital Oedipus complex and the epistemophilic instinct. In so far as these applied primarily to the phantasied interior of the mother's body, 'phantasied' also meant 'physically real' in relation to the internal object. More recent investigations, particularly those related to acute psychotic confusional states in adolescents ('geographical psychoses'), have shown a clear tendency for the maternal claustrum to be sub-divided into at least three distinct areas, each with its own qualities and consequences: front-bottom (genital), back-bottom (rectum) and top (inside chest, breast or head).

The structural qualities of the claustrum can be distinguished quite clearly from the functional ones:

Functions: front-bottom: eroticism, babies, penises, blood-food
          back-bottom: sado-masochism, faecal-penises, faecal-food
          top: oxygen, light, wisdom, knowledge, sensory acuity, romantic emotionality

Structure: portals of entry
          sensory contact with the external world
          texture of the walls
          strength of the walls
          flexibility of the walls
          intercommunication with other internal areas

It has often been argued that the pathological use of projective identification, that is as a mechanism of defence, would better be called 'intrusive identification' since this term catches the essential motive of invasion of an alien personality and body as originally described by Melanie Klein. In that case the term, projective identification, could be reserved for the more Bionic use, as a primitive and largely unconscious mode of communication central to learning from experience. The clinical material, from Mario in particular, shows this latter function in a glorious way, while that from Francesco illustrates the interaction and conflict between the intrusive and projective modes. Antonio, on the other hand, shows us the mind of the child struggling to find the projective mode while still enthralled by the sense of triumph in the employment of the intrusive.

It will be seen that it is being suggested that, for the sake of conceptual clarity the term 'claustrum' should be used when talking of the object of projective and intrusive identification operating at the level of the unconscious phantasy (Row C, Dream-Thoughts and Myths) while reserving the name "container" for a more abstract level of discourse which we must now discuss.

The notion of "container" may, from Bion's description, be seen to be part of a highly abstract and analogical construct aimed at providing a model for thinking about thinking. It is not intended, as far as one can see, for clinical description but rather, like the Grid, for retrospection on the "analytic game". It seems useful to assume that while every claustrum is a container not every container is a claustrum. Mario's "puppy-house" does not appear to have the qualities of a claustrum the representation of which is reserved for the chick in its egg. Francesco on the couch is not in a claustrum, but in the bathroom or on the therapist's lap, he is. Antonio's tunnel is a claustrum when it is dark but not when it is illuminated like the playroom. His feet are in a shoe claustrum when his incapacity to think for himself is felt to be intolerably frustrating.

What then can we say about the qualities and functions of the container as an abstraction which may find a representation in the concrete language that fits with the claustrum of intrusive identification or the 'chamber of maiden thought' of projective identification?

First of all it has to have boundaries which, while they may be concretely represented, are fundamentally the boundaries drawn by selective attention. This appears to correspond to what Bion means by the "facts" which comprise the "evidence" upon which the creative alpha-function can operate to construct the symbols to be used for dreaming and filling with emotional meaning. It is easily imagined that this is an area in which the function of an "experienced" object (like Bion's "experienced officer" of the early work on groups) is essential to creative thought, initially an external object, eventually an internal one. Mario's "puppy-lift" and "animated cartoon machine" would appear to correspond to this object, mysterious in its very essence. Antonio's "lamp-lighter" would seem to have potentialities in this direction while Francesco's God presents its truth-function aspect, juxtaposed to the Devil (Bion's "foul fiend" of the Negative Grid).

Second, the container must be a place of comfort, sheltered from irrelevant stimulation coming from the interior of the body. Although discomfort would initially appear to be sensory its meaningful implications, as anxiety, seem to be its ultimate mode for interfering with the operation of thought. This takes us back to the more Kleinian concept of maternal functions as the modulator of mental pain, the "toilet breast" (Meltzer). The Bionic version would emphasise confusion and its resolution rather than the free modulation-by-sharing of distress through reception of projections. From this point of view it would not appear to be at all surprising if sleep were the perfect 'chamber' for this function, making a somewhat paradoxical link to Freud's ideas about the function of dreaming. Instead of dreams being the "guardians of sleep" we would see sleep as the 'guardian of dream thoughts'.

In keeping with this second requirement we might list a third quality of the container – privacy. This is a complicated and difficult idea, probably requiring a fairly extensive philosophic exploration to delineate it from solipsism, secrecy, withdrawal, isolation, delusional system. As a preliminary it might at least be suggested that 'privacy' in this concept would mean something that is a product of the history of the relationship between container and contained, something that has its inception in a very imperfect way but grows naturally as the history lengthens. Mario's delineation of "our situation" would correspond neatly. It could be suggested that many of the phenomena put down to jealousy would be more profoundly understood if referred to this aspect, say, of the analytic setting as container, or to those internal babies of the mother who are suspected of being able to spy and eavesdrop on the privacy of the baby-at-the-breast.

This might also lead us to suggest a fourth quality for the container, namely exclusiveness. Or do we mean, rather, uniqueness? One might prefer to build a home of one's own but after all it is possible to 'make' it one's own even though it has previously been lived in by someone else. The position of the first child may have its special primogeniture status but it also has its special problems; likewise ultimogeniture. One must suppose that eventually the history of relationship which creates the sense of privacy must also generate the sense of uniqueness where names are better than numbers but not good enough; given name, surname and pet-name almost meet the requirement.

In summary it can perhaps be seen that not only is there a conceptual rationale for distinguishing between the concepts projective (intrusive) identification and container-contained but that so doing offers a rich avenue for differentiation of clinical phenomena, the nature of the analytic method, the dissection of emotions like jealousy, the investigation of social phenomena such as ritual and perhaps some of the central questions in the philosophy of science (Francesco's "ugly thoughts" about the "infinite").

As an aid to the implementation of this sharpened differentiation I am suggesting the following semantic alterations in our habits of thought and communication with colleagues:

Projective identification – the unconscious phantasy implementing the non-lexical aspects of language and behaviour, aimed at communication rather than action (Bion).

Intrusive identification – the unconscious omnipotent phantasy, mechanism of defence (Melanie Klein).

Claustrum – the inside of the object penetrated by intrusive identification.

Container – the inside of the object receptive of projective identification.

This modification of our language elevates to a qualitative level the distinctions, quantitative in nature, made previously by terms such as 'normal', 'excessive', 'massive' appended adverbially to 'projective identification'.

VI

Clinical Use of the Concept of Vertices: Multiplication of Vertices as a Method of Reality Testing: Shifting of Vertices as a Mode of Defence

In that extraordinarily difficult and in many ways unsuccessful book *Transformations*, Bion gave considerable space to the concept "point of view", or "vertex" as he preferred to call it, as a parameter of perception and a creative aspect of thought. His ideas were further developed in *Attention and Interpretation* and illustrated in a kind of Shavian debate in *A Memoir of the Future*, particularly in the third volume, *The Dawn of Oblivion*. But before discussing his formulation of the concept and its diverse points of reference it would be useful to cite a clinical example for the sake of clarity and vividness.

A woman in her forties, five years in analysis and anticipating its termination, perhaps within the next year, had always filled the holiday gaps with interesting activities with her many professional friends all over the world. The phenomenon which appeared in the consulting room, quite against her intention and much to her own disappointment, was a closing down of the material and a diminution in the vibrancy of the contact for several weeks before a break. And so it also threatened to be now as this, perhaps ultimate, summer break approached.

To the Monday of the third week prior to the interruption she brought a listless mood and a poorly remembered dream, something about *it being surprising that the tennis competition continued although the championships had already been decided.* The doldrums were setting in again and she felt rather discouraged.

Tuesday brought a more determined mood and a puzzling dream: *she was visiting one of the subsidiary companies of her group to arrange a shift of personnel. The supervisor was showing her a depressed place in the floor where the previous employee had sat at the time of her nervous breakdown and the patient insisted that the replacement be given a different desk. A tall Japanese man was greeting her.* To this she associated the wonderful performance of the translator in an interview between Malcolm Muggeridge and Solzenitzyn. Her sparkling translation had kept the interview moving.

She had thought Solzenitzyn looked rather oriental. This dream seemed to bring us to a thoroughly familiar position, both as regards her being the indispensable cooperative child who maintains peace in the family and thus keeps it going, combined with her taking no chances of being placed in a position where she might become depressed.

On this desultory background the Wednesday session cast a complete mystification. She had read the obituary of a psycho-analyst and on this basis construed what she perceived as my "grim face" at the start of the session as evidence that this analyst had been a close friend of mine. A prolonged silence followed composed of a ruminative conflict; on the one hand she did not wish to burden me if I were already in distress, while on the other there was great annoyance with herself for this "helpfulness", given the meagreness of her evidence. After about thirty minutes of silence sprinkled with rather scattered associations I felt very strongly that I was being handled with kid gloves as if dangerously explosive, unlike her usually mild and cheerful father. My image of David playing before Saul was strong enough to warrant mentioning it by way of clarification. This brought forward a dream, previously unremembered: *she was in a French delicatessen filling her basket with good things to take back to England but then, doubting the utility, given the prices, she proceeded to replace them on the shelves. The proprietor was offering her a thin slice of ham to sample.*

I made a rather over-complicated interpretation of this material in the closing minutes of the session, something to this effect: hesitation whether to accept the food offered by the breast and nipple (delicatessen and proprietor) because of misgivings about the price (depression after separation) could easily be mistaken for delicacy and concern if mother's worried face was taken to refer to some trouble other than her own lack of appetite. But this infantile behaviour, seen from the adult level (as if, for instance, another customer in the shop might see her taking and replacing items and she could be mistaken, because of this behaviour, for a member of staff rather than seen as a customer). I was thinking of the previous dream in which she appeared as the supervisor's supervisor.

Thursday brought a brilliantly clear dream of a type characteristic of this thoughtful and intelligent woman. In the dream *she had to cross a river by means of a small bridge made of slats of wood laid across narrow supports. She noticed her parents on the other side waiting for her but also that a number of slats were missing in the centre which would make it impossible for her to cross. She thought to herself, without any sense of incongruity, that when she had made the bridge she should have placed the two halves in the opposite way so that the missing slats would then be at either end where this would not matter since the bridge was overly long.*

The main point of the dream seemed clear to both of us: if one looked upon the rhythm of the analytical situation from one point of view, then the week's, or term's, sessions appeared to be preceded and succeeded by separations in the comforting sense that "our little life is rounded with a sleep". But from another point of view the continuity of the sessions from week to week and term to term could be seen as being ruptured by separations of variable dimensions which could not be traversed without some hazard. This would be a simple and clear example of a mental operation which, in the ordinary parlance of argument, would run ". . . but look at it this way . . .". This simple method for altering the meaning of the situation does not violate one's relationship to the truth, but rather it selects a particular vertex for its comforting qualities. It is not the same as denial (denial of psychic reality) nor like negation (denial of external reality). The observations of both internal and external world are accepted but in lieu of a multiplication of vertices for the purpose of reality testing, one particular vertex is selected. It is, one might say, a method for scotomatising thought rather than perception.

In this sophisticated game of find-the-depression the steps outlined could be stated like this: a) why are we continuing this game of analysis when it has already been decided that it must end some time, perhaps next year? b) anyhow it is rather the parents, or breast and nipple, who should be depressed – for the sparkling analytic conversations of the past years have been the result of her skilful translation of the meaning of my interpretations; c) it is better to refuse any further feeding since the cost promises to be very high and to confine herself to being cooperative and helpful at an adult (staff) level; d) at this level the expensive depression can be located elsewhere, either in the past (the former employee who had had a breakdown from the depressive position) or in the analyst (who will be grim faced from losing her as a collaborator); e) anyhow it is quite easy to shift the depression, or at least her awareness of it, by shifting her adult point of view about the sequence of events in the analysis which, after all, is something she constructs in her own mind.

If we may leave our lady bridge-builder for a moment, let us turn to the converse situation, the way in which the multiplication of vertices serves reality testing without the necessity of recourse to experimental action. A young academic, finishing his first year of analysis, found his state of mind increasingly occupied with his widowed mother's depression rather than his own. She seemed to look to him for some help which his estrangement from her, that dated at least from his having been sent off very early to boarding school, could not sustain. But to his surprise he had felt a rush of warm feelings towards her, reawakening a nostalgia for his early years as her pet when together they had visited the home of his childhood. Certain improvements had been made which he noted with approval and they seemed to enter into his dream that night.

In the dream *a new toilet had been installed off the kitchen, which also had a new polished wood floor. A lady's bicycle appeared somewhere.* In fact these are references to recent improvements he himself had made in his present home and the bicycle was the one on which his mother used to come to collect him from his primary school. After his visit to his mother a dramatic occurrence in his sexual relationship had ensued in which he had awakened from an unremembered dream intensely aroused. In the ensuing love-making his behaviour had suddenly shifted from being highly active genitally to his being completely passive, genitally and anally, much to his partner's pleasure, and to his great surprise. It seemed strongly suggested that a reawakening of his early romance with his mother had brought in its wake an enactment of the erotic experience of nappy changing, bisexual in its content.

The following day he brought a dream which moved him greatly, not only because it seemed so closely connected with his appreciation of his wife's beauty but because it somehow carried with it a glimpse of his early enchantment with his mother, in the days of his parents' happiness with each other. In the dream *a large black car was represented, apparently a hearse: but then it seemed to become open at the top with glass sides, like the vehicle used by the Pope for mass ceremonial occasions in his world travels. However, there were rather huge ragged holes in the wooden body which again metamorphosed into a handsome 18th century coach, resting on the stage of an auditorium where a choral concert of mixed voices was taking place.* At this point of the dream he felt powerfully moved. His first association took him back to a childhood event, a concert to which his mother had taken him where they had sat in the balcony and he had been entranced looking down at the heaving bosoms of the young women singers.

This dream, and the events leading to it, would seem to allow their poetry a prosaic expansion thus: when you have an elderly, widowed and depressed mother, the points of view from which you see her are many, all true and all poignant: she is an old depressed woman full of memories of her dead husband and of her disappointments with him; she is the wife who elevated her husband, your "Papa", to appear so grand in your eyes by virtue of his possession of her; she is the original vehicle of your earliest months of life who was later changed; she is the object of your earliest ravishment by beauty, appreciated by eye and ear.

The immediate result of the analysis of this dream was an explosion of anxiety about the approaching summer break but also a new feeling of closeness to his wife and a feeling of readiness for them to have a child.

Clearly the material of both the bridge-building lady and the young academic have their roots in a rich capacity for symbol formation at the dream-image level (alpha-function), Row C of the Grid). In that sense the material is well comprehended at the level of unconscious phantasy in the spirit of Melanie Klein. What does the Bionic dimension add to our understanding? There is the richness of multiplication of vertices in both, but in the first case a particular vertex is chosen, while in the second we have evidence that the plurality of vertices is embraced. In the first instance the motive is defence against depressive pain; in the second the intention seems clearly to be a search for the truth, if possible the whole truth, of the young man's emotional connection with this first most important woman in his life experience.

The question then arises: where in the personality structure should we locate the processes of either selection or multiplication of vertices? In both instances the content is clearly infantile in its orientation to the object, with on the one hand the psycho-analytical experience (also represented by the two parents waiting across the bridge) and on the other the infantile, bisexual experience of the mother's body, historically and in the transference. But is not the choice of how to entertain this richness a conscious and adult function of the personality? Is it not the point at which insight, as distinct from the impact of the analytic process of experience, makes its contribution to the therapy?

The history of speculation about the nature of the therapeutic function of analysis has, from Freud onwards, been divided between opinions in favour of the corrective emotional experience and development of insight. 'Remembering, Repeating, and Working Through' (S.E. XII, 1914) tells the one story, while 'Analysis, Terminable and Interminable' (S.E. XXIII, 1937) tells the other. It would seem that the difficulty about the insight aspect of the therapeutic action is that it was not possible to formulate a conception of its mode of action in the mind without the implication of a rigid psycho-analytic morality.

I would suggest that Bion's concept of vertices gives us a means for grasping the therapeutic action of insight without weakening the concept of the individual. This conception, after all, requires that thought, judgment and decision should rest upon understanding of the moment of life in its uniqueness, not on historical analogies to the present.

VII

The Limits of Language

Psycho-analysis has been left a legacy by Ludwig Wittgenstein which, as yet, has scarcely been investigated, let alone exploited. In his great works, the *Tractatus* and *Philosophical Investigations*, he broached the problem of the limits of language and made two different approaches to it, the first logical-mathematical, the second purely linguistic. He was attempting to define the limits between what could be said and what could only be "shown". In this brief paper I wish to make a purely psycho-analytical approach to the same problem hoping then to see where it has brought us, first *vis-à-vis* Wittgenstein and then to examine the light that it may throw on the psycho-analytical method and process. I wish to start with two pieces of clinical description from two patients, each in the fourth year of analysis but facing the problem of the limitations of language from opposite poles.

Mrs D had come through the crucial struggle with the omniscience which had split her emotional life, and recovered the early and passionate love for her parents that characterised her infancy. The split between an area of dutiful object relatedness and secret perversity had severely restricted her emotinality so that she was coolly devoted as daughter, sister, wife, mother, co-worker and analysand. On the other hand her sexuality had a wildly perverse quality, secret and defiant. The third and fourth years of analysis had undone this split with the result that she had become sexually disengaged from her partner and emotionally cold to everyone while a prolonged struggle took place in the analysis to overcome the omniscience, with its attendant delusion of clarity of insight and independence of judgment, which promoted her resistance to dependence upon the mother and breast at infantile levels and in the transference.

When the omniscience yielded and hopefulness began to return, this brought in its train a flood of dreaming and waking states filled with love for her mother and father, and in the transference. Music, love of nature, a tendency to sing and dance and a restless state similar to adolescence began to occupy her days and nights, marred only by a sense of desperation as the end of her analysis hove in sight. Elements of strong identification with her mother then made their appearance and a strong desire emerged to know all about her mother's childhood, love affairs, courtship and married life. This could fairly easily be gratified for her mother had recently written her memoirs. What had earlier been a rather patronising and belittling attitude towards Mrs D's parents and their marriage was now replaced by a despairing feeling that she herself would never be able to love without reservations, let alone be loved in this kind. The initial object of these feelings was the analyst which the differentiation of the infantile transference from adult feelings and desires gradually clarified and led to an experience of relinquishment, not of the desires, but of the wish for their fulfilment.

Within a few months she fell deeply in love with a man who had been secretly admiring her for years. As neither of them was free to enter a complete relationship they parted, agreeing not to write but hoping to meet again in a year's time. However, neither was able to keep to this agreement and soon almost daily letters of many pages began to fly back and forth. Mrs D had never known such a passion, filled with pain and happiness, different from the wild sexuality of earlier years, for it was so clear that the hunger of their minds took precedence over desires of the body. They were not stronger desires, only more important and in that sense more crucial than the bodily ones. The content of the letters on both sides was of two sorts, the expression of feelings (almost totally excluding sexual desires lest these should be provocative of painful frustration to the reader) and self-revelation. This desire to hide nothing was entirely different from the pacts of honesty made with previous lovers. Those treaties had reference to actions, to have no secrets from one another regarding activities. The present confidentiality had little to do with actions but had to do with mental states. At this time Mrs D also told her mother (at last) that she was having an analysis and that she was in love. Her furtiveness in regard to the analysis, which had caused her agonies of anxiety lest she meet her acquaintances in the vicinity of the consulting rooms, quietly passed away.

Two things now troubled her. One was the question of the distinction between privacy and secrecy, regarding her feelings, and letter-writing to her beloved vis-à-vis her husband from whom she was not formally or legally separated. The other was the vexing question – what was a communication and what was an action in the context of her letter-writing? The two problems were closely linked together for she could recognise that feelings are essentially private, no one had any claim to know them in the external world. But actions were in their very nature public, involved some other human beings and therefore had implication for other lives upon which the consequences of the action might impinge. In theory a communication was a passage of information about mental states from one mind to another. Could this still be considered essentially private so long as no action was engendered? Had not this ideally been the situation in the analysis, assuming that neither the patient nor the analyst acted-in or -out of the transference? She had already had some years of experience in the differentiation of action and communication in the consulting room. Had valid criteria been established? And could they not reasonably be applied to her love letters?

The problem that Mrs D found herself facing in her attempt to preserve the goodness of her new love from being tainted by betrayal of the old relation from which she was not yet properly disengaged, that is with minimal hurt or injury to the lives involved, required that she examine the limits of language as communication. When could it be said that the words with which she described her mental states to her lover had ceased to "say" what she meant and commenced to "show" what she meant? She had seen the problem many times in analysis. When, for instance, was the telling of a dream intended to elicit understanding from the analyst, and when was it calculated to affect his state of mind, to influence him or to evoke some action from him? Could this operational definition based on motivational criteria apply now with the man she loved, or was it necessary to find some linguistic criteria? The trouble seemed to be highlighted by her awareness of the great inadequacy of her language. She was not a poet, though she noticed the trend towards the poetic in her modes of expression. Anyhow it was not really clear whether poetry was "saying" or "showing" since it painted pictures and sang its evocative song. Somehow it all seemed to boil down to being able to say "exactly what she meant" and only what she meant. Yet language was so imprecise, even leaving aside the problem of the reader's interpretation of her "meaning" and the extent of her "meaning it", that is the authenticity and sincerity of her feelings themselves. Finally there was the evidence that so much of her feeling could not even find expression in words in her own mind but cried out for actions, sexual acts, services, gifts, feeding, entertaining one another.

Miss R had, in the second year of her analysis broken out of her intense erotic transference which had prevented her participation in the analytic situation and transformed it simply into an unhappy, unconsummated love affair. Rapid progress had ensued for about six months, with attendant improvement in her general mental state and way of life and relationships. But as her internal situation improved and a long absent father began to appear fleetingly in her dreams, she seemed to be threatened by crushing depression, mainly represented in dreams as freezing, and by whiffs of groaning grief about her father's death. Silent sessions began to occur, now with tantrums at the end when her struggling to speak had been of no avail. It was a different silence from early in the analysis which had been without struggle or pain, a 'belle dame sans merci' kind of silence. Now she felt a dead hand upon her, preventing her speaking, crushing her feelings, accompanied by self-mocking ruminations in which the authenticity of her feelings was ridiculed and juxtaposed to her continued secret masturbatory practices. The formula of contempt was, "If you really felt this or that you would not behave in such and such a way".

During the next year the analysis stood at a standstill while she ruthlessly, with full awareness, acted out her destructive attack on the parents' (and analyst's) marriage in a most dangerous way, abandoned to an astonishing degree to both wantonness and cruelty. It seemed at times that a psychopathic part of her personality had seized control of her identity and that she was out of touch with any but destructive intentions towards herself, the analysis and the analyst. Only after some months did the three-year-old type tantrums of screaming, kicking and refusing to leave at the end of sessions diminish. These had, to some extent, been curbed only by the absolute statement that if she interfered with anyone else's analysis her own treatment would be stopped on the spot. Now weeping and an awareness of helplessness succeeded in shifting her identity back to a more constructive aspect of her personality. Desperation set in as it became clear to her that analysis could not succeed, nor continue indefinitely, under the peculiar limitations of communication that now became evident.

The structure of this extraordinary impairment of intimacy and confidentiality could now slowly be worked out. Although she often lay in silence it was once again the silence of turmoil rather than "waiting-for-daddy-to-take-possession-of-his-incredibly-sexy-daughter". She was flooded with "positive feelings" which she could not express without the most tortuous equivocation. But it was also evident that the vagueness of verbal definition of feelings was not only an external but also an internal phenomenon. Furthermore this ambiguity of expression undermined her belief in the authenticity of the feelings themselves and thus prevented their implementation as an improvement in her cooperation in the analysis. She was able to work now, resumed her education, expanded her social life in an improved way. She felt more in-the-world but could make no headway in the curbing of her compulsive masturbation or sporadic acting out. She realised that the trouble lay in her inability to want analysis if she could not achieve a sincere desire for it rather than for a relationship to the analyst himself, transference or otherwise.

I have brought these two processes into juxtaposition to one another because I think that their opposite polarity can be instructive. Mrs D's intensity of feeling in her love for a man rendered the relationship precious to her, and she found herself in great distress as to the means of preserving its authenticity against betrayal of various sorts. Because she was not free it seemed necessary to preserve the relationship at a level in which its privacy was justified by the exclusion of action. This in turn required the careful differentiation of communication from action in her letter-writing. She needed to discover the boundary between 'saying it' and 'showing it'. Miss R, on the other hand, found herself hampered in regard to belief in the authenticity of her love feelings because she wished only to 'show it'. Somehow the showing was less precise than the saying and thus preserved her from an internal stress, mainly of humiliation before the mockery of the psychopathic big-sister part of herself. While guarding herself from what she thought an unbearable pain, she deprived herself of the means of rendering her feelings convincing to herself in the analytic situation because of the peculiarities of the method. Unlike any other human relationship the analytical method requires of the patient, and analyst, that action be suspended in favour of communication. Intimacy cannot, therefore, be manifest and indeed deepened by processes of 'showing' one's feelings but only by verbalising them. As Mrs D was restricted by the distant position of her loved one and thus unable to utilise services, gifts, sexual activity, etc. to show her feelings, so Miss R was hampered by the analytical method. She could not act them without betraying the relationship she sought to deepen by these means. But the equivocation of her communications undermined her belief in the psychic reality of the feelings themselves so that they faded into a mythical position in her mind. In consequence she could not 'show' her feelings in the only way the method allowed, that of improving her communication.

Wittgenstein puts the problem simply (P.I., p. 507): "I am not merely saying this, I mean something by it. When we consider what is going on in us when we *mean* (and don't merely say) words, it seems to us as if there were something coupled to these words which otherwise would run idle. As if they, so to speak, connected with something in us". In his later work, in revulsion against his earlier attempt in the *Tractatus* to limit meaningful utterances to the scientific molecular statements that could be resolved into atomic ones, he has invented a new and purely descriptive method for investigating the multiplicity of "language games" each of which derives its meaningfulness from its context, the human situation, and can be taken as a "form of life" without the necessity of establishing its relative value to other "games". The requirement of precision is replaced by satisfaction with differentiations that are adequate to their context, regardless of vagueness, and similarities that are composed of linkages of a multiple, "family resemblance" sort. It is in this two-fold use of "meaning" (meaningful-meaningless and meaning it-saying it) that he seems to search out the boundary between what can be said (what is representable in a language game) and what can only be shown, leaving room for the movement of this boundary through the invention of new language games. He has, in contrast to the earlier days, become clear that the structure of external reality cannot be discovered through the analysis of language because language is only a game by means of which man seeks to overcome his solipsistic position in the world, his alienation from other human beings and his ignorance of nature.

In pursuing the problems that Wittgenstein has set us and in trying to adapt them to the things that the psycho-analytical method can reasonably hope to investigate, I have in recent years directed my attention to this "something in us" to which our words are connected when we are able to "mean" what we say. Like Wittgenstein (I think) I have concluded (unlike Freud, I believe, but certainly like Bion) that feelings are the heart of the matter. The authenticity with which we are able to entertain our emotions sets a limit to the sincerity with which we can express them, either by saying or showing. This extends to the whole range of our experiences and communications, from the passionate "I love you" to the trivial "Rather cold today", from the embrace to the handshake, from awe at thunder to irritation that the tap is dripping. There is, therefore, an intimate link between these two uses of 'meaning'; our language game is nonsense when we don't mean what we say. And people suffer from a galaxy of impediments in this regard. Some cannot mean what they say; others cannot say what they mean; in some the meaning-it is so impoverished that it is indistinguishable from nonsense; in yet others it is so shallow as to be useless.

But the other great interference with being able to 'mean' what we say lies in the distinction between communication from mind to mind (vertex K in the language of Bion) and action upon the mind or body of the other. Here we touch on the problem of motivation, or inten-tionality, in Wittgenstein's "language game". In the two women I have described these problems are illustrated, as I have said, from different poles. Mrs D is struggling to preserve the authenticity of her feelings; Miss R is struggling to create this authenticity. Both are confronted with the problem of sincerity in their communications. In both, the discovery of a boundary, sufficient to its context, between saying-it and showing-it on the one hand and between action and communication on the other, is the focus of their struggle. In both, the interference from destructive forces within the personality (Bion's "attacks on linking") aggravates, and in some senses even creates, the difficulty. Who can say but that saintly goodness would find no difficulty at all!

Already, in the context of the clinical descriptions, I have hinted at the more general significance of these questions for the psycho-analytical method and process. Every analyst is, of course, continually struggling with both the Mrs D and the Miss R problem in himself. But can we say anything more than this? Is there a problem here regarding the limits of the analytical method itself? Is the analyst forced, by the strictures of the method, to invent a new "language game" with each patient? What role does the analyst's poetic capacity to express feelings in words play in his interpretive and non-interpretive intervention? Let us examine these questions one at a time.

The critics of psycho-analysis today often cite as grounds for their disparagement that the "talking cure" is so distant from the body and its central place in human intimacy that the whole method can be dismissed as artificial. The sweeping nature of the condemnation coming from T-group, Bio-energetic or Reichian sources may be smiled at but its essential point requires some thought. If we are seeking to rectify the impact of experiences of the pre-verbal period of development how can we hope to do this with a method that relies on language? Are these experiences only historically pre-verbal or are they essentially unverbalisable? The question has perhaps been hedged by the concept of the "corrective emotional experience" which is, after all, an extension of Freud's idea of "working through" carried to the point of tail-wagging-the-dog.

It has been a commonplace, following Freud, to assume that an analyst's limitations were essentially imposed by his own unanalysed "complexes". But "unanalysed" here meant "unresolved emotional conflicts". What of the deeply unconscious levels of mental life which may not have been tapped in the analyst's own experience on the couch but which do not harbour illness? One suggestion might be that his self-analytic work, carried on in the context of the countertransference with his patients, forwards this penetration in some instances. This might be said to follow a dictum that good analytical work is a therapy for both patient and analyst. I would stress in the context of this paper that one element in this is to be found in the exercise of the analyst's capacity not only to observe but to render into language new constellations and nuances of emotionality in himself which hopefully give some clue to the patient's state of mind. It is, in that case, as with Miss R, exactly the strictures of the method that provide the forcing house for this kind of development. It is one of the reasons that we should, if we wish to preserve and extend the technical line of development initiated by Freud, be so reluctant to adopt technical procedures which step outside the boundary of verbal communication. This does not require us to sit in judgment on others whose interests move in other directions.

In the sense implied above, the analyst can be said to invent a new 'language game' with each patient, and indeed this may in fact play an important role in the creation of the sense of exclusive confidentiality which so strengthens the feeling of uniqueness in the relationship and helps it to move into the depressive position, passing beyond the realm of part-object relations. In the case of Mrs D, for instance, one of the factors that helped her to overcome her persecutory anxiety about the analysis being overheard by other people in the rooms of the adjoining houses was the slow realisation that they would never be able to comprehend the "meaning" of what was being said, so idiosyncratic was it and so dependent upon its own unique historical context. Would this not be in keeping with the essentials of the Wittgenstein idea of a "language game", unique to its own context and unintelligible to others outside this setting?

Accordingly, quite a good case can probably be made for considering that this poetical capacity of the analyst, founded on his own experience of discovering and verbalising his primitive emotionality, plays an important role in the analytical process. I would be inclined to place its impact most specifically at the threshhold of the depressive position as we see it, for instance, exemplified in Miss R or in Mrs D a year earlier. It was most noticeable in helping Miss R to curb her end-of-session tantrums by means of verbalising for her the inner rage, and her way of hurting the breast, time and again, by not sucking at it, that the impulse to action was gradually replaced by the shift into weeping and prompt leaving. But in order to do this – and mean it – I had first to feel a most peculiar agony of bursting with a tenderness I could find no means to implement, deeply feminine in its quality and linked with very personal areas of distress in the past.

My point is that this accomplishment, once achieved, was not in itself helpful for the patient, but had to be repeated over and over again towards the end of sessions. Its effect of lessening the rage and impulse to tantrums was clearly visible in the patient's state of bodily tension. I often felt it to be a kind of analytical lullaby I sang to her, like "Rockabye, baby". The meaning of the interpretation was in itself ineffective unless repeated over and over again as a meeting of the minds in which Miss R could discover that I "meant it".

In closing, it remains only to stress the vastness of the region that the philosophers have opened up to the psycho-analysts. Some day a more happy liaison may exist between these two fields as the one becomes more careful in its modes of thought, and the other becomes more emotional in its participation in 'forms of life'.

VIII

Facts and Fictions[1]

All of psychopathology could be said to be the consequence of self-deception, but the detailed study of the mechanics of defensive operations is probably more correctly described, as Money-Kyrle has done, as enquiries into the sources of misconceptions. These conceptual errors can readily be seen to differ from, say, perceptual errors resulting from such pathological states of mind as projective identification – the "delusions of clarity of insight" (Meltzer) or hallucinosis (Bion). The term 'self-deception' seems too valuable to allow it a vague and popular general meaning. We would probably like to reserve it for situations in which we can define, from the evidence, the intention of self-deception. Freud clearly thought that this played a part in the operation of repression, with its consequence of amnesias covered by paramnesias, but the hydrostatic aspects of the Libido theory required that the amnesia be a consequence of a mechanism called into play automatically by the economics of mental pain. Only the filling of the gap by the paramnesia could be taken as intentional, and he compared it with the 'Bowdlerising' of theological texts.

One must accept that it is a great mystery how it is that a person can deceive himself. If it involves matters of judgment it is comprehensible; if it involves distortions of perception, or of memory for significant sequence, one can understand it. But when the facts themselves seem to have been replaced by confabulation, it is difficult to understand how it can command the author's credence. It is not a rare occurrence by any means, in fact the more one becomes alert to its manifestations in others the more one begins to see it operate in oneself. Usually this is at a social level where fidelity to the facts may be of little importance compared with acquiescence in the social ritual. For instance, to entertain one's guests a story is embroidered, distorted, exaggerated, etc., but of course it does not particularly command belief. Similarly when a delinquent tells a lie in court neither he nor anyone else believes it, they are all simply operating under a legal fiction that what cannot be disproved must be accepted as if it were the truth.

For the sake of discussion I am trying to isolate the phenomenon I

[1]Read to the 1st Delphi International Psycho-analytic Symposium, 1984.

wish to call 'self-deception' by saying what it is not, and then to leave it to the clinical material to say what it is. An extremely tall and handsome but ravaged man in his forties, came for what I was led to believe was at least his fourth analysis in various countries. His throwaway and glib manner of speech, his aristocratic demeanour and remnants of military carriage gave little promise of serious intention or cooperation in analysis, nor did his accounts of his completely parasitic 'exotic life-style'. This latter involved no work but only playing at being a writer while he played hide-and-seek about alcohol and drugs with his solicitous and motherly wife. He lived on an allowance from a vast hereditary fortune which had legally been taken out of his control during a period of certification for drug abuse, nor had he any desire to regain control of it.

We had a rather pithy and friendly consultation some three weeks before we began analysis three times per week. This must have made some impact for he announced at the first session that he had started writing a new book in a sudden burst of energy and optimism. He had also had a dream which he not only thought would please me but which was clearly intended so to do. In the dream *he had photographs displayed all over his wall – not very good photographs, perhaps, since they were rather blurred. But anyhow they were all turned face to the wall and on their backs were some brief captions – perhaps a description of the picture.* The dream did not seem to interest him for he went on to talk about his writing: in style he is what he liked to call a "minimalist"; he wished me to read the book, which had just been returned by a publisher, because it contained many of his theories. But he understood that I would not be able to do that so he told me about it while I repeatedly interrupted him to describe the method I used and to explain why telling me about his book was unlikely to prove helpful. He felt quite buoyed up by my being so "scientific".

To the second session he also brought a dream, two dreams in fact and he "could have produced many more if there had been enough time". In the first dream *he and the analyst were sitting on a red velvet couch having an ordinary friendly and polite conversation – but the analyst looked rather like the patient's wife.* The new book he is planning will consist entirely of conversations between himself and his wife. But then he had felt it a bit mean not to include the analyst in it somewhere as its content would undoubtedly be influenced by the analysis as they went along their parallel ways. He would make him a background figure named Jacobovitch; no, that was too aggressive – Jacob Stein – that would do. I will not report what I said to the patient because I was far more concerned to organise the boundaries of the analytical setting rather than to analyse the transference at this moment, but it had to do with the difference between our being pleasant to one another as working partners, and joining together, as he and his wife might be in danger of doing, to ridicule and rubbish the experience he might be having here. If we did that we could only produce a useless caricature of an analysis.

Further thought has led me to other conclusions but before entering into discussion of them I must give an account of an early week of another analysis, this also being a migratory patient who had had multiple previous periods of analysis all with therapists of recognised quality.

This second patient was a doctor from abroad who 'phoned me one day and said that he had been visiting a friend of mine who has written on autistic children and that he was having supervision with her. She recommended that he might also have supervision with me for some of his adult cases because, although he is a child psychiatrist, he does also treat adult patients. He said that he would be in England for two weeks and I arranged four hours with him.

I expected to see him arrive with notebooks and so on. There were no notebooks. He pulled up a chair close to me and began looking at me in a very scrutinising way. I thought, "Oh, oh, here we go!" Then he began to unroll his sad story about his bad experiences with psycho-analysts. He had attempted analysis with at least four analysts, and also with Primal Scream Therapists and Psycho-Bio-Energeticists, and said that really he had been unable to develop any confidence in any of them; none of them had done him any good and that this had gone on for a period of fifteen years. My heart was sinking. Then to my amazement he began to fire interpretations at me, such as, "I see that you have some difficulty with your sexuality and I do not know whether I would want to have analysis with you." That was news that he was planning to have analysis with me! He began to ask me personal questions and began to interpret at me, so I indicated to him that this was not the usual procedure. He decided that I was suffering from premature ejaculation and that I had had serious difficulties with my father. I thought, "Oh boy, what sort of a fellow have we here?" After this had gone on for two and a half of the four hours (I was very patient with him, I think) I said to him that this seemed to be his method of sizing me up to see if I were good enough to be his analyst and I added, "I suppose you realise that I also am sizing you up to see if it is possible for me to analyse you?"

At this he looked startled, scrutinised his watch and said that we only had fifteen minutes left; he hopped on the couch and began telling me his dreams. We had two splendid sessions after that. Then I said good-bye to him and as he went out of the door he said that he would be in touch; he would move to England and have analysis with me. My heart sank again.

Sure enough he 'phoned me up a month later. By that time I had figured out that he was not a psychiatrist. He had mainly worked as a general practitioner and had done some psychotherapy in a free-lance way. He popped up and we had two weeks of analysis in July before the holiday and it went very well – I was amazed. He worked beautifully with me and brought interesting material. He seemed a crazy fellow but he was working very well and I was quite pleased.

After the summer we started again and had our first week of work. I knew hardly anything about him because I could make neither head nor tail of the fragments of history that poured out of him. On Monday the main body of the session was taken up with a dream. This was that *he woke up in the middle of the night and heard a bang down in the basement that was either a gun shot or an electric fuse which had blown. He went down to see what was wrong but it seemed that he could not get deep enough into the basement to find out and as he was coming back he saw at the head of the stairs two naked figures, a man and a woman, they might have been his parents, he could not see for the light was very dim.* I began to explore this with him, saying that it had something to do with things that happen deep inside him and that make him very dim. He does give the appearance that he is almost mentally defective for he talks in so scatty and disorganised a way. It seemed as if it had something to do with his childhood and his feelings about his parents' sexuality. He told me that he had been very dim and had been thought mentally defective until about the age of eight when a school master named Mr Carlson took an interest in him and began to teach him and rescued him from being stupid. Within two years he became one of the brightest pupils in the class and went on to High School and Medical School. I did suggest to him that this bang in the basement probably had something to do with masturbatory orgasm. He absolutely did not hear me when I said that.

The next day, Tuesday, he came back and said that he was feeling very dim again, particularly about his driving. He had bumped into a car when he was backing into a parking space; he almost ran down some people when he was backing out of a parking space; and he had had a dream. In this dream *he was considering going down the road to buy an Amusement Park thinking that he could make a lot of money running it but then thought, no, it is probably illegal. So he went in the other direction and got up onto a chariot with a man who seemed to be very famous because there were crowds of people around cheering him. The patient felt that he was the only one who was clever enough to get up in the chariot with him, all these other people were just standing around cheering. Then a policeman came and arrested him.* We talked about jumping on the bandwagon and thinking that now he was on to a good thing with me and that soon I would get him a proper analytic training and set him up in practice. He was very pleased with that interpretation. He said that he did not really think that I was the kind of man who would have protegés and favourites and he would be quite satisfied if he could just have analysis with me. I was feeling very pleased as well.

The next day he came back and said that it had been a very good session the previous day and that he had had a dream that *he was the proprietor of a cafeteria and was getting food for himself. He had taken a lovely meat pie with something right in the middle of it. As he carried it to the table to eat, the middle part fell to the floor.* He had a second dream as well. He dreamed that *he was assisting the surgeon at an operation, but then it seemed that a skin graft had to be made and that it was going to be his own skin that was to be taken for it. They were going to take an elliptical piece of skin off his thigh to give to the patient.*

Then he launched into a story about a scar that he had on his thigh and how he had got this. It had been the consequence of his accompanying his big brother on a robbery when he was about eight years old. His brother was in the habit of breaking into clubs and robbing the slot machines by breaking the glass and getting all the coins out of the one-armed bandits. Having found his brother's cache of coins, which was kept in the garden shed, he had taken the jar and buried it. But his brother had beaten him up and made him give it back. Then his brother agreed to take him along and teach him his trade. So he took him on his next robbery but the club owners were waiting for them and when they got in through the window, suddenly the lights went on. They jumped out of the window again and he slid down the hill and in doing so some pieces of glass gashed his thigh. They ran home and the doctor came and patched him up and he has a scar there.

It seemed an obvious implication of the dream that if the skin was being taken from his thigh then he must also be the patient who was receiving the skin graft. I questioned him about the elliptical piece and he said that "elliptical" was not the right word. I suggested that "lenticular" was the word he sought. He agreed that this was correct as lenticular is pointed at the ends. I said that the lenticular piece of skin which was on the thigh apparently needed to be transplanted back where it came from, that it represented the patient's mouth. Something that used to be a function of his mouth seems to have become, through the relationship with his brother, a function of his bottom. And that the process of displacement downwards was illustrated in the other dream when the centre of the meat pie fell down onto the ground; that is that something connected with the nipple and his baby-mouth fell down and became connected with his faeces and anus.

He said that he did not know about that. He listened and was patient with me. The next day, a Thursday, he came in and said that he was feeling very dim again, that he could not think and that something seemed to be preventing him from functioning well. He had had an accident. Being early for his session he had parked about a mile away and was just sitting in his car waiting. When it was time he had pulled out of his parking place and had driven up to a T-junction. As he started to turn right, to his amazement suddenly there was a car in front of him and he ran into it.

Then began the following process of argument: that he did not really think that he had hit this other car although there was a dent in it and there was also a dent in his own car, but his car might not have been dented in that accident and the other car might also have been dented anyway. Besides, how was it that he had not seen the other car? It must have been going at a terrible speed for him not to have seen it. In fact when he put his brakes on his car had only moved one and a half feet whereas the other driver put on the brakes and the car had moved eight feet. I asked "How do you know it moved eight feet?" "Well, my car was touching the back of her car and there was eight feet in front." "Oh", I said, "it was a woman then." "Oh yes – she said that I had looked right at her. I did not see her. She got a little cross with me and said, 'Your car hit my car and that is all there is to it.' I don't know that it was my fault, maybe it was her fault. Who had the right of way? There were no signs saying who had the right of way."

This went on for about fifteen minutes. I was thinking to myself that his not seeing the car must have something to do with not paying attention. I said to him, "I think that perhaps you were preoccupied with something and really not paying attention to what you were doing." He answered that perhaps he had been paying attention to the other fellow who had come into the parking place behind him and had parked right in front of somebody's garage although a sign said "Garage in continual use. No parking." Nevertheless this other fellow had parked right there. When he had driven up and seen that he should not park in front of the garage he had moved on and parked in a proper place.

I suggested that when he had pulled out he had been so preoccupied with how virtuous he was that he had not been paying attention. He swept that aside and said that he had a dream to tell me.

In the dream *he seemed to be digging into the bottom drawer of a chest. It was not a fridge but he was looking for food. He found some strips of bacon and some cubes of beef and took them thinking to himself in the dream that his mother would not mind although he was going to be eating between meals by cooking for himself – she only minded if he ate sweets. So he took the bacon and beef and began to fry them in a frying pan and then he put them on a plate and was about to eat when a dog came and tried to grab the meat off his plate. He put his fist all the way down the dog's throat, far enough down past his teeth so that he could not bite – in fact he could not close his mouth.* That was the end of the dream.

It could be said with some justice that my two clinical examples do not immediately seem to supplement one another. My aristocratic author does not seem to be deceiving himself in the obvious way that my dubious psychiatrist does about the car accident. Clearly he is struggling to free himself from the burden of responsibility for its concrete financial, as well as emotional, implications. On the other hand we could say that both of them are revealing in *action* something that is central to their 'exotic life styles' with their peregrinating features, the same essential failure of development, the bizarre but childlike charm. One feels strongly that there is no harm in either of them but rather that something is wrong with their approch to life as well as to analysis.

Having thus equated them I propose now to ignore the fact of their being two distinct, complicated and, in a sense, interesting people. They are interesting because they are different from the well-adjusted, 'average' man of their respective cultures and because neither, despite many disappointments, has ceased to seek help in his struggle to lead a more useful life. As I say, I propose to ignore their individual separate identities and to weave together the phenomenology they have so splendidly displayed.

I want to start with the photographs which festoon the wall, which are "not very good" and, in any case, are facing the wall with their backs displaying a bit of the "minimalist's" art. I suggest that these represent visual data which have so quickly been transformed into language that they have never become available for thought, for integration with other sensa, for sequestration as memory nor for the evocation of emotion. Hence they are said to be "not well focused". But the piece of skin that was to be grafted from the thigh also had no specific destination. It was inaccurately said to be elliptical rather than lenticular. Both of these words have hidden in them the word 'lip' and 'lens' – the latter, I think, being a reference to the large, though not very thick, glasses worn by the patient which give him a rather lemur-like appearance. Both the dropping down of the middle part of the meat pie and the searching for meat in the bottom drawer suggest that the relationship of eye and mouth to the nipple has been dropped, or displaced downward to become a hand-to-mouth relation to the anus and faeces. This is strongly confirmed by the story of his brother's raids on the slot-machines by breaking the glass, and the patient's stealing of the glass jar with the loot and burying it. The scar on his thigh, also from glass, would correspond to the scar on his personality, as seen in the rubbishy ideas he dredges up to ward off the experience of the car accident, with Jacobovitch and the silenced analyst-dog hovering impotently in the background. The book of conversations between the patient and his wife is intended to evolve in parallel with the analysis and to constitute an analysis of the therapist. In both cases the feeling engendered in the initial contacts, of being on to a good thing, arouses the desire to capitalise on the experience in some parasitic way, by jumping on the band-wagon/chariot, for instance, in lieu of buying an amusement park that would be illegal. Fortunately a policeman arrests this move, as does the dog which grabs the food stolen from the bottom drawer.

May we assume that the trouble lies somewhere in the region of the deployment of attention? If you drive away from your analytic parking place full of self-adulation because you have respected the no-parking sign, unlike the next analytic baby-driver, you may very well not notice the problem at the T-junction any more than you noticed the policeman when you were feeling so superior to the groundlings who hadn't the wit to climb on to the chariot of fame. Similarly you will not get a well-focused view of the facts of your experience of analysis if you are so busy writing "minimalist" accounts of it for your mythical reading public or your putative guests at the next dinner party.

This brings us to confrontation with the thesis of this paper which I will state in terms of the psycho-analytical experience. As psychiatrists we are accustomed to take a history as part of the process of determining whether some form of therapy is called for. As psychoanalysts we are almost sure to hear, during the early weeks of an analysis, the story of the patient's life compounded of memory and family mythology. By the end of a useful analysis the story is quite different, not necessarily because different facts have emerged, but because the meaning of events and their importance for the patient's development have changed. Above all, what has changed is the interest in this history as an explanatory hypothesis.

I would suggest that this is one of the central gains in an analysis and a hallmark of movement from the paranoid-schizoid to the depressive position, namely a move away from explaining, and therefore of apportioning blame, towards trying to understand, and therefore to accept, the uncertainty inherent in the infinite complexity of human relationships and development. But what is the basis of this shift in mode of thought and value system?

Let me start to answer this by telling the second dream that my decadent aristocrat brought to his second session and reserved for the very end of it. In the dream *a man with a soldering iron which, however, also had a flame like a welding torch, seemed to be cutting off his clothes, starting at the feet and working upwards. It did not hurt but he did somewhat mind that it involved stripping away a green tweed suit which he does not at all like but for which he has a sentimental attachment.* It is the suit his father used to wear on the rare occasions that he attended the House of Lords.

The patient himself recognised that this was a representation of his experiences of the first session in which he had felt the analyst to be somewhat aggressively "scientific", but that it had not hurt and that he had rather liked it. It seemed very different from what he had expected on the basis of his earlier experiences of psycho-analysis.

In contrasting the two dreams, the "sitting on the red velvet couch" and "the man with the soldering iron", I am struck by the enormous difference between them. The former depicts a preconceived plan for using the analysis to write a story about his conversations with his wife in which the analyst is to be placed in the background, just as the photographs are turned face to the wall. In the second dream an unexpected experience has made an impact on him and has given a representation that is full of meaning and full of hope. Could we say that these two dreams are also a consequence of the splitting of his attention during the session, perhaps also indicated by his insistence on smoking although it is clear to him that no ash-tray being in evidence is meant to discourage this distracting practice? It is not such a deviation of attention as was seen in our psychiatrist at his T-junction, but is enough to render his experience of the session a rather passive one.

We should now be in a position to state the thesis in more theoretical terms thus: according to Bion, thinking about an emotional experience is necessary if there is to be any learning which can alter the structure of the personality in the direction of growth. This thinking has to start with the unconscious operation of alpha-function upon observations, the sensa, of the emotional experience. From this process comes the meaningful representations in symbolic form from which dream thoughts can be made as the first step towards their transformation into words or other symbolic forms as well as elevation to higher levels of abstraction and generalisation. If the assimilation of the experience into the unconscious is diverted by a splitting of attention to the facts or to a premature verbal transformation, then what results is a story or fiction embodying preconceptions. The essential emotional experience becomes unavailable for the evolution of a new idea. Meaning of an already elaborated nature is suffused into the facts, often requiring a distortion of the facts to fit. Such a construction is available then for recall in a mechanical way but not for the reconstructive, and far less certain, function of memory. Such recalled stories therefore carry with them a sense of certainty which cavalierly ignores the question of the factual accuracy of the original fiction.

By contrast, emotional experiences which are worked upon by unconscious processes and distilled for their meaning become learning experiences which alter the personality, what Bion calls "becoming O". Such experiences are not factually recalled but may be reconstructed, always with a sense of uncertainty about the facts, which, stripped of litigious significance, are not valued in themselves but for the meaning that was distilled from them.

By this same token we may consider that the so-called history that a person entertains of his development – and perhaps we should rather use the word 'autobiography' – will be seen largely to consist of events which have never been assimilated unconsciously, and thus have never contributed to his development. They constitute what could be called the 'personal myth' of his life, more or less correct factually but empty of what might be called 'autogenous meaning'. Instead the story is suffused with received meaning, usually of themes from popular culture. It is not surprising, therefore, if the story is full of 'traumatic' events, if we take this term to mean those events which so took the personality by surprise that they could not be assimilated, as Freud suggested for the "war neuroses". In this paper we are adding a more banal category, namely events in which the attention to the experience was so split or so diverted to fiction-formation that the unconscious processes were forestalled from operation.

Needless to say, what I have described is immediately recognisable as a ubiquitous phenomenon, starting quite early in childhood. But the extent to which it is deployed for the purpose of mastering emotions instead of experiencing them may place it as a serious deterrent to growth of the personality.

IX

An Enquiry into Lies, their Genesis and Relation to Hallucination

with
Dr Francesco Scotti (Perugia)

In giving us the Grid and the Theory of Thinking to enable us to think about thinking, Wilfred Bion has set us a hard task to fill it out with psycho-analytical clinical realisations. Even more difficult is the exercise that he has only hinted at, namely forming a Negative Grid to describe the genesis of lies, or *misrepresentations* of the truth. In this enquiry I will assume that the truth with which we are concerned is the immediate state of mind of the subject and its primary representation in dream and unconscious phantasy (Row C of the Grid). It is necessary at the outset to exclude the category described by Roger Money-Kyrle as the "misconceptions" derived from the mating of a preconception with an inadequate realisation. I am not concerned with *errors* in conception or, if they exist, of *errors* in representation. Rather I wish to approach the problem which Freud sometimes thought lay at the basis of repression, namely tampering with the truth, 'Bowdlerising' as it is called in relation to history and its documentation.

The method of exposition I wish to pursue is as follows. First, I will present the material brought by Dr Scotti to the seminar in Perugia in October, 1982; then there will follow an exposition of the theoretical model for organising our understanding of the material; and finally the discussion. But as a preliminary, in order to help the reader to focus his attention on the salient phenomena, we must mention one particular aspect of Bion's model of the mind as an organ of thought. In framing the hypothesis that the first step in thought formation is essentially a mysterious, unobservable mental function which he has termed alpha-function, Bion has followed the great tradition in philosophy which assumes that objects are not directly knowable but only construable from the phenomena they generate. This unobservable alpha-function may, under certain circumstances (or perhaps always, in parallel) operate in reverse, cannibalising the partially formed alpha-elements. The products of this reversal of function Bion has described as "not beta-elements, but rather beta-elements with traces of ego and superego". A mind-boggling suggestion.

Clinical material

A woman of thirty-eight had had a tormented history of some fourteen years of mental illness, made worse at its outset by hospital treatment with drugs and electro-convulsive therapy. During the last ten years she has been under psycho-therapeutic care and eventually a systematic psycho-therapy with slow but unmistakeable progress in being freed from delusion and hallucination. At the time of the sessions to be presented she was married with a one-year-old daughter and was working in a large factory.

The session of the Wednesday before had been cancelled owing to my being ill.

Session I

She begins by asking me if I am better.

I reply that I am. The patient comments that, unlike her, I get better quickly.

She tells me that last Wednesday not even the cleaning woman showed up. The patient telephoned her and the woman was cross. Today she had her come to the house to explain and found out that the woman had had heart trouble and wanted to reduce her working hours. So she felt wicked.

I tell her that she has felt herself to be abandoned twice in the same day.

She replies that she had a dream the previous night. She dreamt on the Wednesday too. *She finds herself in the presence of Fratello Gino together with many other visitors. The scene occurs in a large building like a school. Many people have brought presents and among these is a statue of Fratello Gino. The name of the person who gave the present is written on it but nobody knows who it is. The patient says, "It's the name of somebody from my town. I'll go and see and find out who it is." She goes to see but finds she is mistaken because it is the name of a shop and not of a person.* In the second part of the dream *she is walking along a road by herself.*

In commenting on her dream she explains that Fratello Gino is a saintly man like Padre Pio and has replaced him in popular worship since Padre Pio's death; he too has the stigmata. He is a spiritual man, different from Padre Gabriele who cures people. She does not go to him to obtain a cure but only to ask that he should pray for her.

She has been to Fratello Gino several times, sometimes with her first fiancé, at other times with her brother. Fratello Gino discovered the sexual things she did with her fiancé and scolded her. But the fiancé did not listen. He is dead, and her brother is dead. She says that the presents are associated in her mind with Christmas: last Christmas her father was still with them. In the last few days she and her husband went to see her mother-in-law. She is afraid that her mother-in-law is going to die too.

When I draw her attention to the part played by the statue in the dream her face changes and she looks into space. She says that she now sees the statue in the dream twined round by a serpent which is the sign of the Devil . . . She adds that Fratello Gino is a deacon and also has the power to exorcise . . .

She reverts to talking about the cleaning woman who was cross. Afterwards she felt badly not to have thought that there might have been a good reason for her not coming. I tell her that she cannot stand being abandoned even for good reasons by the cleaning woman or by me.

We talk about the next session. She has some difficulty because she does not know with whom she can leave the baby and she has to give up going to work to come to me. But she does not want to interrupt the therapy at this moment.

Session II

There is a long silence at the beginning.

I suggest continuing to examine last Friday's dream.

She says that the statue was, in fact, ugly and has been exchanged in her mind, at the moment, by a wooden statue of a serpent. This deals with Fratello Gino being tempted, a temptation of a sexual kind. She sums up the reading from yesterday's Mass (the Immaculate Conception) as Adam's sin and Eve who blames the serpent.

I comment that the sin that the Bible talks about is connected with the desire for supreme knowledge, accessible through the fruit of the tree of the knowledge of good and evil. Perhaps the reference to temptation of a sexual kind can be attributed to the idea that impulses of this kind coming to the surface in her might bring about destruction.

She says that in this period she does not feel like making love with her husband. She feels like working for her daughter and in the house. When she has to make love she feels tired. She thinks that this is the effect of drugs.

I comment that she seems able to do what is asked of her as duty rather than what causes her pleasure. The fact that she connects lack of pleasure with the effect of drugs could be interpreted like this: that sexual pleasure should be controlled because it comes from an internal stimulus felt as dangerous and destructive, the same kind as those held at bay by drugs. (I took the liberty of talking about the drugs mentioned by the patient as if they were a mental event and not a biological one, which they usually are, for two reasons: the dose of thiordazine that the patient was taking at the time was a minimal

95

10mg.; she herself complained bitterly every time I suspended the drugs that I left her at the mercy of her bad thoughts).

She says that it is true that she finds it easier to choose duty rather than pleasure. She talks about the disgust she sometimes feels when making love.

I ask her to tell me more details about these unpleasant circumstances.

She says that the seminal fluid disgusts her. Then, with some reluctance, she adds that it makes her think of many children. She adds that she is afraid of falling pregnant although she would like another child.

I comment that what she says should probably be taken literally, that in the seminal fluid there are a lot of children who attack and destroy her.

She receives this idea in silence. A moment later she seems relieved. She says that today she felt very depressed and only the idea of coming to therapy gave her the urge to move herself. She talks in a more involved way about her daughter and husband.

Anamnesic elements connected with the dream

The first element concerns the patient's religiosity. Both she and her husband are involved in religious experiences felt very deeply from an emotional point of view and they regularly seek charismatic figures. She feels that I am critical of this kind of religious behaviour although I have never expressed anything about this. She had never told me about Fratello Gino before. He lives in a convent some thirty kilometres distant from Perugia and attracts many patients from the clinic. On the other hand she had talked much about Padre Gabriele. I suggested that the mention of these visits to the priest was intended to encourage me to offer more of my attention and time. My intervention irritated her very much and she answered that Padre Gabriele did not compete with my therapy even if he cured her temporarily. As can be seen, the patient is still intolerant of interruption but this is slight compared to her aversion to my talking during the first two years of therapy when she arrived and talked during the whole hour with strong emotional participation without leaving any time for my own words. At that time she devoted herself to the ill will that everybody, but mostly her parents, entertained towards her.

The second anamnesic element concerns the three deceased figures, the fiancé, brother, father. I was somehow involved in their fatal history. At the time of her fiancé's death from leukaemia, in 1972, the patient was already being treated at the centre. Although I devoted much time and attention to her, for instance I went with her to talk with the doctor who was treating her fiancé and who warned her of his imminent death, she does not retain any memory of me in that period. She also denies having felt the violent emotions I saw her express. During these years of therapy she talked a lot about her dead fiancé and built up a more and more rigid and poor image. There he appears as a vulgar man, merely interested in the erotic component of their relationship; she suffered his sexual initiative owing to her naïveté or because she was ill, never because of a voluntary acceptance; this would constitute an intolerable fault for her. She seldom admits to having felt genital emotions and, even more rarely, feelings of tenderness.

The history of her brother is even more tragic. In 1973 he presented a psychotic crisis and was treated at the centre but died owing to a fall during a flight from the hospital. After her brother's death the patient, who was under psychiatric treatment, kept on coming to the centre but after six months she decided to give up for she had realised that she felt in a dilemma about her brother's death; it was either my fault or hers.

As regards the third deceased person, her father, she was severe in her judgment; either he appears as violent and suspicious (she said that he wanted her to be a prostitute), or she feels that she has not done enough to return his love.

Discussion

It would appear that Dr Scotti's patient has not only made very considerable strides in the organisation of her life but that progress in the recovery of her capacities for thought based on self observation has in all probability made these strides possible. But her relation to the analysis and the analyst is highly ambiguous. On the one hand she feels herself in great need of its continuity and appears to make ample use of it, in contrast to the early years which were largely devoted to the outpouring of her anguish. On the other hand the positive therapeutic role in her life is played by her religion and its representatives. There is much to suggest that Dr Scotti, who is held to be an atheistic communist with a preoccupation with sex, stands for the satanic forces which the patient feels that she must confront and resist as she had failed to resist the seductions of her fiancé due to her youth and "naïveté".

This splitting of her objects produces states of confusion when separations, as with both the cleaning woman and Dr Scotti, make her aware of the harsh judgmental quality which is "wicked" in herself. The central material of the two sessions from December 1981, develops this theme of evil wrapping itself around good until its quality becomes indeterminate (the name of the person who sent a gift of a statue to Fratello Gino). Although Fratello Gino is meant only to pray for the patient rather than to cure her, we learn that he discovers her sexuality with her fiancé (and by implication with her brother and father) for which he scolds her. But fiancé, brother and father die. This is her theory: God punishes people who take advantage of her virginal innocence, although Dr Scotti seems "to get better quickly". Nonetheless one has the impression that, like her mother-in-law, he is listed for destruction.

It is in this context that an attempt to explore the dream further brings a vivid phantasy, almost hallucinated ("flashes", some patients call them). The close connection between the cleaning woman and Dr Scotti leaves little doubt that he, or rather his wicked sexual tongue, is the serpent. The following session bears out the thesis that resistance to her husband's sexual demands represents an identification with Fratello Gino's resistance to sexual temptation. Likewise it stands in opposition to Dr Scotti who is felt to be enthusiastic for pleasure rather than duty in sexual activity. Conflict now appears openly. The desire for another child versus her fear of pregnancy and disgust for semen. But the relief she feels towards the end of the session seems to be less the result of interpretation than of her successful resistance to the satanic voice of pleasure.

A session six months later, by showing the progress she has made in discerning her own misrepresentations of the truth, throws a bright beam on this interesting dream. The patient is now in mid-term of her second pregnancy.

Session III

The patient's gynaecologist has suggested that her maternity leave from work be prolonged. One of the reasons he has mentioned is the patient's mental state but she needs a certificate from her psychiatrist. She does not want to ask me for it at first but then she does. She does not want me to certify anything false but is worried about the certificate on headed paper from the Mental Health Centre because it could damage her reputation and that of her children. She expresses a series of phantasies on this subject: if she should die suddenly and they discover this certificate? This had happened in the case of her father when after his death his children found out about the illnesses that he had had (presumably luetic).

She tells me that she has destroyed all the clinical files of her admissions to hospital. She was worried that her husband might read them. She adds, "Terrible things, not true! They talked about my homosexuality." (In fact the records had merely mentioned, in passing, a sexual incident at the age of five.)

I comment that perhaps she is not the first not to accept the bad image that comes from the files. Now she is afraid of my certificate because I might give her an image of herself which she will have to keep in front of her. I tell her under what conditions I agree to write the certificate; not that its content be true but that it be opportune; and provided that it does not interfere with the therapy which cannot be based on a certificate. I refuse to reply to her questions about the certificate – I shall write "state of depression" as that is what the gynaecologist wrote on the previous certificate.

She tells me that she has collected all the clinical files of her admissions to hospital and that her first fiancé had helped her. She adds: "He has not read them either", but then, as if she had just made an effort to remember, "My fiancé then died."

Discussion

Six months later we see that the transference situation has changed. In the interim the patient became pregnant once more and presents Dr Scotti with a double bind situation regarding the psychiatric certificate entitling her to have additional maternity leave from her job. Either way he is in danger: on the one hand of lying, and sharing the fate of her father, brother and fiancé and, on the other, by letting the truth emerge he would be "damaging her reputation". But clearly her reputation has been built on lies, as her marriage seems to have been, since she destroyed all the hospital records to hide her history of mental illness from her prospective spouse. Or were the records untrue ("talked about my homosexuality", an incident from when she was five)?

Dr Scotti takes the position that he may tell the truth, but not the whole truth, as this would not be "opportune", provided that he thinks that his so acting will not interfere with the therapy. Then something very interesting happens: the patient tells a lie about her former fiancé, makes an effort to correct it, and is moved, evidently by tender and grateful feelings towards this man about whom she has built up such a vulgar, even sinister picture. But the next moment she swings back to her theory that the wages of sin is death and the logical fallacy *post hoc-propter hoc*. We see the struggle between truth and lies enacted before our eyes.

During the seminar, at this point in the discussion, Dr Scotti was reminded of an hallucination that the patient had had four years previously when her psychotic manifestations were still frequently in evidence during the sessions. At one certain point when the therapist was attempting to intervene with some interpretative comment the patient became hallucinated and subsequently reported that she had seen a figure swathed in bandages from head to foot – Lazarus, probably. In a later session she was able to give further information regarding the development of this figure and relevant associations to it. It seems that at the moment Dr Scotti began to talk, her attention was drawn to his short cuffs which were showing beyond his coat sleeves. The hallucination was not a momentary 'flash' but rather developed by a slow process, presumably occurring during the duration of his talking to her: these cuffs seemed to emerge from his sleeves and gradually wrap themselves about his body until he became an anonymous figure completely swathed in bandages. While "Lazarus" was her spontaneous exclamation her later associations ran to her brother whose death had been from a head wound sustained on his flight from mental hospital. The last time she had seen him his head had been similarly swathed.

It seems strongly suggested that the Dr Scotti who "gets better quickly" in 1981 is connected with the Lazarus figure of 1978, for Lazarus certainly 'got better quickly' thanks to Jesus. What Dr Scotti recovers from is the tissue of lies with which he tends to be wrapped, like her father and former fiancé, being made into a satanic figure of vice, atheism and seduction. The patient's attempt to maintain a severe splitting of self and objects, whereby her own destructive impulses can be projected onto the "bad", that is, absent cleaning woman, Scotti, dead father-brother-fiancé, to form satanic objects (Bion's "super"-ego), has clearly lost force. She has begun to recognise that the Fratello Gino who prays for her and the Dr Scotti who thinks about her, are conjoined in some way against what is "wicked", demanding and uncompromising in herself, represented earlier by the hallucination of the cuffs which emerge to swathe Dr Scotti, and later by the image of the serpent which enwraps and eventually replaces the statue of Fratello Gino.

While the imagery of the patient's dreams and 'flashes' of phantasy suggest that a wicked Lilith-tongue is busy perverting the truth, it seems more likely, judging from the "Lazarus" episode, that the chief agent of misrepresentation is the patient's organ of vision. I do not say 'eye' because this would imply that vision, the capacity to form visual images of one's experiences, was restricted to the ocular apparatus, while what I wish to convey is the broader visual function of the various senses. The adage that 'seeing is believing' expresses the common sense view of reality testing, but it does not take into account the extent to which our visual image of an event is compounded of all the senses available (the Bionic "common sense").

The central point that this material illustrates so beautifully is this: the compounding of the data of an emotional experience is not merely mechanical, like fitting the sound track to a film; rather it is this mysterious alpha-function which Bion has named for us. By a mysterious creative act of mind the data of the various senses are introduced into the container (Keats's 'chamber of maiden thought') where the thirst for knowledge (K-link) and the dynamism of concern for one's love objects (Ps←→D, with the catalyst of a "selected fact") can produce a dream image in which meaning is trapped, like light in a diamond, to borrow Bion's image. And it is this mysterious process, he suggests, that can also be reversed in mid-stream, as it were, to produce a tissue of lies, misrepresentations. These are the stuff of which hallucinations are made. In the patient's material, starting with the 1978 experience of the "Lazarus" figure and culminating in the decay of the dream image of the statue of Fratello Gino, we see the step-by-step process, as if in slow motion, like the fading rather than the blossoming of a flower, whereby the tissue of lies winds itself about the true dream-image until it is no longer recognisable.

But this extraordinary material, so carefully observed and faithfully reported, suggests something further and goes some distance to demonstrate it in action. It suggests that, armed with this Theory of Thinking which Bion has given us, we have a conceptual tool for unravelling misrepresentations, stripping them away to reveal the dream image, the true representation of the meaning of the emotional experience. I will not say that this is a new dimension of psychoanalytical work, for in fact we have unwittingly been doing it, albeit clumsily, from the beginning. For instance, one can see Freud doing it with Dora. Perhaps it looks a bit too much like Sherlock Holmes, but we learn from Bion's *A Memoir of the Future* that Conan Doyle's character made a deep impression on Bion's ways of observing and thinking. After all, we can, in our consulting rooms, be Counsel for the Defence of the loving and creative aspects of the patient's personality rather than the Prosecuter of his criminal side.

The Concept of a Negative Grid

The particular model of the mind which emerges from the line of development of psycho-analytical thought, from Freud through Melanie Klein to Bion, presents a Platonic and theological picture or metaphor of how the mind operates to generate meaning. In this sense it steps forward from the endless mind-body debate to suggest that, in fact, we live out lives at both levels – symbolic and asymbolic. At the animal level of gratification of physiological need we are able, almost like protozoa, to gravitate towards suitable sources of satisfaction and away from unsuitable or threatening sources. In *Explorations in Autism* we named this the "one-dimensional" level, for we felt that its operations were richly displayed in "autism proper". Bion and Esther Bick, in their explorations of groups on the one hand, and skin-container functions on the other, described the level of mindless conformity and mimicry implemented by forms of deeply narcissistic identifications, whereby two-dimensional adaptation to the environment, particularly the human milieu, is achieved.

These developments threw a new light on the suggestion, implicit in all of Melanie Klein's work, that the internal world of objects is experienced in an absolutely concrete sense in the unconscious, and is primary for the establishment of the emotional meaning of our intimate relationships. This image of a threefold adaptation to the external world provided a powerful model for construing the events of the psycho-analytical consulting room and has, indeed, been eagerly taken up in some quarters for elucidating the phenomena of social life in humans (and perhaps in higher animals as well).

It was against this background that Bion's Theory of Thinking made such a powerful impact, and I must admit that my own comprehension of its revolutionary significance had to wait until *Attention and Interpretation* made clear the correlation of his theory with the formulation of levels of dimensionality. An entirely new background for the classification and comprehension of mental development and mental aberration has emerged allowing, amongst other matters, a first comprehensive view of psycho-somatic processes.

But what concerns us in this paper is a first attempt to take up Bion's suggestion that, in so far as truth is the food of the mind's growth and development, and lies are its poison, it is essential that, in parallel with a theory of thinking for the elaboration of the truth, there must be a theory of unthinking for destruction of truth or the elaboration of lies. Clearly we are not intending to enter upon any philosophical debate of the "what is truth?" variety, for the meaning we are oriented towards is unambiguous. We mean, of course, truthful-*ness* versus *un*-truthful-*ness*, or what Bion calls the plus and minus K-link in emotional human relations. And we are not, in the first instance, concerned with how people represent their states of mind to others but with how they represent, and *mis*-represent, these states to themselves, to their own "organ of consciousness".

In his periodic table for the growth and use of thoughts, the Grid, Bion had included the function of mis-representation only in Column 2, a misuse of thoughts, known to be untrue, for hiding our ignorance from ourselves. But further on in *The Elements of Psycho-analysis* he suggested that a more comprehensive format for the investigation of untruth would be a Negative Grid, the negativistic mirror image of the Grid as it were. Within this model for describing the processes of thought (formation, growth and use) the first mysterious step is symbol-formation, or alpha-function as Bion calls it. It seems essential, in attempting to explore the phenomenology of a Negative Grid, that we start at this point, the formation of true and false symbols for representing the meaning of our emotional experiences.

Stated in this way the problem of primal lies or misrepresentations poses us a critical problem. The Kleinian hagiography of the internal world seems to throw up, in accordance with the theory of envy, an image of a rather satanic aspect of the personality, the 'root of all evil', we might say. It is a simplistic picture but a useful starting point, much more functional in the consulting room than the theory of life and death instincts. Our initial problem is this: granting that this satanic part of the personality often presents itself as highly intellig- ent, does close examination of its mental processes bear this out? Examination of the techniques of the pamphleteer and pornographer, the demagogue and the propagandist, suggests that what looks like high intelligence is in fact a compound of speed and negativism that 'dazzles' the mind and interferes with rational honest thought.

In keeping with this comforting realisation about the "enemies of promise", we find Bion's suggestion of "alpha-function in reverse" generating "beta-elements with traces of ego and superego" – a formulation which left us aghast with incomprehension at first – to be a most pregnant proposition (see Chapter XI). The present paper is the next step in the utilisation of his idea that a simple process (from the point of view of mental operations) destroys the incipient alpha- elements (symbols) and reduces them to a rubble which cannot be used for thinking but only for evacuation as action, hallucination, somatic disturbance or Basic Assumptions Group behaviour. This, Bion's ultimate theory of the formation of "bizarre objects" and their place in "soma-psychotic" disturbances, seems to me to be the bril- liant addendum to Freud's amazing description of the formation of delusional systems spelled out in the Schreber case. Such are the leaps-in-the-dark that genius can make!

On the other hand, along with its comforting aspects, this formula- tion presented a gloomy picture of the irreversible destruction which such a process of 'cannibalisation' must wreak. In keeping with the idea of "minute fragmentation" which explorations of schizophrenic processes by such workers in the field as Hannah Segal and Herbert Rosenfeld had added to Melanie Klein's concept of splitting processes and Freud's idea of the "world destruction phantasy", restoration of the destroyed objects, or, in Bion's terms, the truth *about* these objects, seemed an impossible task. Accordingly some people, myself amongst them, felt, on the basis of long and intensive therapy of such patients, that a part of the personality caught up in the delusional system could never be recovered for integration within the operational personality. The present paper calls this pessimistic view into question, for it suggests that the reversal of alpha-function does not perhaps consist of a destruction of the forming alpha-element (which may be inde- structible once it has become formed enough to be available for memory) but only a covering over by the 'tissue of lies' which Dr Scotti's patient illustrates.

Thus the dream image of the "statue of Fratello Gino", an expres- sion of gratitude which we can recognise as really Gino-Scotti, becomes enveloped by the serpent, and is eventually replaced by it, just as Dr Scotti had become swathed in the elongating shirt cuffs of the patient's hallucination of some years before to form the "Lazarus" figure. The origin of this swathing in her image of her brother's injured head (and by extension with her dying father and fiancé) gives particular poignancy to the moment of insight into her former fiancé's kindness and loyalty to her which had been swathed in such accusations of ruthless sexual corruption of her sexual innocence. At that moment-of-truth the patient would have to recognise her own "wickedness" as she had had to do about the cleaning woman's heart trouble as the cause of her absenting herself, and by implication the fact that Dr Scotti "gets well quickly" like Lazarus. If this is the situation in the mind, that the true symbol cannot be destroyed but only covered over, hope must exist that the truth will shine through, that it can 'dawn' on the benighted mind.

X

Clinical Application of Bion's Concept 'Transformations in Hallucinosis'

In every field, science or art, the vision of the genius requires a backup from workers in the field to give to the "imaginative conjecture" its practical realisation. In psycho-analysis this takes the form of discovering the clinical phenomena which correspond to the theoretical formulation derived from inspired reflection. Freud did much of this "field-work" himself, while Melanie Klein's strength lay in the discovery of phenomena for which precise theoretical formulations had to be achieved later. Bion is different from either, for on the basis of clinical practice a massive conceptual framework was gradually constructed, from *Experiences in Groups* to *Attention and Interpretation*, for which clinical reference was largely implicit rather than explicit. It is certainly from no preconceived plan that I find myself, in the last five years, giving lecture after lecture and writing paper after paper illustrating Bion's ideas with clinical material. Clearly his ideas are the current diamonds in the cutting head of my tool for exploring the unconscious with myself, my patients and supervisees. I confess without shame that the concept "transformations in hallucinosis" left me blank for years, while Bion's more specific ideas about the phenomenon of hallucination proper seemed immediately to link with my clinical experience. Only recently has its meaning dawned, no, burst upon me with a particular patient, lighting up an obscure area from many clinical experiences in the past.

Bion's theory seems to be this: when there is an impediment in the process of transformation of the perception of emotional experiences into symbolic form, or what he calls alpha-elements to be used in dreaming, something has to be done to get rid of this stimulation of the mental apparatus by the emotional experience. His idea is that the evacuation of the stimulation is mainly in one of two forms: either it is transformed into group behaviour of the type described as the Basic Assumption Group mentality; or it is transformed into somatic disturbance. This latter is the basis of his theory of psycho-somatic disorders. But there is a third method of evacuation which is through the sense organs themselves, by reversing their functions so that instead of taking sensa in, they give out the data as beta-elements which form hallucinations.

Related to hallucinations there is another type of disturbance in thinking that Bion has called "transformations in hallucinosis". As I have said, this is a concept which I have found extremely puzzling. On the other hand I have long been convinced that it is an important concept because I could see that it had a reference to clinical phenomena which were inadequately described and linked by existing ideas of psychopathology. It can be applied to people who seem to have a disturbance in their perception of their environment which takes the form of absolute conviction about what is in other people's minds and the meaning of their behaviour. Thus instead of forming opinions about what other people think and feel on the basis of the evidence of their behaviour, what they say – and this is apparent from their deportment – is that they have convictions of *knowing* what the other person means. This is not even experienced as intuited but as 'given', 'obvious'.

In the past I had assumed that this was a variant of omniscience and that omniscience was a consequence of states of projective identification of the sort I have described in a paper called 'The Delusion of Clarity of Insight'. The phenomenon that I described there seemed to be the consequence of a state of projective identification with the mind and the sense organs of the internal object (being inside Mummy's or Daddy's head, looking out of their eyes, listening with their ears and so on). But that type of disturbance does not involve a falsification of the observed data, nor is there an incapacity to think about them. Instead of convictions we see the operation of judgment-forming opinions which are held with unusual force considering the data available. The phenomenon which Bion describes as "transformations in hallucinosis" involves a falsification of the data of perception of the external world as well as the incapacity to think about them to form opinions. The meaning of things seems just to be given – that is the perception of the data and the meaning are not differentiated, things *mean* what they *seem*. Yet again it is different from the flatness of a two-dimensionality where the meaning of perceptions is purely conventional and in that sense 'given'. Transformations in hallucinosis seem to be most apparent in people with a paranoid disposition. Because ideas about paranoia tend to combine ideas about omniscience on the one hand with concepts of poverty of imagination on the other, I had assumed that these patients somehow could not construct alternative hypotheses about the meaning of things in order to exercise judgment. However, it was very difficult to support the idea that paranoid personalities were lacking in imagination because, in fact, they seem extremely imaginative. An alternative hypothesis suggests that their thinking is perhaps similar to the thinking of the Basic Assumption Group mentality, that is that all ideas are derived logically from a basic paranoid assumption. On the other hand it is often clear that the same rigidity of thought may exist in the paranoid personality quite outside any area of paranoid feelings or system of ideas. The rigidity is there even without the paranoia.

This then was the clinical problem to which Bion's hypothesis about transformations in hallucinosis seemed to commend itself as a rich idea. Since I do not feel at all certain of Bion's meaning, I must report on my own thinking as it has been stimulated by his writing. My thought goes something like this: the transformations in hallucinosis are different from hallucinations in that they do not involve the perception of objects that are not there in external reality, but they involve the perceptions of relationships that are not there. That is hallucination involves the sensory experience of bizarre objects, and these are bizarre for the reason that they exist outside the system of meaning – they are meaningless objects and therefore they belong to the general world of delusions and delusional systems. But although transformations in hallucinosis are within the world of symbol formation, thought and meaning, there is something disordered about the quality of the thought that has gone into them. And this produces something similar to poverty of imagination and rigidity. Bion's idea seems to be that the transformations in hallucinosis derive from processes in which the emotional experiences have begun to be transformed into alpha-elements, dreamed and thought about, but that then the process is reversed and the dreams and alpha-elements are cannibalised back to a primitive state, similar to beta-elements, which are then evacuated by reversal of the function of the sense organs and taken back again as new perceptions.

We may see something analogous to this when we observe a child trying to build something, say with Lego. He starts constructing something and then, at a certain point, he becomes discouraged or anxious and he smashes it to pieces. But the smashing does not just disintegrate the construct into the individual pieces of the Lego but rather into partial structures. There are a few little pieces stuck together, the wheels and axle of a car, part of the bonnet and windscreen and so on. These little pieces are not meaningless primary shapes for they retain traces of 'automobile-ishness'. In Bionic terms the alpha-elements which are reduced to debris by destruction do not revert to being beta-elements, but to beta-elements "with traces of ego and superego", i.e. shreds of meaning. The debris is then evacuated through reversal of sensory function as with hallucinations. When they are taken in again they are perceived as already having shreds of meaning bound to them. Therefore the patient does not perceive events and objects that he needs to think about in order to derive meaning – he perceives objects with the meaning already contained. Moreover he is quite unaware of having any difficulty thinking about them because he experiences things as implicitly meaningful.

I would like now to present some clinical material which may illustrate this theory. Professor A is a successful academic in the field of the political sciences who has come to England on a sabbatical from his university in a Commonwealth country. He is accompanied by his wife, who is also an academic, and their three children. While his main purpose in coming to England was for study in relation to his research, he had also decided to use the opportunity to have the experience of analysis, for its theories had come to play an integral part in his professional equipment. He is a tall, good-looking man who wears spectacles and sports a short beard. He looks, perhaps, a little younger than his forty-five years. This may be a matter of demeanour for he is faultlessly polite and meticulous of speech, but with a touch of subservience, suggestive of a public school boy. The flatness and blandness of his speech does not immediately strike one as in excess of the customary accents of his country, but there is something rather arresting in his use of local colloquialisms, with mock innocence, often followed by apology and translation. The impact of this is clearly patronising and reflects upon his demeanour in a way that suggests general insincerity.

The first two months of the four-times-weekly analysis were full of surprises for me which I shall try to cull from what was otherwise an orderly and systematic review of his past life and experiences which he assumed I expected. I shall not discuss the history itself but will concentrate rather on the observations which led me to the conclusion that I was seeing, in pure culture as it were, the phenomenon of transformation in hallucinosis. The first surprise was when, one day in the first few weeks, he described how surprised the family was at the dirtiness of the English atmosphere. He said that, of course, he understood that so highly industrialised a country as England must suffer from smog, with pollution and inversion of the atmosphere, as occasionally happened in his own native city. I was somewhat amazed at his unquestioning acceptance of both his observation and its presumed explanation – that is dirtiness – since he was living, not in a city, but in the heart of Oxfordshire, and it was early autumn, a time of damp and of stubble burning from the harvest. When I raised the question with him he replied blandly that he recognised these other factors but that both his wife and children agreed with him that the air was filthy and smelly and that one need only wipe a finger over any surface to verify this. I should say here that his judgment, which was not given as an opinion but as a statement of fact, had an extraordinarily insulting impact on me.

The very fact of my having raised some question about the accuracy of the Professor's observations evoked a series of dreams in which his exuberance and friendliness were cut short by rebuff or disaster. He became very touchy and irritable with me and clearly felt that he was being scrutinised in an unfriendly way. Then he brought a dream: *that the house across the street from his parents' home had been burnt out in the upper floor and that the two windows were just black holes.* It turned out, upon investigation, that in fact one of the sons of the family that lived across the street had committed suicide. Furthermore the patient revealed that his own birth had been straddled by two dead babies, one before he was born and another baby soon after.

After my interpreting that I seemed to him to be this burnt-out mother with very persecuting eyes, he became shallow and chatty for several sessions and I had great difficulty in bringing him back to the evidence of depression. Finally he relented and admitted, near to tears, that he had always felt that he needed, as he called it, to "keep himself alive". By this he meant that he lacked *joie de vivre*, he had to force himself to take an interest in things, to seek any pleasure or to form any plans. It then appeared that the present trip to England for study was in fact one of a series of rather inexplicable flights to foreign lands: there was one after finishing his doctorate; another after the birth of his first child; and this present one was in fact on the heels of the death of his mother.

Following this, in an atmosphere of mixed resentment and relief, he produced two very interesting dreams which are at the heart of the matter of this paper. In the first *he was attempting to enter a cave from which a torrential river was pouring forth.* In the second *there seemed to have been some disaster and wounded people were pouring through the doors into the emergency department of a hospital.* In the first dream then the river was pouring out, and in the second wounded people were pouring in. His only association was that he had dreamed of this cave many times before but the only specimen that he could remember was of one in which he was the member of a choir that was singing inside the cave. All I could suggest to him at that point was that these dreams had something to do with the way in which he talked and listened, and had some reference to the experience of the analysis. A series of "disasters" followed in succeeding days. First there was an episode of severe chest pain; then he had an accident in the home. He was injured by a tin of fruit falling off a shelf in the kitchen damaging his nose quite badly. This happened while he was seeking food, naked, at three o'clock in the morning in the dark. Such foraging turned out to be his usual habit. Finally he missed a session because he had left his car lights on so that the battery was flat when he came to drive to me. I tentatively linked this flatness of the battery with the flatness of his voice and the unmusical torrent that can pour out of his mouth when he becomes shallow, chatty and tangential. He became quite explosive and almost rushed from the room. But he quietened down and finally told me that he was "sick and tired of people getting at me about my voice" – something I had never heard about before.

The incident of the missed session proved very interesting and helpful. When he had telephoned he had been at the railway station only five minutes walk from the consulting room, but he had elected to wait for a man whom he knew to have jump leads because he had allowed this man to take a lead from his own battery the week before. Since he had not joined the AA or RAC he was convinced that no emergency service would be available. It was during this session that he had acknowledged that he was a "frightened" person and that he had been "sent to analysis by friends for the sake of my family". Why? He did not know. But being sent to analysis was somehow linked in his mind with an incident when he, an inexperienced rider, had been put by friends on a mare which promptly ran away with him, "rushing over ditches and fences to get to the stallion". It seemed that his mother had become pregnant with him one month after the death of the previous child and again became pregnant of a stillborn child one month after the patient's own birth – "rushing to get to the stallion".

After this piece of work he seemed to settle into a more comfortable relationship with me and to take more interest in my comments, but he began to feel persecuted at the university where he was sitting in on various seminars. In the context of a tirade against a certain lecturer named Mrs Santini, he evoked a vivid and totally imaginary picture of what her husband must be like: a little, greasy-haired Italian, a little cock of the walk with no accomplishments but his military fascist manner. Thereupon he dreamed *that a nasty traffic warden gave him a £10 fine not because his car was incorrectly parked but because he had failed to report a man whose car was wrongly parked.*

There was little doubt that I was this Mr Santini-Traffic-Warden-Daddy, small, aggressive and unjust, punishing him for failure to report material about the part of himself which broke analytic rules by missing sessions and withholding material. I was accused of "ordering" him to remain in Mrs Santini's seminar, like his father who had "ordered" him to join the scouts. He acknowledged that the only way to deal with his father was "dumb insolence" and could not be certain that he had not practised the same technique with me. And the strife became even worse over a dream *that his adoptive daughter, a sick looking squaw, was to married to a sweaty, fat African politician and he, the patient, had to arrange the ceremony. But he had lost the ring. Eventually it was seen to have been stolen by a sparrow which was perched with it in its beak on the rooftop.* We seemed to fall into a hopeless conflict over my suggestion that this was a denigrated picture, like the one of Santini, of myself and my wife: he had never suggested that these people were inferior; I was accusing him of racial prejudice. True, they were not a beautiful couple: the bride certainly looked more fit for the casualty department than a wedding; of course he would not wish his actual daughter to marry such a man, etc. Again he was near to tears and accused me of trying to find justification for throwing him out of the analysis. I was stunned by this accusation, for the material was so enthralling that I felt deep regret that the patient would only be with me for a year.

I would like to try to describe the following session in some detail. It was the last session of the week, prior to a week in which I had needed to move one of his sessions, but caused him no actual inconvenience. He was on time, looking a bit more friendly I thought; he immediately reported that on leaving the day before, he had seen that I looked old and puffy, clearly suffering from heart disease. It had come as a direct, undoubted insight. Only on the way home had it struck him that I had looked quite well at the beginning of the session and had, in fact, a minute before run up the stairs to fetch him from the waiting room. I promptly began to pull together the material – the dirty air, the burned out eyes of the mother-house, the gushing cave and the torrent of people coming into the casualty department, the heart disease – emphasising the way in which both what comes out of his mouth and what goes into his eyes and ears seems to be subject to some mutilating attack or disaster. I said, by way of amplification, that this process of hallucinatory contamination of perception seemed a ubiquitous but variable process, less noticeable in the less crucial senses like smell. He immediately launched into a description of his extraordinarily acute olfactory sense and the strong emotions evoked in him by reminiscent odours, for instance the smell of toast, marmalade and hot milk that strikes him when he comes to his early morning sessions, presumably from our breakfast.

Like the "heart disease" this seemed to be a perception, not a conclusion. I was then in a position to tell him that none of these items was correct, that this was an experience connected with coming into the parents' bedroom in the morning, of the Mummy-mare who throws off the children to rush to her stallion for her breakfast. It then transpired that the grievance about the scouts covered a whole line of complaints about his father for cutting him off from his protective older sister by sending him to a boys' school, by moving from the first home where he and his sister had had a secret oasis in the nearby quarry amongst the enveloping foliage.

After this interpretation and outpouring the patient was silent for several minutes and then reported that his body felt thick and heavy, as if turned to stone. I suggested that he had had a feed of concrete reality which had petrified him, as concrete as the toast, marmalade and hot milk of the parents' meal but calculated to put him in a state of suspended animation for the week-end so that he should not interfere with our pleasures.

It subsequently appeared that this first home, so nostalgic in its recall, was a cottage in the grounds of a children's hospital where the patient's father was an administrator. One can construe that his mother's depression had driven him early on to attach to his protective older sister the meaning of this oasis-cottage-breast. His mother, on the other hand, took on the meaning of the hospital-body full of sick and suffering children, like the home of the suicide son, with its burnt out windows.

The thesis thus far developed might be stated in this way: when the patient's sense organs operate in reverse and project images from the disasters caused to his perceptions by the reversal of alpha-function under the sway of his burning resentment, his renewed intake through his senses cannot be used as data for further thought, for it is felt to constitute fully developed thoughts already. Consequently what pours out of his mouth are not ideas that have been produced by thinking, but the regurgitation of the hallucinatory pseudo-thoughts that he has 'perceived'.

Two weeks later he brought a dream which rounded off the process: *he was travelling in a coach, he did not know whither, and he seemed to be alone, whereas the other people in the coach seemed to know one another. But in spite of his being alone somebody else said that he was accompanied by two orphans. The coach stopped at what he called a "hamlet", but which was, in fact, only a single building where they were stopping for refreshments. To his astonishment someone came out of the building and brought him a big paper bad saying that it was a gift for him. It seemed that it was a birthday present from his father which had been sent ahead to await him at this refreshment stop. When he opened the bag it turned out to be something which quite thrilled him; a flash gun for his camera. He was particularly pleased because the flash part had one of those types of lenses that softens the light so that the pictures that are taken do not have a hard chiaroscuro but a soft one. It also had another feature that he could not understand at all. The flash part was at the top and then there was a metal column at the bottom of which was something made of amber-coloured glass.* He had no idea what its function was, nor did he have any associations to it except, of course, that in his country the yellow light in the traffic signals is called amber. Also there further came into his mind a door knob of amber-coloured cut glass, for the amber gadget on the flash gun also had a cut glass pattern on it. And he had a very vague idea that perhaps the internal door knobs of the first house that he had left at the age of six were of the same kind (in subsequent sessions it became quite clear that these were in fact in his wealthy grandmother's "bijou" house).

The gift from his father was associated with another gift, not for himself but for his elder daughter, that had been sent along with them when they came from their native country as a present to be given to the daughter on her birthday. This was a camera, not from his father but from his wife's father, a very kind and thoughtful man. For the first time he talked of his father as he had never talked before, with affection and warmth, and described other aspects of his father's personality: his generosity, orderliness, efficiency and Christian ethics.

I was very interested in this piece of photographic apparatus which clearly seemed a gift from the analysis to rectify his perceptual equipment, to soften his perceptions, as it were, to add a note of caution to his interpretations of perceptions, as he had been able to do regarding the perception of my "heart disease" on his way home in his car.

Regarding the two crucial dreams we need to go back to the analogy about the child playing with Lego. The cave could be taken as his mouth which has ordinarily been used for singing with the choir – that is, for sincere speech, in keeping with the cultural modes of communication, with all the music of the voice, gestures and facial expression. But the mouth can also be used for pouring out a noise which has a resemblance to speech and communication while really it is a means of evacuation of the debris following some destructive process in his internal world. We might describe this in terms of Bion's concept of the reversal of alpha-function, or the analogy of the child smashing the Lego to pieces. One might take the doors of the casualty department as his eyelids through which comes pouring the mutilated percepts of this previously evacuated disaster. This could be seen as a circulating process – something pours of of his mouth and that same something pours back into his eyes – as exemplified by my looking old and puffy with heart disease. Or the alternative process can take place: the mutilated thoughts which pour out of his eyes come back into his ears as my threats to throw him out of the analysis, or into his nose as the smell of "our breakfast".

The problem is where does the disaster take place? In his transformation in hallucinosis the patient experiences the disaster as taking place outside himself – my having heart disease or wanting to throw him out of analysis, whereas in fact the disaster takes place inside himself (like the child kicking the Lego to pieces); something that was about to be constructed in his mind is destroyed and the debris from this reversal of alpha-function is evacuated in one way or another.

The question that now arises is this: in what way is this disturbance of perception different from Melanie Klein's theory that attacks on internal objects in dreams, phantasies, masturbatory processes, etc., affect our way of experiencing the external world? I think that the difference is to be found in the rigidity that derives from the hallucinatory element and the momentary operation of the process. The perceptions are in no way doubted for the meaning of the perception is implicit. In the processes that Melanie Klein has described, the person has experiences with external objects which must be thought about. In thinking about these experiences conclusions are reached about their meaning in the light of the momentary internal situation. Thinking enables judgment to form opinions which are held with greater or lesser conviction. But the thinking has to take place.

In the transformation in hallucinosis the abortive thinking has already been done, so that the perception contains these abortive bits of thinking. Take for instance the incident about my heart disease: from what the patient said later it seems clear that I looked quite healthy to him at the beginning of the session. Something had happened to him inside himself during the session so that when he looked at me at the end of the session he saw me in a hallucinated way and with absolute certainty. It was only later on, on the way home, when he thought about it, that he began to wonder.

How does this differ from the sort of thing that you might find with many patients? It is certainly a common experience after difficult sessions that a patient sees the analyst as older, more tired and so on. But a patient in that condition would report to you in the following session that at the end of the previous one you had "seemed" to him to have been older, more tired than you had appeared at the beginning. He would not "see that you had heart disease". Another way of putting it is that in our relationships with people we always realise that we are seeing things "as" – that is we are infusing the meaning so we use words like "it seemed", "she appeared to be", "I saw it as". We are always aware that we are adding the meaning except when we are in a state of hallucinosis which, I think, is much more common than we realise.

But clearly in non-psychotic people it is an occasional aberration. In Professor A it occurs under the sway of strong emotion. For instance, on a Thursday the patient before him, a woman, had been held up in a traffic jam and came forty minutes late for the session, so I had taken her into the consulting room for fifteen minutes, leaving no time between her session and the Professor's. When he came into the consulting room he lay down on the couch and said, "I suppose it is not very polite to say this but the smell of her feet is in the room." On enquiry it became clear that he had smelled her naked feet. It was not that he smelt something that he thought might be her feet, and that perhaps it was strong because she had taken her shoes off – no, he had smelt her unshod feet (incidentally she does not take her shoes off – and neither does he). In a way this example is more impressive than the "dirty air" or my "heart disease", for it demonstrates the speed with which the process of transformation in hallucinosis takes place. If we return to the analogy of the little boy who breaks up his Lego, what is it that has happened at that moment that changes the direction from building Lego to smashing it to pieces? This is the crucial moment, but is it the crucial question for psycho-analysis? Description of that moment does not have any explanatory power for our understanding of what happens afterwards; it helps to describe the turning point but it does not describe anything about the nature of the mental events that follow.

In the history of psycho-analysis there has been a strong tendency to utilise the recognition of emotional conflict in an explanatory way, as if to say "because of this conflict such-and-such happens". But the mental mechanics are not necessarily related to the structure of the conflict that precipitates it. The implications for therapy are far-reaching. For instance, suppose that I had not been analysing the transformations in hallucinosis but was simply analysing the emotional conflicts of the transference. In time the transformations in hallucinosis might disappear, but there would have been nothing in the way of insight to prevent the *tendency* for it to come back the moment a new conflict erupts. Although the afterthoughts about my "heart disease" may have come late, they did come and did correct the hallucinosis. Similarly with the breakfast and the smelly feet: the process became amenable to correction. Compare this with the adamant conviction about the "dirty air". The birthday gift from the Professor's father is not perceptual equipment, it is insight which illuminates his percepts, softens his judgment and adds a note of caution to his sense of certainty.

XI

Clinical Application of Bion's Concept 'Reversal of Alpha-function'[1]

When a new theory is proposed in psycho-analysis it can be said to undertake two functions: one is to organise in a more aesthetic (beautiful?) way the clinical phenomena that have already been observed; the other is to provide a tool of observation that will open to view previously invisible phenomena of the consulting room. Bion, beginning with his papers on schizophrenia, sought to amplify the model of the mind which we employ in psycho-analysis so that processes of thinking and disturbances in this capacity could be investigated. The first systematic presentation of this effort, *Learning from Experience*, formulated an "empty" concept of alpha-function by means of which the "observation of the sense impressions of emotional experiences" were converted into elements, building-blocks for dream thoughts, which could be used for thinking, might be available for storage as memory, and whose continuity formed a "contact barrier" that separated conscious from unconscious mental processes.

The "emptiness" of this model was stressed over and over again by Bion, along with a caution against over-hasty attempts to fill it with clinical meaning. He himself, almost single-handedly, explored its possible meaning in the series of books which followed, namely *Elements of Psycho-analysis, Transformations* and *Attention and Interpretation*. It is with a certain trepidation that this paper is offered as a tentative exploration of his fascinating idea that alpha-function can perhaps work backwards, cannibalising the already formed alpha-elements to produce either the beta-screen or perhaps bizarre objects. It is probably best to quote rather than to paraphrase. He writes (page 25, *Learning from Experience*) in evaluating the analyst's and patient's separate contributions to the situation in which the beta-screen is being formed: "The analysand contributes changes which are associated with the replacement of alpha-function by what may be described as a reversal of direction of the function." And here he adds a note: "The reversal of direction is compatible with the treatment of thoughts by evacuation; that is to say, if the personality lacks the apparatus that would enable it to 'think' thoughts but is capable of attempting to rid the psyche of thoughts in much the same way as it

[1]Previously published in *The Kleinian Development*.

rids itself of accretions of stimuli, then reversal of alpha-function may be the method employed."

He continues: "Instead of sense impressions being changed into alpha-elements for use in dream thoughts and unconscious waking thinking, the development of the contact-barrier is replaced by its destruction. This is effected by the reversal of alpha-function so that the contact-barrier and the dream-thoughts and unconscious waking thinking, which are the texture of the contact-barrier, are turned into alpha-elements divested of all characteristics that separate them from beta-elements and are then projected, thus forming the beta-screen."

Further: "Reversal of alpha-function means the dispersal of the contact-barrier and is quite compatible with the establishment of objects with the characteristics I once ascribed to bizarre objects."

He points out that there is an important difference in his conception of the beta-element and the bizarre object; the latter is "beta-element plus ego and superego traces".

Before we can embark upon the clinical material through which meaning may be poured into the "empty" vessel of thought, it is necessary to remind the reader of an historical item. Bion has amplified Melanie Klein's concept of sadistic and omnipotent attacks upon internal objects and the structure of the self to include also attacks on individual functions of the ego and upon "linking" in general as the basic operation in thought – its prototype being the link between infant and breast. To test the usefulness of Bion's formulations it is necessary to demonstrate that they make possible an integration of observations not possible by previous formulations. The particular question that will arise in connection with the following material is this: does the formulation of alpha-function and its possible reversal extend the range of psycho-analytic observation and thought beyond that made possible by Melanie Klein's formulations regarding sadistic attacks, splitting processes and projective identification with internal objects?

Clinical material – a thirty-five-year-old man

The session begins perhaps two minutes late: no comment. He has had a horrible dream which it takes him some considerable time to tell against strong resistance in the form of a "what's the use" attitude. The background of the dream collects before the dream is actually presented, including some material of previous sessions which had dealt with his feelings of ingratitude to his mother's friends whom they had visited together in Germany during the summer. He had never sent a thank-you note but yesterday had received an invitation for Christmas. He hates ingratitude in himself or others and yesterday's material had centred on a Fellow of the college (his initials,

D.M.) whose furniture he had helped to move; D.M. has never thanked him nor invited him to dinner. Today's material then veers off into a description of his sensitivity to his surroundings and how he will lose his room in college next year and have to find one in another which he hates. It is connected with the Institute in the USA where he spent two miserable years and he also feels at loggerheads with X who tried to bully him into accepting the "great honour" of being a Fellow at his college.

In the dream *there was a huge L-shaped room like the one at the American institute but also, by virtue of the grey lino, like his present room as it was before he had bullied and cajoled the authorities into carpeting and decorating it, and had exchanged all the horrible furniture for a rather nice settee and chairs.* (Yes, he says as an aside, he realises that this excessive dependence on external comfort implies a defect in his internal sense of security.) In the dream *someone was talking about an old woman who had been dreadfully deformed by an accident. Then she seemed to be there on the floor alive but so deformed that she was hardly recognisable as a human. One extraordinary and particularly horrible feature was that originally she had had extremely long fingernails, extending not only outward but also up her fingers, and under the skin of the arm. These seemed to have been struck and driven up her arm so that their ends stuck out near her elbows. The point seemed to be that she was suing for compensation but this was refused on the grounds that she was so completely deformed that one could get no idea at all of what had been her original state. This applied particularly to the fingernails for, although they did not protrude from her fingers but only from her elbows, the intervening nails did not show through the skin. The impression of horror did not seem to be accompanied by any emotion other than aversion.*

I suggested to him that the background of the dream indicated that the problem was one of guilt and reparation, neither of which can be set in motion unless the mutilated object can be recognised and connected with its former undamaged and perhaps young and beautiful state, i.e. his mother as a young woman in his childhood as compared with the old woman equated with her friends in Germany who kept being generous to him despite his ingratitude, thus becoming old and empty. In order to get rid of this tormenting sense of guilt it is necessary so to attack the old mother that her disfigurement defies connection with the original object, becoming "some old woman" rather than "mummy". But is there not a mathematical technique that he mentioned yesterday called "transpositional equations" connected with analytical geometry, whereby if the distortion of the grid of reference can be demonstrated, two objects which seem grossly different can be shown to be identical basically but projected on to different grid systems like distortions in a picture on a piece of rubber? He agreed; his work deals with the mathematics which makes such crude analogies unnecessary. (I was thinking of the pictures of fish and skulls in D'Arcy Thompson's *Growth of Form* and he confirmed this reference.) The long fingernails therefore represent the lines of the grid and if they can be made visible and the grid rectified to its basic axes, the image of the beautiful young mother can be rediscovered in the dehumanised old woman. The motto of the defence would be, "If you damage mummy and the sight of it causes you guilt and remorse smash her beyond all recognition until you feel only horror and revulsion."

Discussion

We were approaching the first holiday break of this man's analysis which had been arranged at an interview just prior to the previous summer holiday when he was expecting his mother to come all the way from Australia to visit him and take him to see some aristocratic friends of hers in Germany. The patient had not seen his mother for some years and was disturbed not only at finding her looking much older than his image of her, but also at finding his former devotion to her much cooled. He is the eldest of her children and the only "successful" one, having been rather arrogantly independent since early childhood.

From the Kleinian point of view it is a rather ordinary dream that illustrates the thesis that retreat from depressive anxiety referrable to damaged internal objects follows a route whereby the depressive pain is felt as persecutory depression and opens the way to further attacks on the damaged object as a persecutor. The parallel material of his associations suggests that the room in college, which he had made cosy by "bullying and cajoling" the authorities to carpet, hiding the old lino which reminded him of the "two miserable years" in the United States, was to be taken away: that is, that the analysis was threatening to return him to a state of misery (the analyst being from the USA) as revenge for his not feeling "honoured" at being accepted for analysis (as with X's invitation). The analyst, like the Fellow with the same initials, D.M., is to contain the split-off attribute of ingratitude.

But what could a Kleinian formulation make of these fingernails which, instead of growing out, had been driven in in the reverse direction until they stuck out at the old woman's elbow? What could it make of the refusal of compensation on the grounds that the old woman was so horribly deformed that no idea could be established of her previous state? Perhaps we can assume that the imponderable nature of the deformed old woman is exactly the quality that makes her a bizarre object in Bion's sense rather than a mutilated object in Melanie Klein's. In the courtroom of the dream no one seemed to doubt that she had been a human, that there had been an accident, that her fingernails had been driven up her arm. But somehow the *frame of reference* of thought had been destroyed, a framework having a particular connection with the patient's overriding professional preoccupations. One might say that his work has to do with getting at the truth about problems of analytical geometry through formulae which would be far more precise than the 'crude analogies' of grid-distortion.

Not only could Kleinian formulations before Bion have made no headway with such a problem; they would not even have been able to state the problem itself, namely the attack on thinking. They could approach the attack on feeling only, where, of course, they go quite some distance. In contrast, a Freudian formulation would probably get hung up on the castration anxiety which most certainly is an element in the dream (are the woman's nipples the remnants of her penis, smashed up and driven inward and upward until they stick out of the breasts?).

Bionic recapitulation

The patient is facing the first holiday break of his analysis and feels that his jealousy of the other analytical children is going to drive him to attack his internal analytical mother with a view to lessening his devotion and its consequent separation pain. But the return to analysis would hold him to a state of mind of misery about these attacks, hating himself for ingratitude, perhaps even reducing him to having to beg, rather than bully, the daddy-authorities to redecorate the mummy and make her cosy once more. That would be unbearably humiliating to such an independent baby. Although he has spent years developing a mode of thought for seeing the truth with precision, in such situations he is prepared to destroy that mental capacity (alpha-function of a particular sort) by making it run in reverse (instead of growing outward to form the lines of a grid of reference, the fingernails are driven backwards to disappear under the skin appearing only at the elbows). The consequence is a beta-element "plus-ego and superego traces" (the distorted old woman having only traces of the mother and of his discarded ego-capacity for thinking with transpositional equations). She is now a bizarre object, uncontainable in thought, suitable only for evacuation.

Implications

Let us take the 'crude analogy' of a geometric grid on a piece of rubber as a model of a piece of mental equipment, a particular bit of alpha-function apparatus. Place on it a picture of an old woman and pull the rubber in various ways until the picture of a beautiful young woman appears. Take this as a model of alpha-function operating on "the sense impressions of an emotional experience". Such a bit of apparatus may be essential for the creation of an image that makes it possible to connect the old woman who visits you from Australia with the beautiful young mother who insisted on having other children against your sage advice.

Postscript

The analysis progressed very well through the next term bringing forward memory after memory of the catastrophic reactions to the births of his next siblings, reactions which progressively relegated his father to a position of negligible importance in his life and consolidated his status as mother's little husband and adviser. As the second holiday break approached he became rather restive, left early to go to Australia to visit his family on the grounds that his next sibling (who had the same first name as mine) needed his help and advice. While there he had a group-therapy "experience" during which he developed a manic state, thought he was the Messiah, and returned late to break off the analysis, full of "gratitude" that the analysis had laid the background for his total cure in the group. He was, however, willing to see me once a week to help him to understand how this transformation had come about. Over the next two months he gradually slipped into a state of depression after breaking off completely in a rage at the analyst's "stupidity". He finally returned to analysis in time to make a more satisfactory preparation for the long summer break. It was of interest that he could not bring himself to pay his fees until the last day, by which time the four months of work came to almost the precise amount he had paid for the five-day group "therapy".

Bion wrote me a kind and interesting note when I sent him the paper, referring to my phrase, "aesthetic (beautiful?) way". "Now I would use as a model the diamond cutter's method of cutting a stone so that a ray of light entering the stone is reflected back *by the same path* in such a way that the light is augmented – the same 'free association' is reflected back by the same path, but with augmented 'brilliance'. So the patient is able to see his 'reflection', only more clearly than he can see his personality as expressed by himself alone (i.e. without an analyst)."

XII

Psychotic Illness in Early Childhood
Ten years on from *Explorations in Autism*[1]

with
Doctor Anna Sabatini Scolmati (Rome)

The clinical work and seminars of the research group (John Bremner, Shirley Hoxter, Doreen Weddell, Isca Wittenberg and Donald Meltzer) which eventuated in *Explorations in Autism*, took place between 1965 and 1974 in an atmosphere of enthusiasm about the illumination shed by the conceptual tools made explicit in Melanie Klein's paper, 'Notes on some Schizoid Mechanisms'. It was largely by the extrapolation of her implicit model of the mind that we developed such concepts as dimensionality, dismantling of the senses, and primitive obsessional mechanisms. Bion's ideas, which had stunned us but had as yet not been assimilated, played a very little part in our conscious conceptualising but were already at work, underground as it were, as was Esther Bick's idea of skin containment.

In the last ten years no such formal research study has been carried on, but a different type of experience has given rise to new ideas which now seem 'ripe' to be shared. But I wish to make it clear that they do not have the same status scientifically as the earlier work and will require clinical confirmation to assess their usefulness. They derive from the conscious use of Bion's Theory of Thinking as a clinical tool and have proved, in my opinion, to be astonishingly clarifying and therapeutically effective. The experience of which I speak, which I have shared with my wife, Martha Harris, has been one of teaching analytical child psycho-therapy at various centres in Europe, North and South America and India, following cases over periods as long as ten years at a frequency ranging from one to five times a year. The main centres have been in Oslo, Paris, Novara, Rome and Pisa. I would estimate that we have followed about twenty cases fairly closely and seen another thirty cases in a more diagnostic way. This experience, of course, has taken place on a background of regular supervisory work once a week or fortnightly with young colleagues in

[1]Read to the Colloque, 'Approche Psychoanalytique de l'Autisme et des Psychoses Infantiles Precoces' – Monte Carlo, 1984.

London and Oxford. But I mention the foreign teaching in particular because the long-term but infrequent contact, the carefully prepared material of those occasions and the cross-cultural data have conspired to form very clear-cut conceptual ideas.

The central impression derived, as I say, from following the psycho-analytical process as it unfolded over the years, has been one of differentiation of the group descriptively covered by the term 'Early Infantile Autism' into four distinct categories which I would name: a) autism proper and post-autistic states; b) geographical confusional psychoses; c) primary failures of mental development; d) failures of post-natal mental adjustment. In order to make this differentiation clinically vivid without the lengthy exposition of material which the present limitation will not allow, I must first describe the conceptual tools with which the clinical phenomena have been dissected and construed. I will state them in the form of a story of infantile development.

When the neural system of the foetus has reached a point of anatomical complexity sufficient for integrated functioning (three months? six months?) behavioural responses to internal and external stimuli commence with the purpose of maintaining a tolerable (pleasant?) level of excitation alternating with non-REM sleep. As the complexity of the patterns of stimulation and responses increases, excitation of the apparatus begins to give way to a new level of cognition characterised by proto-emotions, the observation of which by consciousness, the organ for the perception of psychic qualities and attention, sets in motion the first proto-mental processes, alpha-function. This function correlates formal gestalten of the sensory organs to the observed emotion to make symbolic representations of the meaning of the emotion.

But in the confines of the womb all these proto-mental experiences are 'muffled', vague and impossible to coordinate. For this reason the symbolism is primarily auditory and rhythmic in form with a bodily dance-like aspect. So long as there is no foetal distress the dream processes which now ensue are peaceful and no reversal of alpha-function results. Hence the foetus is not burdened by accretions of stimuli nor by the production of "beta-elements-with-traces-of-ego-and-superego". These, if they occurred, would require evacuation as hallucinations or psycho-somatic disturbance since they can neither be thought about, nor stored as memory, unless evacuation into a receptive-containing object is possible. But as gestation approaches term and the confines of the womb begin to narrow, various types of distress begin to ensue and reversal of alpha-function begins to produce disturbing mental products. Hallucinations and psycho-somatic disturbance result and an object for evacuation and containment begins to be sought. The placenta fails to perform this function but auditory impressions suggest that 'extra-terrestrial' objects exist which might be capable of such services. A desire to seek such objects generates efforts to find egress from these narrow confines which are ultimately successful in rupturing the claustrum.

But the world outside comes as a great shock because of the intensity of stimuli which impinge on every sense, accustomed as they are to only minor muffled increments of stimulation. Some are painful in a primary way and others in a way that is secondary to the intensity of emotion they arouse. These latter could be called 'aesthetic stimuli' of the 'brave new world' of colour, sounds and tastes-smells. They are delicious, enchanting, intoxicating – and emotionally painful because their meaning is obscure. These intolerable stimuli, evacuated as beta-elements-with-traces-of-ego-and-superego (shall we abbreviate them as b-e-t-e-s, betes?) in the form of screams and other evacuations such as urine and faeces, seem to find a containing-receptive object which is able, moreover, to restore the betes to their symbolic (alpha) form and return them to the infant in a way which enables it to have *interesting dreams*.

I wish to remind you that this is a 'story', an 'imaginative conjecture', not a theory. It is a model to be used for exploration of clinical phenomena. In order to erect it into a theory (supposing that were an important or useful thing to do), a huge amount of work would be necessary: systematic evaluation of cases in therapy, infant observations, observation of foetal behaviour, correlations with neurophysiological behaviour, etc. I have found it extremely illuminating with regard to the delineation of the three categories that I would consider to be non-autistic infantile psychotic states (see b, c and d, p. 123). But in order to expound them it is necessary to augment the 'story' by what can now reasonably be called the Klein-Bion Theory of the Infant-Mother Relationship.

Having found this receptive-containing object which enables it to resist the inclination to turn away from the pain of its mental experiences by reversing its alpha-function, the infant is beset by three problems: 1) the object is not always present when needed; 2) it sometimes fails to perform its services satisfactorily; 3) its beauty is both thrilling and agonising. The baby's natural tendency (derived from primitive one-dimensional tropism levels) is to split the object into good and bad, but this also splits itself into segments which are attracted to, and identify with these objects, either when they are internalised (introjective identification) or entered (projective identification) or both. The development of personality *structure* has begun.

Before we can turn our attention to delineation of the three additional non-autistic types of infantile psychosis, it is necessary to review the findings put forward in *Explorations* in the light of the Bionic 'story' of foetal life and the "caesura of birth", as well as the Klein-Bion theory of the mother-infant relationship. We suggested in that book the following view of early infantile autism and its sequellae, "post-autistic states". Infants of high intelligence and powerful emotional potential, when confronted with the near ubiquitous postpartum depression in their mothers, develop a technique for defending themselves against this intensified depressive pain by dismantling their sensual apparatus into its components through abandonment of the act of concentration of attention (consciousness). The result is return to a one-dimensional world of uni-sensual objects with only tropism qualities, muting of emotional responsiveness and failure of interest in objects, interest being bound up with emotional meaning. But this is a highly reversible state and does not generate personality structural deformities. It does, however, by avoiding mental pain and conflict, reduce the rate of personality structuring to a minimum. As its use is diminished the dismantling tendency is replaced by its natural successor – obsessional separation and omnipotent control of objects.

I feel that this formulation is still completely tenable but further observations of autistic children and the course followed by them in the psycho-analytical process allows for the following Bionic additions: these children are not primarily affected by the absence of their maternal object but by its presence. The pain it produces derives from its failure of emotional response and attention but also from its beauty to which these children are highly responsive. The problem of how a present beautiful object can cause pain that overwhelms the pleasure it engenders leads them towards an intense preoccupation with the inside of their object (body and mind of the object being in no sense distinguished at this point in development). It is from this three-dimensional problem that they flee by dismantling their senses since the depressed state of the mother makes her seem so impenetrable to projective identification that no means is felt to be at hand for investigating the problem of disparity between external beauty and internal uncertain benevolence. They retreat from interest in the problem by abandoning emotional life itself, under the theory – the only one that they can imagine – that the mother contains another baby who is so precious to her that she will not risk being penetrated. Their consequent overwhelming emotional state is one of feeling 'thrown away' and it is with this 'throwing away mother' that they are fundamentally narcissistically (adhesively) identified.

There is nothing more that I can add at this point to our understanding of the essential nature of the autistic disturbance proper though much could be added to our view of the course of the therapeutic process if time permitted. Let us turn instead to our central task of delineating the other three distinct types of infantile psychotic disturbance in their genetic order, starting with *failures of post-natal adjust-ment.*

Certain babies, probably for reasons connected with foetal distress in the last month of pregnancy (infarction of the placenta for instance), experience the "caesura of birth" as being driven out of, or dragged out of Eden – but not a garden of earthly pleasure but rather of absence of pain. They are insensible to the beauty of the outside world and experience its sensa only as a bombardment. They reject it and seek only to be sequestered once more, to be wet, inert, protected from the force of gravity. Their attention becomes centred on serving themselves with their tiny capability by curling up, licking themselves, stroking themselves. They resist tenaciously the demands of their body to be used, both sensory organs and motor equipment alike. Their cry is feeble and their evacuations leak out rather than being forcefully projected. In fact they evince so little distress that it is difficult for their mothers to take an emotional interest in them.

The children who exhibit a *primary failure of mental development* present a far more complicated picture, for a real maternal failure seems to be involved, in conjunction with certain qualities in the child which predispose it. When the pregnant mother has so little contact with phantasy that the baby in her womb is only an idea in the minds of other people about the growing protrusion of her abdomen, the baby's protomental life, as expressed in its dance movements, evokes no attention or phantasy or emotional response from the mother. (Imagine the impact of dancing, not before an empty theatre that you could people in phantasy, but before an audience of whose blindness you had not been informed.) The rigidity of the container crushes the emotional thrust. To such babies the urge to break out of the container is increased by persecutory feelings; the outside world, in its beauty and intensity, breaks upon them with unbearable power. They desperately seek the containing-receptive object, but, regardless of her willingness, the mother is handicapped by shyness for this baby is a stranger to her. Thus deprived of spontaneous emotion and phantasy with which to implement her care of the child she becomes mechanical in response, aided by all the advice she seeks – and gets. The baby's attempts to confront its dilemma by splitting and idealisation result so quickly in a fusion of the bad part of itself with the bad object (paranoia) that it retreats from the emotionality and the attempt to understand to a two-dimensional adjustment utilising omnipotent signals to control the object for the purpose of obtaining services. The mother responds with relief and feels no stirring of phantasy to enable her to talk to the baby any more than she could when it was a non-presence in her womb. Things usually begin to go smoothly as the mother becomes well-trained and the baby content. Motor development, sphincter control and feeding habits seem satisfactory. Only when language fails to develop is retardation noted, unless, because of the absence of the mother (going back to work for instance) strangers to the baby's system of signals recognise the failure to achieve emotional contact. Thinking and dreaming, thus also emotional conflicts, fail to develop but the computerised two-dimensional mimicry and recall systems prosper. A very odd child results – toneless voice, expressionless face, agrammatical speech and idiosyncratic interests (and often displaying prodigious virtuosity of recall), hallucinatory tendencies and motor peculiarities. Help may not be sought until pressure from the school insists on the child's essential ineducability.

A somewhat similar bafflingly paradoxical situation exists with a child of obvious high intelligence and near total ineducability caught in a *geographical confusional psychosis*, but the history of the illness is definably different from the others. The baby seems to make an easy transition to life outside the womb, seems to find its containing-receptive object and to make good use of the mother both for evacuating its distressed states and for taking in comfort and interesting ideas from a mother full of phantasy and emotional vitality, but perhaps torn somewhat by the mutually exclusive demands made on her by other members of the houshold, economic problems or health. Since the baby seems well satisfied its pleasures are often sacrificed to placate the demands from other directions. The baby is confronted by the disparity between the degree to which the mother reciprocates his adoration of an aesthetic object and her rapid slipping away, seeming rejection of his more passionate communications, vocal, faecal and urinary. But since the mother is so inviting of penetration for brief periods, the baby plunges inside her in phantasy to discover the source of her unfaithfulness. Perhaps his external rivals also penetrate and control her from inside. But because this intrusion is made secretly no web of Ariadne leads him out and he is lost in the labyrinthine interior of his object. Depending on the space he has entered he may find himself in the foul, frightening dungeon of her rectum, or the constantly eroticised interior of her genital parts, or in the balmy and spacious cathedral of her head-breast from whose windows a sophisticated view of the world is available and sweet music fills the air. Or the imprisoned child may move among these spaces and show a constant oscillation in his state of mind, from persecution and distrust to erotic excitement to peaceful compla-cency. But whichever of these states predominates, the claus-trophobic atmosphere abounds and creates a resistance to any educa-tional influence whether because of distrust, excitement or compla-cency. Again the result is impeded language development of the 'private language' type, usually with correct grammatical music. Idiosyncratic obsessive interests and activities, often highly evolved and complicated, occupy much of the child's time, while interest in other children is either absent or clearly phobic. The story of the illness and of its therapy is strongly suggested in the traditional story of *Jack and the Beanstalk*.

At this point in the exposition it becomes necessary to illustrate this differentiation of diagnostic categories with clinical material. The choice lies between trying to describe the clinical picture as presented at consultation through history and observation, or rather to illustrate the evolution of the child as seen in the psycho-analytic therapy. I have given my opinion that in fact the descriptive picture is so variable, so overlapping, the parents' observations and recall of the development so unreliable, and the age at which the child is presented so scattered, that diagnostic impressions are far from distinctive in the four different categories. However, the course that they follow in their development under the influence of the analytic setting and transference is quite different for the four types, and it is largely from that experience of the therapeutic process that our understanding of them has been drawn. This method of exposition will, of course, be of very little help to workers who are not in a position to carry on such a therapeutic type of evaluation, but, on the other hand, since the prognosis of the four categories seems to be so different, it should encourage therapists to make the attempt, even where the child arrives at an advanced age, or the family seems unsupporting or even where organic factors seem to be contributory.

It seemed that it would be necessary to illustrate these distinctions with three separate case histories, necessarily of unsatisfactory brevity. But good fortune delivered to hand an extraordinarily suitable case illustrating, in sequence, all three categories – failure of postnatal adjustment, primary failure of development, and geographical confusional state. Dr Anna Sabatini had been working with this little girl of six and a half years for only two months, three times a week, at the point of presentation to seminars of the Rome Tavistock Child Psychotherapy Course. Sara was the only child of a very intelligent and united professional couple for whom the child's history was a tragedy which had exacted great sacrifices from them. The child had been born four weeks prematurely and was said to show evidence of foetal distress despite the delivery having been very rapid. Because of this and her small size (four pounds) she was placed in an incubator for the first twenty-five days and kept in the hospital nursery for an additional twenty-five days completely without parental contact. The mother's only effective rebellion against this regimen was to insist that the child be fed on her expressed breast milk, hoping to continue on the breast once the child was home. But in fact Sara then refused the nipple and would only take the mother's milk from the bottle in a slow, listless and incomplete fashion.

This listlessness and calm continued, lying quietly with her little fists closed, and no striking evidence of disordered development imposed itself on the parents until it became clear at one year of age that she was unable to sit up, could not take solid foods. Extensive neurological investigations, including brain scan and EEG, failed to reveal more than suggestive evidence of brain damage of a diffuse sort, but a course of physiotherapy and muscle training was instituted. By fifteen months Sara could sit, by twenty-eight months she could walk but her gait remained insecure and ungainly, with small steps, feet scarcely lifted from the ground, and she had great difficulty in ascending and descending stairs. Speech did not develop beyond one or two syllables of a general indicative sort, and sphincter control did not arrive until five and a half years. The failure of development seemed all the more puzzling as her general demeanour was rather elfin and seductively pleasing both to adults and to the children in the nursery which she had attended from the age of two and a half years. Vague indications of autism were bruited much to the parents' discomfort. Therapy was decided upon in no great spirit of optimism.

The following is a translation of Dr Sabatini's presentation to the seminar.

Summary of Sara's behaviour in the first twenty-eight sessions

Sara presents herself as a well-developed child, perhaps a little overweight, with dark hair and big black eyes with very long lashes. Only her mouth is out of proportion, being very small, with tiny spaced teeth. Her little breasts are quite definitely formed, as if in a pubertal child. All in all the initial pleasing impression is marred by these jarring features, along with the peculiarities of her behaviour. For instance, her mouth seems to play no part in her activities except for the repeated drinking of water; her general muscular coordination is uncertain on her spindly legs and she either walks on tiptoe if she is hurrying or otherwise shuffles slowly about. Her posture is usually bent forwards and slightly rotated with the right shoulder advanced and head bent over it giving a peculiarly elderly outline. She emits sounds which vary from a gloomy sustained note to a cry something like a seagull, haunting in quality. Only rarely do single syllables escape her – na, ba, la, ma, pa – and only latterly do they seem in any way specific to objects or actions.

From the first session onwards passing flatus, urinating and defecating have played a prominent role, characteristically done in a curled up squatting posture with her eyes crossed while straining. This developed into the primary contact with me, sitting on my lap for some period and then being moved, with her acceptance, into the lavatory as the premonitory signs became recognisable. Other than this she almost never sits, but is on the move, her eyes darting at, into and along every object and surface save the person of the therapist from which they slip away or dissolve. It is only in more recent sessions that phantasy themes have become recognisable in any sequential form to be described or interpreted; initially I was confined to making interested noises, giving bodily care and describing evidence of fleeting emotions or anxieties. However, her readiness and even eagerness for the sessions is apparent to the parents and to me alike.

Twenty-ninth session, Tuesday, 6 p.m.

Even before she emerges from the lift Sara's sounds can be heard, but this time their clear tones fill me with hopefulness. From her right hand there hangs her usual amulet, a plastic bag full of carefully folded papers and, on this occasion, instead of the usual unused tea bags it also contains some rather dirty cotton wool (which I later discovered she had found in her father's car en route to the session). Pulling me by the hand she leads the way into the playroom, her little head bent over her right shoulder and thrust forward.

Once in the room she can hardly wait for me to remove her coat before thrusting her hand into the toybox, also taking my hand to put into it. When I put the box on the floor Sara first empties the sack of little animals on to the table and then one of the family dolls. She searches quite purposefully among the animals until she finds the horse which she places in a standing position; then she finds the grandfather and, with my help, places him astride the horse. In one ecstatic movement she brings her hands to her chest while hunching over and thrusting her bottom out to indicate that I should take her on to my lap, which I do.

I tell her that the grandfather has found a place on the horse and she has found hers on my lap. When people are united, near each other so that the gaps and empty spaces are filled, this makes her happy.

She gets down from my lap and, again with my help, tries to put other doll figures on to the horse until finally the mummy, daddy and baby girl are astride together. She laughs joyously and nestles, puppy-like, in my lap so that I will take her in my arms.

I tell her that Mummy, Daddy and Sara are on the horse together, which makes her happy because it is just like being on the Dottoressa's knee or in her arms or their all being together inside Sara where she can hold images of them in her mind.

She gets down from my lap again and this time tries to put the figures on the back of the sheep, but soon turns to the bear family in its little transparent plastic case where there is a proper sized niche for each one, daddy, mummy and baby bear. She takes out the baby bear to put it on the back of the sheep, laughing.

I tell her that she wants to be the only one on the Dottoressa or inside her where she feels safe.

She now begins a slow repetitive operation rotating the three bears among the three different sized niches.

I tell her that Sara is trying to understand why one house is small and why another house is big, and why a big daddy bear cannot go into the little house of a baby bear.

When they have all found their proper places again she closes the plastic box carefully pressing the edges tightly together.

I tell her that she is afraid that if the house of the bears is not closed tightly some of them can fall out the way her caca, pee-pee and vomit fall out of her body sometimes.

Holding the box tightly and staring into it she places it in the toybox which she then closes only to open it a moment later to remove a little plate of plasticine balls which she had made in a previous session. She brings them to the table where she begins to roll them, one after another, between her fingers.

I tell her she is thinking about her caca in her bottom, that when caca is hard like these balls it hurts when it comes out, but at other times it comes out like water and then she feels she is losing something from inside her.

She again begins to roll the balls between her hands and places one ball on top of another of the same colour but then separates them again. She puts them down and, holding her little amulet, begins to stare into space.

I say to her, "Sara, do you want to go to the bathroom?" She does not answer but lets me take her there where she does her caca and pee-pee.

I tell her that Sara knows she has some things that are solid and some that are liquid. She can hold them inside herself or make them come out. When they come out no part of Sara is lost. Sara is still all there (I had my hands on her shoulders); the only things that come out of her body are those that do not help her to grow and are not part of Sara.

She helps me push the toilet button and watches the water carry everything away, almost putting her head down into the toilet bowl. (At the beginning of therapy she was still afraid of the toilet and the noise of flushing.) Sara then returns to the room, takes the pitcher and returns to the bathroom with it. At first she wants me to hold the pitcher under the tap in the bath tub but then decides on the tap under the sink which she turns on full by herself. When the water fills the pitcher to overflowing she looks on ecstatically.

I tell her that Sara watches the water come out as she had done when she made pee-pee and caca so that the toilet should hold what she cannot hold in herself when she feels overflowing.

She slows down the flow of water, then turns it on full again, as she has learned to do recently. While it is flowing, as if taken by a sudden impulse, she goes quickly to the room and returns with the daddy bear. I am astonished to see her immerse the bear repeatedly, pushing right to the bottom of the pitcher. When I comment on this she laughs and seems somehow satisfied, but a moment later she leaves off this activity to return once more to the room, this time to fetch the box with the two remaining bears. I anticipate a similar fate for them, but am surprised by her directing me with a gesture to fetch a towel. Then without my help she rescues the daddy bear from the pitcher, dries him carefully (with my help at this point) and returns him to his rightful place in the box. Looking intently into the transparent box she now returns to the room to replace it in the toybox.

I tell her that Sara had wanted to drown the daddy with the water because he takes up so much space of the mummy's body with his penis, filling up her tummy.

But as if to correct what I have said she does something she has not done since the earliest sessions, namely to go almost skipping to her father in the waiting-room to demand a sweet with a well-known gesture. But he has none with him and she returns disheartened.

I comment that she wants to go to her daddy to see if he is angry with her for trying to drown him. He is not really angry although he has no sweets to give her.

We return to the room where she now puts the family baby on the horse's back. Her success in doing so seems to excite her particularly. Then she does something she has never done before which quite astonishes me. With a glance at her amulet she goes to the toybox where she finds the sack with the little houses. She empties the sack on to the table in order to take possession of it, for she then places her amulet inside it and seems ready to go away.

I ask her, "Are you taking part of the Dottoressa with you again today? Some of the things we do here? Are you taking away one of the Dottoressa's skins?"

She looks at me and nods, "Yes" and, clutching her double-skinned amulet turns towards the door. I agree that the time is up and put her coat on, which she allows, en route to her father. He tells me on the way to the front door, "This morning she chattered a lot".

Commentary

Without a doubt this child had had a disastrous start to her extra-uterine life. The mother says that what began as a belly ache turned into a premature and precipitate labour and delivery of a premature child. We do not know what were the signs of foetal distress but must assume that there was a considerable anxiety about the survival of the child to warrant such a prolonged incubation and stay in the hospital nursery. The reasons for keeping the parents at a distance during this period may have been to spare them attachment to a damaged child whose viability was in doubt. But the mother's insistence on providing her own milk in the hope of continuing breast feeding may very well have contributed the item of continuity which enabled the child, after the "caesura of birth", to begin to emerge from a failure of post-natal adjustment in which the tiny creature seemed to resist the transition from "an aqueous to a gaseous medium", with all the alterations of sensation and physiology that this implies.

Certainly tender and patient care by these intelligent and sensitive parents, along with the physiotherapy and motor training, made some headway in bringing the child's attention to some focus on her body and the object world. But much precious time was lost in fruitless neurological examination and forlorn optimism. Finally it was decided that attention must be paid to the failure of Sara's mind to develop since evidence of latent intelligence was amply provided by her engaging demeanour. By the age of six and a half, when she arrived for a trial of psycho-therapy, she presented a discouraging picture of apparent mental deficiency, with possible organic and autistic features. But her plunge into the relationship, bottoms first one might say, found a sensitive and bold response in the therapist. Certainly the finding of the toilet-lap set in motion a stream of phantasy from which her undersized mouth was extraordinarily omitted, for the item of drinking water seemed quite unintegrated in the other content. The amulet with folded scraps of paper and unused tea-bags would seem to have represented her concept of self as a faeces-and-urine-producing contraption, body and mind as yet finding no differentiating representation.

In this twenty-ninth session of the therapy, to which her amulet has been brought, mysteriously substituting cotton wool for tea-bags, her approach from the very start is highly purposeful, beginning with the emptying of the little sacks of animals and family dolls, just as it ends with the emptying of the sack of little houses which she appropriates as a container for her amulet. For the theme of finding a container for herself as a container for her family is certainly the thread that runs unbroken through this amazing session. The horse, representing the Dottoressa's lap to hold herself and family, metamorphoses into the experiment with discrete spaces using the bear family and their transparent niched container. Clearly she is concerned that the quest for *lebensraum* should not lead to a conflict within the dotteressa-container, just as a more sophisticated child would be concerned that its attachment to the therapist should not arouse problems of jealousy or envy from parents or siblings.

One feels that up to this point the phantasy represented in Sara's play has been worked out to some extent before and is being given a new definition in the present session. But from this point on, a highly original move takes place. Having replaced the bears in their respective niches and the container well sealed in the toy box, she shortly takes out some previously formed plasticine balls to represent the way in which her objects seem to her to turn to faeces the moment they are internalised, presumably a source of deep pessimism. An attempt to bring them back to life by placing them in some conjugation fails and the urge to defecate asserts itself. The toilet-lap, now the dottoressa-toilet, receives her evacuations quite joyously, apparently, and is transformed into the pitcher-dottoressa that receives the water and runs over in the form of talking. But this marvel of a talking-toilet is not enough; its greatest virtue is yet to be revealed. If, in the course of a forceful evacuation of liquid substances, Sara happens to lose her internal daddy, this dottoressa-toilet knows how to rescue him and restore him to life and sweets-giving generosity (one doesn't, after all, expect sweets from the toilet itself, not even a talking, daddy-rescuing one).

But Sara senses the approach of the end of the session. The problem of separation from such a valued, perhaps even a little loved, dottoressa-beast-of-burden, threatens to overwhelm her. After all she is still, as her amulet declares, unable to control her evacuations in the sense of psychic reality, that is, to evacuate what she wishes to be rid of without her precious objects tumbling out as well; obviously the thing to do is to internalise her dottoressa-toilet containing herself, containing her family; a sort of internal nappy.

Let us now restate Sara's progress in therapy within the theoretical framework of this paper. The complex of unfortunate factors surrounding her birth seems to have left her with no zest for life in this gaseous world, clinging perhaps to the one thread of familiarity in the taste-smell of her mother's milk. But gradually, with care, her sensory equipment began to respond to the pleasant aspects of this milieu, if not yet to its aesthetic qualities. By the time she arrived for psychotherapy some three-dimensional concept of herself, represented by the amulet, appears to have developed, but a purely "skin-container" self, in the terminology of Esther Bick. So inadequate a container did this seem to be that her objects were virtually felt to pass through her and emerge as excreta in a moment. Consequently her method of establishing security remained virtually two-dimensional, 'sticking' with her bottom in particular.

It is in this twenty-ninth session that Sara, with the help of her dottoressa-talking-toilet, evolves a new and more satisfactory three-dimensional concept, of taking inside herself this containing and rescuing object. She has now achieved a new structure for herself, passing from an "invertebrate" to a "vertebrate" personality structure, in Bion's terminology. But it will remain to be seen whether she is able to employ this method of projective identification with her internalised object in a flexible way. If she becomes entrapped within this containing object she will evolve a geographical confusional phase which the therapy will have to help her escape from. In my experience this is rather the rule than the exception in the therapy of primary failures of mental development.

XIII

A One-year-Old Goes to Day Nursery – A Parable of Confusing Times[1]

with
Dr Maura Gelati (Rome)

The assumption of the unity of the mind must have had, one would think, a fatal blow from Charcot and the hypnotists had it not been rescued by Freud with his view of the stratification of consciousness. But in his last years he came round to the view that the mind does in fact 'split itself' into segments so isolated from one another that health and illness, for instance, can exist side by side in the individual personality. When Melanie Klein, in 1946, gave a new firmness to the concept of splitting in the personality, and thereby promoted the phenomenon of narcissism on to a structural rather than an instinctual plane, the consequences for the psycho-analytical model of the personality were extensive. First of all it brought the function of 'attention' into focus, and limited consciousness to what Freud had called "an organ for the perception of psychic qualities". Consequently 'narcissism' could be viewed as an organisational phenomenon, bringing infantile parts of the personality into collusion against the authority, experience and values of the parental figures (internal, external in the family, or cultural representations of such figures). The directional implications of narcissism under the earlier Libido Theory were now transformed into 'egocentricity', a view of the world in which the self stands at the centre.

The social and political implications of Freud's findings underwent a drastic change. His ideas of Group Psychology, which had viewed the wide world as an extrapolation of the family and its dynamics, was no longer tenable. First, Melanie Klein's picture of narcissistic organisations brought the 'gang' into view, and then the momentous formulations of Bion on Basic Assumption Groups revealed tribal mentality at work in civilised forms. The result has been a widened and far more complex view of man, and with it the realisation among psycho-analysts that the method they were pursuing in their consulting rooms was too narrow in its range.

This narrowness, that is the psycho-analyst's preoccupation with individual relations rather than group phenomena, and within this limited theatre a preoccupation with intimate emotional processes

[1] Previously published in *The Journal of Child Psychotherapy* (London), 1984.

thrown up by the more easily recognisable aspects of the infantile transference, can perhaps largely be blamed for the disappointment of its followers and their turning to other methods. Only the final work of Bion's life, his extraordinary fictionalised *A Memoir of the Future*, brought these late findings about phenomena of human beings in groups, the tribal dimension, back into touch with the basic model of the mind as an un-unified structure. In this complex scenario he has dramatised the interaction and failure of interaction of the various structures and organisations which comprise the complex mind of modern man. The deep clefts in the personality are illustrated and the difficulties of communication are made apparent. The pre-natals cannot talk to the post-natals, the children are cut off from the parents, the group-creature lives in a different world from the individual. We may wish to see it all as roots, trunk and branches, but the differences in premises, point-of-view, means of communication, availability of symbol formation and the poverty of language for expressing emotional states – all of these make the individual's mind a mirror of the community.

These newer ideas will certainly guide psycho-analysts to discover the phenomena in their consulting rooms which reflect this complexity. Work with children, amplified by the newer experience of observation of infants in their families, may lead the way, as it has for half a century. The problems of harmonising the many sides of the individual and his many-faceted participation in the world must find a language. As always the unusual sensitivity of the artists and poets must supply it to the social scientist. He in turn must mould it into a tool of enquiry and observation, which is the essence of therapy.

What is at least clear is that the individual does, and must, live in multiple worlds. If he confuses the meaning, the values and modes of operation amongst these worlds he will fall into confusion and perplexity, be attacked by anxiety from which he must seek relief by mechanisms of defence of one sort or another. This is the substance of what we still call 'mental illness', utilising our old medical model. This model has dictated the search for therapies, but the history thus far makes it all too clear that the expense in human resources can never hope to meet the need. If psycho-analysis is to make a significant contribution to the evolution of our culture it must be in the area of prevention and this surely means some radical alterations of our child-rearing methods and pedagogical principles.

The confusion in the minds of educated and devoted parents faced with this complexity was brought home to me recently in some sensitive and moving observations of the experiences of a little boy and his parents surrounding his introduction to a crèche for the purpose of allowing his mother to return to her work as a teacher. Seven observations over a five-month period were presented to a

Child Psychotherapy Training Course in Rome which was founded by Mrs Gianna Henry of the Tavistock Clinic. I will present Dr Maura Gelati's observations with comments and then review them in order to present a particular point of view. Simone was eight months and twenty days old when the series of observations reported commenced, although the child's development had in fact been under weekly observation since his birth.

First Observation (at home) – 8 months and 20 days

Unexpectedly Simone's father comes into the room and the baby (who is walking with the help of his mother) goes towards him and stops between his legs. His father picks him up, throws him in the air a few times and Simone laughs happily. Mother says, "I don't understand why he prefers his father. In fact he does not do anything different with him from the rest of us. But his father is something special to him. He is in love with him." She stretches out her arms to take back the baby but Simone, who at first had stretched out his arms, suddenly, on the point of being taken, throws himself on to his father's shoulder and puts his arms tightly around his neck. This scene is repeated two or three times.

Mother says, "Little rascal, you're teasing me, eh? You want to make me angry. You know I'm jealous."

Simone's father puts the baby into the playpen together with some toys, and taking the newspapers covers himself with them. He places himself so that Simone cannot see him and says that if the baby doesn't see him he lets him read in peace, but that otherwise he wants to stay in his arms.

While not in any sense turning against or away from his mother, Simone is using his affection for his father to project his jealousy into the mother. Probably this has been aroused by the restless situation and uncertainty of the parents who have been agonising about whether to put the child in a crèche or leave him at home in the care of grandparents.

Second Observation (at the crèche) – 10 months and 20 days

Today is the first day in which Simone will become part of a 'scholastic structure' and the mother tells me that she had wanted to bring the child here not so much from necessity (as either the paternal or maternal grandmother could have taken care of the child at home in her absence) but because she believes it is the best solution for the baby himself. In this crèche there are not many children. In Simone's group there are only twelve other babies of which ten are, like him, starting at the beginning of the year. Simone is with the very youngest.

I arrive at nine o'clock (they have been there since eight o'clock this morning) and find the baby in a room that is not very big, carpeted wall-to-wall, with a mattress in the left corner on which is seated a nurse[1] with an infant in her arms. There are some mothers seated around the room and two or three children are playing or crawling on the floor. The mother sees me and smiles her welcome. She too is seated on a very low chair while Simone is standing by himself, supported, or rather, fiercely holding on to the window sill which, being very low, permits him to look outside. He turns around immediately when he hears me ask where he is and he smiles fleetingly at me.

Today he is dressed in a pair of overalls that I have never seen before and he is shoeless, as are all the other children. I go over to him and pay some compliments. He immediately grabs my hand and begins to walk. He emits joyous little cries and goes towards a mattress in the corner of the room attracted there by some coloured toys (plastic rings which are to be fitted on to a wooden base). I let him sit down and he begins by taking a big blue ring. But he lets it fall immediately in order to grab hard the wooden base which he starts to whirl around as if it were a club. His mother warns him to be careful not to hit the other children. She appears worried that he might either hurt himself or some other child but the nurse does not manifest any signs of worry in that respect.

Simone tries to put the wooden base in his mouth. He rubs it against his gums then starts to whirl it again. The nurse goes over to him, takes the base from him and shows him how to slide the coloured rings on to it. She urges him to repeat the movement. She then offers him a big blue ring but Simone, instead of sliding it on to the support, starts to turn it deftly between his hands always directing it towards himself. The mother says, "Simone, not like that. Slide it on to the wood, slide in like the lady did." But the baby doesn't even make the attempt and bangs the toy against the floor.

A little girl of twelve months, Miriam, comes over to him, takes away the ring and tries to escape by crawling quickly away. Simone becomes serious, looks on the point of crying, then sticks his thumb in his mouth and sucks on it furiously. His mother says, "It's useless to console yourself with your thumb! Come, silly, go look for another toy." She laughs, but seems almost a little embarrassed.

In the meantime another nurse comes into the room with some new toys that she has just bought. She puts them all on the mattress and blows up a fish which is bright red, about forty centimetres long. Then she throws the fish on the mattress among three or four children. Simone, who is now on the floor on hands and knees, is only a short distance away but he does not immediately succeed in

[1] 'puericultrice'; a speciality in Italian hospital paediatric departments.

coordinating his movements in a forward direction and bumps against the mattress. Then, stretching himself without having completely by-passed the mattress, he succeeds in grabbing the fish by the tail and pulling it towards himself. He appears to be happy with his prize but immediately Miriam comes and takes it away from him.

Simone sits down angrily and begins to protest both verbally and frowning, until he becomes red in the face. As the toy doesn't 'come back', he begins to hit himself with both hands on the thigh. His mother says, "Hey, look how angry this baby is! But do something! What sense is there in hitting yourself?" She takes him by the hand and makes him walk.

Simone walks in the direction of Miriam who is seated a little further away holding the fish tightly in her hands. Simone, on reaching Miriam, doesn't bend down to take the fish but instead pulls the little girl's hair. His mother, pulling his hand away says, "No, don't hit Miriam, look what pretty toys are over here". She sits him on the floor giving him two comic books to look at. Simone takes one in his hand, turns it over, bringing it up to his mouth.

Instantly Miriam comes over and takes it away from him. I give him the other comic book, but the little girl takes that away from Simone as well. He gets very angry, becomes terribly red in the face and begins to hit himself, this time on the knees. This scene lasts a few minutes and then, holding his mother's hand, he goes towards a balloon with a diameter of about sixty centimetres and leans on top of it, hitting it lightly with the palm of his hand, but as he is leaning too heavily he finishes by falling on the floor when the balloon moves and he hits his head on the wall.

Here we see Simone's entrance into the world of his peers, presided over by kindly and protective adults. But it is also apparent that the adults are confused in their values and as a result give conflicting indications; conflicting with one another and from time to time inconsistent in themselves. The mother starts out by being concerned that Simone should not hurt other children and should meet the expectations of the adults, but soon realises that the presenting problem is one of meeting the aggression of the other children. She counsels disengagement but realises that this results in his rage being turned against himself. However she is even less pleased when his violence comes out more directly, and both counsels and provides a substitute for the stolen prize. But when he does find an even more desirable, that is bigger, prize he still ends by hurting himself.

Third Observation – 10 months and 4 weeks

Elena, who seems to have moments of gloom similar to those of Simone, is on the carpet. She had already come to the crèche a little last year and is now one year old. She happens to find herself near Simone during one of her sad moments and Simone, who until that moment had been playing, throws his toy away and quickly grabs the little girl by the hair. I, who am near him, try to hold back his hand and say, "No, you are hurting the little girl." But every time I let go of his hand Simone grabs Elena's hair and pulls hard. The little girl's cries become more desperate and Simone stares at her very seriously, obviously ready to repeat the action.

Holding his hand I guide him towards another corner of the room, but just as we arrive there a baby of six months, who had all this time been quiet, begins to cry; immediately Simone goes over to him and starts to pull his hair. The nurse stops him and tells him that it is not nice to do so, but Simone looks at her with a serious expression and repeats the gesture. The nurse says that they are all like that; the moment a child is crying the others are ready to hit him. Taking the baby into her arms to protect it from Simone, she rocks it to and fro.

After only one week we see evidence of a change in Simone's adaptation to the crèche. The hair-pulling which began as an enraged attack on Miriam for stealing the fish has now become a serious disciplinary measure towards crying babies. Simone has both projected his helplessness and identified himself with the disapproval with which his helpless thumb-sucking and crying was met by his mother.

Fourth Observation – 11 months and 3 days

Simone is seated in his special car seat next to his mother who is driving when they arrive. She gets out, walks around and opens his door, saying, "Come, darling, we've arrived." Simone, frowning heavily, pulls back and becomes rigid when his mother tries to take him out of his seat. When he realises his mother is succeeding in lifting him he bursts out crying with his fists in his eyes.

His mother says to me, "Yesterday he began to cry when we went to the crèche. Today he doesn't even want to come out of the car". She appears sad and upset. She goes towards the crèche saying, "Let's hope he will get used to it and stop crying, otherwise we'll have to think of some other solution. Every morning when we leave, for example, my mother-in-law, instead of encouraging me, says, 'You're right, Simone, to be unhappy. Here you have a nice home and they send you away'. You can understand what my feelings are on hearing this. How can I feel serene? However, we'll just have to see".

While talking we've reached the entrance to the crèche. In the meantime Simone has calmed down; he is seated on his mother's forearm and has his right arm round her shoulder; he wears a very serious expression.

His mother says to him, "Simone, darling, don't you want to greet the lady, don't you even want to give her a smile?" Simone stares at me a moment and then bursts out crying. His mother says, "Don't you know her any more? Look it's the nice lady. But surely you recognise her?" Simone stops crying but remains sulky.

We've entered the building and in front of the baby section the nurse comes forward to meet us, saying, "Ah, there you are Simone, good morning." As soon as he sees her he desperately bursts out crying. He has become 'all mouth' and in a few seconds his face has become quite wet with tears. His mother, still holding him in her arms, says, "Come, Simone, be good, don't act like this. Come, let's take off your sweater and see if there are some nice toys around. Look, look, how many children! Come, let's play".

The nurse tells her, "Yesterday he stopped crying almost immediately", and turning to Simone, "Come, come, Simone, don't cry. You see that you are making Mummy feel bad". She takes him in her arms and tries to take off his sweater but he bends himself backwards, leaning towards the floor instead of against her shoulder.

His mother looks on in silence, appearing very pale. The nurse says to her, "It's better for you to leave now. I'll take the child in and, you'll see, he'll calm down right away". The mother replies, "Why can't he be like that child there, that one never cries", pointing out a child of six or seven months who is playing on the floor. Saying goodbye she leaves us. Simone still in the arms of the nurse continues crying but more softly. I go over to him with a ball and hold it out to him. He takes the ball, lets it fall and holds out his arms to me. I take him and he leans against me, holding his head on my shoulder with his face hidden in my neck. He cries with big tears and I can feel my neck becoming wet.

Simone goes on crying like this some little time, his heart beating very hard. He has put his thumb in his mouth and I can hear him sucking. I keep one hand on his back, caressing him gently and, little by little, he calms down.

It has been worthwhile describing this scene in some detail to place it in vivid counterpoint to the little serious-faced hair-pulling disciplinarian of crying babies. It also brings out very clearly the pressure to "be good", not to cry or protest at being "sent away from his nice home." The child's physical weakness in the face of adult determination is illustrated in the resistance alike to being removed from the car and divested of his sweater.

Fifth Observation – 1 year and 4 days

The nurse lets Simone watch as she shakes the cup with little stones in it, emitting a rattling noise. He laughs on hearing the noise, stretches out his hand and takes the cup. He too shakes it and, succeeding in making the noise, he then shakes the cup too hard and all the stones fall out. The little boy continues to shake the cup without obtaining the hoped-for result. He looks at the cup in surprise and, putting it into his left hand, puts the thumb of his right hand into his mouth.

The nurse says, "Now he rarely sucks his thumb, only in moments of unease or sadness. He really has adapted himself very well. He is a well-balanced child both with the other children and with adults". A little boy, seated next to Simone, bends towards him. Simone grabs him by the hair, pulling it hard. The nurse says, "No, that isn't nice", and, addressing me, "He's always ready to pull the other children's hair, almost as if studying their reactions".

While we have been speaking Simone has picked up the cup again and has put the stones back in it. A little girl near him all at once puts a stone into his cup instead of into her own. Immediately Simone grumbles his disapproval and takes out a stone to throw it away.

It seems an acute observation that Simone pulls the other children's hair "as if studying their reactions". The disciplinary grumble of disapproval and rejection of the little girl's stone certainly seems an insistence on protocol. Note that the nurse's praise for Simone's "good adaptation" does not appear in her eyes to be refuted by his pulling a child's hair the very next moment. In fact it is part of what "all children do", as brought out in the third observation.

Sixth Observation – 1 year and 17 days

The nurse sees Simone's father through the glass door and says, "Look, it's your father, Simone". The child goes towards the door and stretches his arms up to his father who picks him up, puts him on his own head for a second and then embraces and kisses him.

Simone has remained still, with his arms wide open against his father's body. For a few more seconds he remains in this position and then bites the biscuit in his hand. He then offers it to his father who also takes a bite. With his free hand he seems to caress his father's face, though a little vigorously. His father says, "Gently, gently, little one. Not so hard. Caress me, come, that's a good boy."

This interesting bit of observation takes us back to the tender scene between father and son in the first observation, but something different has been added, namely the roughness, in which the caress and the blow have become a bit difficult to distinguish. Similarly the matter-of-fact way in which the biscuit is shared suggests that Simone has become 'one of the boys'. We will see the implications of this biscuit biting in the next, lengthy observation.

Seventh Observation – 13 months and 12 days

I arrive at the crèche at eight o'clock in order to observe Simone's arrival. He is usually accompanied by his mother whom I haven't seen for some time. At 8.10 he arrives in his father's arms. He is well-seated on his father's right arm with the upper part of his body leaning against his father. He is wearing a blue wind-cheater with a hood, long corduroy trousers and 'men's' shoes with rubber soles. The tip of his nose has a little scratch.

His father sees me first and says, "Simone, look who is waiting for you." The baby watches while I go to meet him, smiles slightly and leans his head on his father's shoulder, always however keeping his face towards me. The nurse, who comes out to meet the child says, "Simone, don't play bashful; you're really not the type".

Simone lifts his head and looks me full in the face, smiling more widely; then twists a little, wanting to come down from his father's arms. His father immediately puts him down and Simone directs his steps determinedly towards the door of the kitchen and adjoining pantry. His father is blocked from following by the nurse who wishes to complain to him as an official of the Commune about the staffing situation. But Simone is stopped at the door of the kitchen by the cook who tells him, "No, Simone, you can't come in here", and then turning to me, "You know what we discovered? He goes into the pantry to bite the apples. We found the whole first layer of a crate marked by his four front teeth."

Simone, hearing the "no" of the cook, makes an about-face and returns to his father who is still talking with the nurse. Going near to him, rising on his toes and stretching his arms he grabs onto his father's jacket. Still talking, father bends down immediately to pick him up. The baby leans his head on his shoulder, then straightens up, waves "bye-bye" with his hand, kisses him rather loudly on both cheeks and then, twisting and turning, indicates his wish to be put down.

The nurse says, "What a good boy; you said bye-bye to Daddy." And the father, having kissed the baby also, confirms this. "Yes, Simone is really good. Show the lady how you cry when you get a spanking." Simone, however, now on the ground, does not pay any attention to his father who continues to explain, "He has learned to make believe he is crying. He goes aah! aah!"

I tell him that Simone is really growing up. The nurse takes the child's hand and says, "Come, Simone, let's go and get some biscuits." They head towards the pantry while, turning to me, she says, "Simone is easily bought off with a biscuit. Even during the worst moments of saying good-bye a biscuit usually resolves his pain."

This part of the observation strongly confirms the link between Simone's 'good adjustment' and his camaraderie with his father. The ease of separation and the play-acting about spankings show the strong bond against 'babyishness' which binds them, linked with evidence of his becoming a man-of-the-world who can bargain and accept compromises. After all, to paraphrase, biscuits don't grow on trees.

Seventh Observation (continued)

Simone trots by the nurse's side into the pantry and emerges with a biscuit in his right hand, already bitten. His father has already left but Simone does not seem to notice or mind. He is concentrated on eating his biscuit in little bites, passing it from hand to hand. He walks about the room confidently, although it has become almost dangerous because of the older children who are riding up and down on their tricycles at some speed, avoiding those on foot only at the last moment. I feel a little anxious but neither the nurse nor the children seem in the least worried.

Here we have a glimpse of the 'world' that Simone is now so well-adapted to, a world of dexterity and self-assurance, where the smaller ones are accustomed to being harassed by the larger and one must not cry until actually hurt, and then it is only to be 'make-believe' crying to call down upon your assailant the aggression of a still larger member of the hierarchy.

Seventh Observation (continued)

A two-year-old boy comes near me, pulling my skirt, asking me to take down a little truck which is high up on a shelf at the other end of the room. I go towards it and the little boy takes my hand. Simone, who seemed to be ignoring me completely, walking casually about the room, follows me quickly and attaches himself to the opposite side of my skirt. I give the toy to the little boy who goes away happily. But Simone pulls me by the skirt towards the slide. On the way he sees a little girl with a *grissino* in her hand. He goes up to her and breaks off half the bread stick in spite of her protests and begins to eat it, moving away with a calm expression but looking back at her every once in a while with detached interest.

As soon as he has finished the *grissino* he proceeds to the slide, five steps high, which he mounts on his knees rather than on his feet. He does not look at me until he is standing at the top, smiling triumphantly. Then, seating himself, he slides down holding on to the edge. The smile of happiness makes his eyes shine as he slides down and stands up at the bottom, only to repeat the whole operation immediately.

Clearly it is a man's world, but you must know your place in the hierarchy. Yield quietly to a bigger boy but the girls are fair game. The main thing is to improve your skills and thereby your status, to make yourself more attractive to the big girls.

Seventh Observation (continued)

All at once the delivery boy comes in with a sack of bread which he gives to the nurse. The bigger children greet him with cries of joy and run to get their share. But as Simone does not come near she calls him and he goes to her and holds out his hand. Putting the bread into his mouth for a bite Simone returns to the slide and prepares to mount by his usual method. However, the bread in his hand prevents his exerting the necessary lift so he places it on the step above. In this manner he proceeds upwards, placing the bread ahead each time. Satisfied with his achievement he sits down at the top and bites his bread, stuffing the last bit into his mouth before he slides down.

Once back on the ground he spies a piece of bread dropped by another child, in the centre of the room. He goes over to it and is about to pick it up when the nurse who is watching says, "Simone, you don't want to become a garbage can, I hope!" She emits a little cautionary cough, Simone looks at her, touches the bread lightly and appears to make a slight retching movement, emits a similar little cough and moves away leaving the bread.

Again one is impressed by the subtle adjustment to the culture of the crèche. Simone does not compete with the older children for the bread but waits for a 'hand-out'. His ingenuity is in full spate and he easily masters the task of returning to his slide-performance along with his bread-impedimentum, waiting until he is safely at the top before devouring it. We could be observing monkeys at this point, except that the monkey would probably hold the food in his mouth. But most striking of all is his submission to the values, as enunciated by the big girl, the nurse. Not only does he agree that the piece of bread on the floor is to be looked upon as 'garbage', as indicated by the little retching movement, but he also clearly identifies with her in the little admonitory cough.

Seventh Observation (continued)

The nurse calls the names of the children in her group and says, "Shall we go into our room?" Simone, who is near her, is taken up in her arms. I say good-bye to her because my observation hour has passed and she says to the baby, "Say bye-bye to the lady who has to leave." Simone stares at me very seriously but does not make any move. The nurse raises his arm to wave it a little in order to encourage him, but his hand remains limp. So I must leave followed by Simone's serious, perhaps accusatory, eyes. A strikingly different leave-taking from the cavalier manner in which his father was dismissed! For the observer to leave after such a virtuoso wooing on the slide seems difficult to forgive.

Now we can return to the most intriguing item of all, the presumptive apple-biting reported by the cook. Note that it is not alleged that Simone has been greedy, taking a bite from the apples, nor wasteful, biting many and eating none. No, it is suggested that he has gone through the entire top layer on the tray of apples marking each one with his four front teeth. What are we to make of this behaviour? Would it be too exotic to suggest that the meaning of the behaviour was indeed 'marking'? Each of the biscuits would, after all, be marked with the name or emblem of its manufacturer. Might the little stickler for protocol of the stone-and-cup incident, the egalitarian of the enforced *grissino*-sharing, have noted the absence of an identifying mark on the apples, equivalent to 'G.I.', government issue? Far from being a thief he may have been representing the Inspector General's Office.

Nothing of this analysis of this weekly sampling of a one-year-old's behaviour can be convincing, but it is very evocative and suggestive by virtue of the extreme youth of the child. I have called it a parable for this very reason, that the limited number of salient facts dove-tail so tightly that one has almost the impression of a preconception generating an invention as a literary form. I have taken the text as presented to me by a relatively naïve observer to whom the formulations reached at the seminar came as a surprise. So no tampering with the material for the sake of theoretical exposition is possible. I say this more to convince myself than the reader, for I was quite dazzled by Simone's performance. I found in his adaptation to the crèche and his parents' dilemma a parable of our confusing times, in which the avowed aim of raising our children in gentleness and an atmosphere of love and trust must be suspected of sending them disarmed into a rough-and-tumble world. This rather sporting definition certainly fits the crèche, but in Simone's adaptation one can see the outlines of a far less benign system, at once political and brutal, or at least incipiently violent.

It seems strongly suggested by the text that Simone's virtuosity in adaptation had its roots in a process already in operation at home, namely of using his affectionate and exciting relationship with his father to project jealously into his mother. We can only guess at the motives which may have prompted this, in all likelihood the residual grievances about weaning and the awareness that his mother was preparing to leave him during the day, either with a grandmother or at some strange place. The fourth observation makes clear the underlying suffering about separation from his mother, while the contrasting ease of separation from the father in the seventh observation shows how strongly structured is the new defensive system against these pains of babyhood. Yet there is not an item in the parental behaviour, as described by the observer, which could arouse our concern, let alone our criticism. Their affection for Simone and concern for his development is sincere, intelligent and informed. They could serve to epitomise the educated, sensitive and united parental couple which psycho-analysis holds to be so vital for creating the atmosphere in which children can develop.

Yet we find ourselves looking with misgivings on Simone's adaptation, far less pleased with him than are the father, nurse or observer. We seem to see the beginnings of a severe division between the social relationship's sphere and the realm of intimate family relationships. A sense of hierarchy, identification with authority, sanctimonious punitiveness, arrogant exhibitionism and male chauvinism are all suggested, at the expense of tenderness, gentleness and sensitivity of which he is clearly capable. Simone is certainly not unarmed nor long perplexed by the structure of the crèche and its social order. His initiation by Miriam confronted him with confusing instructions from his mother, but he soon threw these off and placed his reliance on primitive social impulses of a clearly tribal sort. We may not see him as Golding's 'Jack', the incipient demagogue, but neither is he a 'Ralph' or 'Piggy'. No, he gives promise of being a good organisation-man, and that is what we are determined to be worried about.

In terms of the structure of the personality the organisation-man would conform to that level of functioning which Bion identified as group-mentality founded on the operation of the Basic Assumption. By this he meant that primitive or tribal grouping takes place at a level at which creative thought is not in operation, but is stimulated by mental processes of logical deduction from the Basic Assumption. He named and studied three of these which he called Fight-flight, Pairing and Dependence. The central aim of the group is security and stability, and all meaning is derived from the Basic Assumption by logical operations. In the realms of individual mentality its paradigm would be paranoia, where the Basic Assumption is that an arch persecutor exists. All events are interpreted in this light. To the organisation-man his status in the group constitutes his security, and the stability of the group is the foundation of this status.

Individual mentality operates on entirely different principles, namely the internalisation of parental objects of admiration, trust and dependence. With the help of these internal objects thinking transforms emotional experiences into symbolic representations by borrowing forms from the outside world as containers that can be filled with meaning. Dreaming becomes the basis for transformation of introspective processes into language, while abstraction and generalisation carry the processes of thought forward. Emotional experiences, and therefore, as their most intense matrix, intimate relationships with other individuals change the individual so that the organisation of his personality develops. This development is guided by the admiration for the internal objects and the aspirations, essentially ethical, which they generate.

The organisation-man does not develop in the structure of his personality, he merely becomes more skilful in manipulating his group in the interests of advancing in status and security. Obedience to the Basic Assumption is the only virtue for the organisation-man. This means obedience to those higher in the hierarchy and exacting obedience from those lower. Rights do not exist; these are ethical concepts of the individual mentality. For the organisation-man these are replaced by privilege. A system of stratified privilege implies the turning of a blind eye by those lower down the scale to the activities in which those higher up indulge themselves while forbidding or preventing them to those lower down. It is essentially collusive, even conspiratorial in regard to the lowest stratum. But in fact the lowest of the lowest are the children of the lowest (omitting the domestic animals, insects and toys over which children may tyrannise).

How then do we in fact operate our family lives? How does Simone's family operate in comparison with the crèche? In order to explore this we would need to be able to make a whole galaxy of differentiations whose subtlety, in action, is still beyond our means. When does a principle change into a rule? When does a warning become a threat? What distinction can be made between a consequence and a punishment? What is the quality of the love that "does not alter when it alteration finds"? When does forgiving become excusing? How do we foster learning rather than engage in teaching or training? Though we may escape the hypocrisy of failing to practise what we preach, how can we avoid the even greater hypocrisy of preaching what we practise? If we are determined to "turn the other cheek" how many times must we do so? If we intend to mean what we say, does this commit us to action rather than only to communication? What is an enemy and should we kill him?

These subtle questions do not exist for the organisation-man. But the world outside the walls of our family home is very largely made up of organisations. Within them there may exist, and often do, small 'work-groups' operating in which the ethics of individual mentality prevail, under rules of procedure, the sub-world of contractual relations and cooperation. But experience suggests that this sub-world which Rousseau so greatly over-valued is fragile, breaking down into the politics of the Basic Assumption as soon as conflict and stress arise. Clearly we cannot exist without these organisations, short of returning to the caves. We, as individuals, need organisations – and they, of course, need us. How can we operate without compromise, without degrading the character which we must show to our children, for it is the most important thing we have to offer them as aid towards developing themselves? Is it really conceivable that Himmler was a good husband and father? Willy Loman then?

Clearly the answer is that we do not know; we do not know how to accommodate to the requirements of the organisations without compromise; we do not know how to raise our children; we have not the powers of introspection nor the conceptual tools for making the necessary ethical distinctions. No one knows – as yet. But perhaps watching children like Simone can teach us. It would, however, be unfair to Simone's qualities to leave the impression that these few observations give a rounded picture. Nor on the other hand would it clearly illustrate the thesis of this paper if the impression were to be left that tyrannical tendencies were a strong feature of this child's make-up. In fact this period of marvellous adjustment to the group culture was short-lived indeed, as an observation a few weeks later will clearly illustrate.

Eighth Observation – 15 months (six weeks after the last one reported, a two-week winter holiday having intervened)

Simone arrives in his father's arms. The child's posture is upright and he lowers his head towards his father's only when he encounters my eyes. His father says, "Aren't you going to say good-morning to the lady?" Simone stares at me very seriously and when his father puts him down on the ground in order to take off his jacket he attaches himself with both hands to his father's left leg and looks upwards without cooperating at all in the operation of divesting him of his jacket. His father takes him by the hand and guides him towards the classroom, trying to interest him in the children's games and in the numerous toys scattered all over the floor.

Simone picks up a rattle with three little bells, shakes it and brings it to his father; then he picks up a toy drum and shakes this too and again brings it to his father. His father says, "They all make a noise, these toys, Simone! You see how pretty they are!" And he too shakes one of the toys. While Simone moves a few feet away in order to pick up a new toy, Miriam comes close to Simone's father and inserts herself between his knees. Then the little girl turns her back on him and tries to support herself with her shoulders pressed against his knees. Simone's father maintains his position with his arms on his knees; Simone immediately, without stopping to pick up another toy, comes close to him and puts a hand on his father's wrist, looking alternately at his father's face and at Miriam's face.

Simone's father says to the little girl, "Little kitten, you like to be cuddled, eh?" and turning to Simone continues, "Come here, Simone, let's see if Miriam would like to play with you." He then pushes the little girl towards Simone, who, when Miriam is near him, changes direction and bends down to pick up a little rattle which has the form of a lolly and emits a sound when compressed in the mouth. He puts it in his mouth many times making it squeal, but when he realises that his father is going towards the door he bursts into tears and tries to run after him.

The nurse picks him up in her arms and says, "Come, Simone, come let's go get a cracker." And she goes with him towards the pantry. When they come out again Simone is holding a cracker in his hand but he doesn't eat it. I notice that another ten minutes pass before Simone takes his first bite of the cracker and even later he bites absent-mindedly, at intervals, and he finally leaves a last little piece on the edge of the table.

Simone, with a tiny yellow box in his hand, goes towards the window. He looks out and his eyes follow the few cars that pass by. Every once in a while he goes, "Br-br", but this sound doesn't coincide with the passage of the cars. I am not able to understand on what basis he makes his selection.

Miriam comes to him and, taking the little box away from him, begins to pass it through the window knob. She repeats this move-ment four or five times until Simone leans against the window and takes the little box away from her the moment it comes within his grasp. He turns it around between his hands and then sticks it in his mouth.

Miriam protests against the theft of the box and Simone lets her 'grumble' for a bit (it sounds as if the little girl is talking because she gives the right intonations with her voice but the words themselves are incomprehensible); then he extends his hand and offers the box to her, grumbling and frowning at the same time.

Miriam takes the box and again begins to pass it through the window handle. The whole scene is re-enacted four or five times, including the grumbles and exchange of the toy. Simone then again puts the toy in his mouth and, using my skirt as a support, tries to climb up on a chair. During this action the box falls down and finishes up underneath a round table a little distance away. Simone crawls under the table, picks up the box and gets onto his feet all smiles.

The nurse comes up to the children and says, "Come, Simone, let's go play with the building blocks." She picks him up in her arms and goes towards the shelf full of toys.

It is quite clear that Simone has recovered from his brief flirtation with the group culture and the Basic Assumption of "Only babies cry!" But his parents have also recovered from their anxiety that he should be well-adjusted. They are now dividing the bringing and fetching of the child on the basis of convenience rather than political principle, and the grandmother fills in at times. Simone regularly registers his grief at being left and his impatience to be collected. In the crèche he is rather isolated from the other children, preferring to concentrate his attention on some learning operation. But he is not unfriendly to the other children; perhaps more tolerant than convivial, as in the case with Miriam.

Perhaps most impressive is his recovery of incorruptibility by biscuits, which he now accepts graciously but without compromise and he nibbles without enthusiasm. Things on the floor are no longer 'garbage' but may be put into the mouth as part of his infantile equipment of reality-testing. His accomplishments, both in motility, dexterity and knowledge are more private in their satisfaction, not to be used for display or seduction of the 'big girls'. He is prone to invent games which have a separation-reunion theme in them and clearly has in mind his parents, perhaps especially his father who more often collects than brings him to the crèche. This he demonstrates not only by his behaviour at the window but also by saying "Daddy-Daddy" a few weeks after this observation. The general impression is now one of cooperative acquiescence rather than obedience towards the staff in matters of eating, being cleaned, lying down for a nap. He is no longer disciplinary towards other children nor is he subservient or self-punitive. Rather, as with Miriam and the yellow box, he waits his chance to recover stolen toys and even spontaneously converts the conflict into a process of turn-taking. Quite remarkably civilised! On the whole his relation to the equipment of the crèche has become imaginative and experimental rather than conforming. The nurses are clearly less proud of him, more puzzled and troubled, but on the whole admiring. As are we!

In summary then, the brief period of conformity to the Group Basic Assumption culture can be seen as regressive and its primitive automatic quality stands out with great clarity, along with its essential function, defence against the pain of separation from his parents and his "nice home". The recovery has been accompanied by a forward thrust in his strength, imaginativeness, urge to language formation and respect for the space of others.

XIV

Family Patterns and Cultural Educability

with
Martha Harris (Oxford)

When in 1977 Beresford Hayward, of the Organisation for Economic and Cultural Development (OECD) asked us to prepare a psycho-analytical model of the relation of the family to the community, he had in mind an instrument for use in an international study of educational processes, a model which could be used to integrate findings of a multidisciplinary approach. This request was timely for us as we had embarked on a plan to produce a revised diagnostic system for child guidance clinics which would bring together knowledge and methods of study directed variously towards the individual, the family and the community. The result was called 'A Model of the Child-in-the-Family-in-the-Community'.

This chapter aims first to display the classification of family patterns we described in the 'Model', and then to explore the relation of these patterns to learning processes and corresponding educational conflicts. The theoretical model employed was the Kleinian-Bionic model as described in *The Kleinian Development*. Family life was envisioned as a more or less stable organisation of three general types: 1) the family proper (couple family), 2) the narcissistic gang, 3) the Basic Assumption Group (BA). Within these three types of organisation we made the distinction between individuals occupying special *roles* and fulfilling particular *functions*. The roles are assumed to comprise culturally defined prerogatives, responsibilities and privileges, and therefore variable from culture to culture. The functions, however, we named as follows:

1) generating love
2) promulgating hate
3) promoting hope
4) sowing despair
5) containing depressive pain
6) emanating persecutory anxiety
7) thinking
8) creating lies and confusion.

On the basis of this three-type organisational model and eight pattern dynamic concept we were able to describe in outline the structure and functioning of the individuals-in-the-family-in-the-community, sub-dividing each disturbed organisational type into six sub-types, or thirteen sub-types in all.

The avowed intention of any family grouping is to nurture the development of its members for the preservation of the group either through harmonious integration with, destructive attacks upon, or parasitism on, the surrounding milieu, human and non-human. This nurturing must involve its members in learning, and this learning may take place inside or outside the family grouping; it may be formal or informal, noticed or unnoticed. Acquisition of knowledge and skills may contribute to development of the personality and thus to status, or it may confer *de facto* operational status, or status may be acquired by other means as if the status itself conferred skills and knowledge which do not in fact exist (hereditary status for instance). Thus roles and functions may coincide, overlap or diverge. Skills and knowledge always have both internal world and external world significance but particular aspects of skills and knowledge vary in their balance with regard to these two types of significance, or they may be confused with one another (as in the case, say, of a tribal medicine man or a present day bank manager).

Psycho-analytical studies of the life of individuals suggest that there are a large number of ways in which alterations in the skills and knowledge may come about, some of which we can describe with some richness and precision. These various methods of organisation are probably all, from the most primitive to the most sophisticated, used to some degree by every individual of at least minimum intelligence, but psycho-analytical experience shows clearly that the character is deeply etched by the preferred modes of learning and that these preferred modes are in turn deeply influenced by the modes current in the nurturing family group and its state of organisation. We will now try to describe these modes of learning and in so doing make explicit the learning theory which is implicit in the Kleinian-Bionic Model-of-the-Mind.

1. *Learning from Experience* Following Bion's classic description we would emphasise that learning from experience modifies the person because it is the result of an *emotional* experience in which the chaotic sense data and the persecutory anxieties pursuant to the confusion are submitted to an object, either an internal object or an external object carrying a parental transference, for sorting. The learning consequent has therefore *the meaning of an item of introjective identification* since not only is the immediate problem resolved (secondary learning of knowledge or skill) but also something is learned of the modes of thought employed in the resolution (primary learning: Wittgenstein's "now I can go on"). The dependent relation to the internal or external tutor

requires a struggle from the paranoid-schizoid to a depressive orientation (Bion's Ps↔D) since the meaning and significance must be entertained as an aesthetic experience.

2. *Learning by Projective Identification* Ranged in order of increasing primitiveness the next mode of learning would be through the employment of the omnipotent phantasy of projective identification first described by Melanie Klein in 1946 ('Notes on Some Schizoid Mechanisms', International Journal of Psycho-Analysis). Since the motivation for this type of learning is often envy of the object's superior capacities, and since the aim is the immediate acquisition of these skills or knowledge, the result is often a delusional overestimation of the desired acquisition. Nonetheless projective identification does enable the subject to 'go through the motions' of the admired skill or knowledge and thus to achieve some degree of mechanical reproduction of the performance of the object's human (or animal) capability, albeit a caricature. This caricature aspect derives from the lack of authenticity of the emotionality intrinsic to the performance and may, in the case of children, appear comic; in the hands of the comedian it becomes satire.

3. *Learning by Obsessional Collecting* Since the obsessional state of mind employs omnipotent means of controlling its objects in the service of evasion of oedipal conflict, it is given to sorting, cataloguing and collecting, but in so doing deprives objects of their freedom and vitality. Such lifeless collections of objects, facts and recollections have no utility in themselves but may become a source for non-obsessional utilisation having, so to speak, a secondary value. The obsessional person may be highly prized by his community for his performance of this type of donkey work but is inevitably replaced by some mechanical contraption. It is important to stress that obsessional sorting and collecting of objects and facts can only employ an index of manifest qualities since deeper meaning and significance always require a creative conjunction scintillating with oedipal significance, and thus of anxiety, for their apprehension (i.e. the aesthetic level).

4. *Learning by Submission to a Persecutor* Much of the learning to which children are submitted is experienced by them in this mode, sometimes called the 'stick-and-carrot' method of pedagogy, more or less benevolent but structurally tyrannical. While the mechanics of the learning may be so achieved, rebelliousness and negativism are engendered so that the consequences tend to be of two sorts: either the acquisition is jettisoned from the mind as soon as the tyranny is escaped; or a projective identification with the persecutor leads to the

skills and knowledge being used in an aggressive and tyrannical way. It is not certain whether the more primitive form of learning by conditioning does actually take place in human beings, as it clearly does in lower animals, since momentary and seemingly automatic (unthinking) obedience can simulate the phenomena of conditioning seen at submental levels (autonomic).

5. *Learning by Stealing and Scavenging* The senses may be utilised in a secretive way for the acquisition of skills and knowledge. This produces secondarily a considerable inhibition of the utilisation of whatever is acquired since its display is felt tantamount to confession of guilt. This stealing can be modified by a phantasy of scavenging for valuable things that others foolishly throw away. Inevitably this tends to be confined to items of recherché or dubious value, the exotic or anachronistic. The sense of lack of social integration verging on tramp or pariah often accompanies activities built upon such a method of acquisition.

6. *Learning by Adhesive Identification* Esther Bick in her 1968 paper on skin function (International Journal of Psycho-Analysis) described a second method of narcissistic identification more primitive than projective identification and based upon very different motives. She described people whose internal objects were such poor containers and thus provided so little emotional endoskeleton to the personality that they were forced to hold their personality together by other means, one of which was through the phantasy of adhering to the surface of external objects. This seems to correspond closely to what Helene Deutsch described in her famous paper on the 'as if' personality type. This adhesive phantasy produces a type of identification with the superficial, socially visible qualities of the object but not with its mental qualities or states of mind. The behaviour that results is so immediate and so contingent on the presence or vividness of the external object as to deserve the description 'mimicry'. Its manifestations in the behaviour of autistic children has been described in *Explorations in Autism*. It is suitable for the learning of social roles but cannot foster the capability for social functions.

Our next task must be to educe some general principles governing the relationships in family groups which tend to favour the utilisation of one or other of these six modes of learning in the members of the family. We will then attempt to relate these general principles to the chief sub-types of families that have been described in the 'Model'. The course we have chosen for the elucidation of general principles is to apply our eight categories of emotional functions to the six types of learning to see if they have any discernible relationship. It would then be an almost mechanical task to apply these conjunctions of learning type and function type to the family sub-types.

1) *Generating love* Where love is generated or diffused in the social atmosphere either by an individual through his relation to internal objects or by coupled relationship, security and therefore the possibility of dependence is fostered. But the richness and generosity displayed also evoke envy. Therefore a delicate balance is set up between tendencies to introjective and projective identification in the dependent members. This balance seems to be particularly affected by the loving person's capacity to allow the dependent members to experience the mental pains of their inferiority and neediness, to allow both space and time before helpful intervention.

2) *Promulgating hate* This function, which consists in attacking the living links within the group by playing upon the feelings aroused in frustration, tends always to generate a gang, either by direct leadership or *eminence grise* activity. Such gangs are intrinsically tyrannical and utilise threat and seduction to bind their internal organisation. Since the destructive skills are essentially simpler than constructive ones, the learning process by submission to the leader is rapid and gratifying to dependent members of the family sub-gang.

3) *Promoting hope* Hopefulness as an emotion, and optimism as its characterological attitude, seems to have its roots in a sense of the positive balance between constructive and destructive forces in the individual and group. It is easily disturbed by external events of a tragic nature, even more so when these are imponderable strokes of fate rather than when their human agency is clear. Therefore the maintenance of hope as a quality of family atmosphere depends upon some member being able to maintain a sense of proportion, both in the longitudinal and global sense. An atmosphere of hope fosters aspiration and willingness to risk positions of safety, to deploy vitality and resources, and thus stimulates the thirst for knowledge and skills. Its manic simulation in complacency, religiosity and denial of tragedy has an opposite effect. No quality so draws the dependent members towards introjective identification as resilient hopefulness in a parental (or even a child) figure, for it displays courage in the face of consequences, a more convincing stance than courage in the face of danger.

4) *Sowing despair* Pessimism, born of a sense of either impregnable rigidity of the system or overwhelming destructive forces, poisons the atmosphere of a family group and drives its members towards security operations. This tendency favours obsessional mechanisms of learning but also the type of leaving-the-field characteristic of scavenging. In its more extreme forms this retreat may extend to external as well as psychic reality and favour the quasi-theological

clinging of the Basic Assumption Group. The learning of irrelevant skills and the acquisition of delusional knowledge may then alienate the family and its members from the culture, with the exception of items useful for a parasitic or destructive relation to the community.

5) *Containing depressive pain* The modulation of depressive pain in a family group is characteristically a function of the parents but with surprising frequency is found to be exercised by one of the children, sometimes in a way which has the appearance of an emotional illness (as for instance after a death in the family). Since this modulation within tolerable limits is a precondition for the employment of learning from experience by dependent members, its failure tends to set in motion fragmenting forces within the group as persecutory depression circulates and irritability increases. When unity of the family declines egocentricity flourishes and engenders delinquent attitudes. Scavenging and stealing, and the modes of learning stimulated by them, replace identificatory learning processes in the 'every man for himself' atmosphere. The materialistic ambitiousness of the children in a disorganised immigrant family would exemplify this state. But where psychopathology in the mother takes the form of extreme fragility, adhesive processes are set in motion in young children and can persist even in the face of subsequent recovery or strengthening of the mother.

6) *Emanating persecutory anxiety* Any member of a family who has a sense of present terror may serve as a focus for this emotion, either by exuding the anxiety into the atmosphere or by projecting it through terrorising younger or weaker members. The sense of supra-parental forces of catastrophe so undermines both the roles and functions of the parental figure that an atmosphere of incipient panic, of apocalyptic dangers, can pervade. Whether the dangers be medical, financial, social or political, the atmosphere of helplessness paralyses learning functions of all but the most mimetic type. Adhesive identifications with figures outside the family can be seen when such situations make contact with community facilities.

7) *Thinking* While this function can be performed by anyone in the family in default by the actual parent, the capability soon runs out if the problems become complex, or when the family is in a dislocated relation to the community, or if the community itself is in disarray. A member who displays a capacity for thought quickly accrues transference significance, quite irrespective of age, and thus undertakes parental functions with or without usurping parental status. In the absence of this function the family must depend on traditional values, modes of behaviour, or seek advice outside its structure. In the face of

the disintegration of traditional patterns of family life (in immigrant groups or where Church affiliation has withered), professional thinkers-about-family-matters come into great demand with as yet inadequate equipment to fulfil this task.

8) *Creating lies and confusion* Since the creating of lies and confusion seems to develop as a talent in quite young children while the capacity for thought is still sparingly existent in their elders, family organisation is constantly threatened by the liar in its midst. The detection of lies, except for factual ones, being so difficult as still to evade the skills of psycho-analysts, it is not surprising to see the havoc that lying can wreak in a family. The uncertainty it throws into the atmosphere easily metamorphoses into cynicism about the value of truth, and poisons the ethical quality of family life. This has a destructive influence on the impetus to learning since confabulation seems to be so powerful. This essentially psychopathic tendency, asocial where it is not antisocial, seems even to make a game of un-learning what has already been acquired and perhaps corresponds to what Bion has called "alpha-function in reverse".

Any one of these eight functions may be implemented by actions or communications, open or covert; by truth or lies (that is by actions or statements whose meaning is known to be false). At any one moment any of these eight functions tends to be delegated to individual members, bringing them into functional conflict with their opposite number. Where individuals are at the moment attaching themselves to someone else to perform a function for them we will speak of functional dependence. Functions may be assumed by the individual or may be imposed upon him by other members. Functions may be in abeyance, being carried out by no one, thus forming a focus of chaos with implicit catastrophic anxiety. We may now turn our attention to the description of the Family Proper (the Couple Family) and some of its various types of imitations, caricatures, distortions and perversions.

The Couple Family

It must be remembered that we are not intending to present a concept of the ideal and its variations. We are attempting a highly dynamic model which assumes some degree of flux as a constant factor in the life processes of individuals, families and communities. Therefore the following descriptions of organisation must be taken in two senses: as the description of a momentary state, and as a general tendency.

At the moment when the family is presided over by a couple (not necessarily the actual parents) this combination will be seen to carry between them the functions of generating love, promoting hope, containing depressive pain, and thinking. The capacity of the couple to perform these functions will be felt to require their periodic withdrawal into privacy, supposed to be sexual and mysterious. The times when they are obliged to be apart produces a hovering sword-of-Damocles atmosphere while their conjunction arouses a constant expectation of 'new baby' members of the family. The history of their courtship is of mythological interest to the dependent members giving form to their hopes of the future.

The four introjective *functions* of the couple, generating love, promoting hope, containing pain, and thinking, are not felt to subdivide into masculine and feminine aspects but rather to be arranged in a more linear way, with the maternal person taking the brunt of the children's projections and the father being the end of the line for these mental waste products (Harry Truman's "the buck stops here").

All the catastrophic anxiety of the dependent members tends to centre on the mother, regardless of the intensity of love that may be felt for the father and the depressive anxieties that may accompany it. Therefore any evidence of debility in the mother tends to be blamed on the father's possible or suspected inadequacies. On the other hand debility in the father is taken as evidence that the system is being overloaded with hate and projected persecution and encourages polarisation among the dependent members, with a scape-goating tendency.

The growth of all members of the family, as evidenced by carefully monitored and frequently discussed indicators of physical, social, intellectual and emotional development, is necessary to maintain the sense of security which is intrinsic to the family and is felt to be utterly independent of the community despite the overall optimistic and benevolent view taken of the natural and social milieu. Thus the family is felt to be mobile potentially, even though it may be tenderly attached to the home or landscape or community of friends and neighbours. If opportunity glows on the horizon a pioneer atmosphere begins to scintillate, akin in feeling to the times when the mother is pregnant.

The overall relation to the community is felt to proceed through the individual members moving about: at school or at work or shopping, etc., as representatives of the family. Their individual identities (given name) are secondary in significance to their family identity (surname), not as an indicator of status but as a burden of responsibility. It is not so much a matter of "what will the neighbours think?", as of "letting the side down", in the business of contributing to the general ethos of the community.

The great vulnerability of the couple resides in the unique identity of each individual – for the death of a child seems to be the one unbearable stress (Wordsworth's *We Are Seven*). Even a miscarriage or a stillbirth can have a shattering effect upon the joyousness and commence a deterioration in ethos, relationships, cohesiveness, from which recovery may seem impossible. It has a more devastating effect than, say, the impact of a defective child, the development of a schizophrenic illness in a child, or the delinquency or defection of a member.

The Doll's House Family

A benevolent and not obviously ugly caricature of the Couple Family can be seen to arise through the mating of young people who have, out of the rigidity of the latency period, been unable to experience identification with the adolescent community. Out of love, respect, insecurity or lack of imagination, they have continued beyond the latency period to seek to fulfil their parents' expectations of them, including the injunction that they should be fruitful and multiply. Where intelligence is good and opportunities not utterly lacking, such couplings prosper economically through conformity and a good eye for opportunity, within timorous limits. The underlying timidity betrays itself in a slavish conformity to community standards or parental ones where these are not too aberrant.

The atmosphere of the home thus created is 'on show' while being at the same time withdrawn and seclusive with regard to emotional involvement with neighbours or community activities. The facilities of the community are submitted to rather than being employed or exploited, officials of the community (teachers, doctors, police, etc.) being held in awe, often involving some degree of idealisation regarding efficiency, honesty and knowledge.

Thus a paradoxical ethos of particular inferiority and a general moral superiority reigns in the family. They are good people and expect their children to be good children, which they usually are in a somewhat muted way. Consequently neurotic symptomatology claims parental notice while the character pathology, as long as it is not antisocial or eccentric, passes unseen. The first native generation or successful upward social mobility favour this pattern of family life, and security is its overriding value. Consequently illness generates panic, and economic setbacks promote feelings of shame and humiliation. Secrecy, which is meant to govern the intra-familial processes *vis-à-vis* the surrounding community, gradually creeps into the relationships within the family as well, introducing an element of increasing furtiveness to the atmosphere, with special reference to sexuality.

The Matriarchal Family

Where the mothering person (generally a woman but not necessarily) seems to arrogate to herself all the introjective functions, the difficulty may lie in the inadequacy, absence or debility of the fathering one, or it may reflect the force and vitality of the woman. Where this force has a hostile anti-masculine flavour the matriarchal shades into the girl-gang family of delinquent type. But in some cases the mothering person combines in herself such bisexual attributes of character and outlook, skills and strength, that the matriarchy approximates to the Couple Family in its ethos.

In the aspects of the community where the matriarchal family is traditional (the Jamaican immigrant population, for instance), the paternal function is fulfilled in a split way, by a combination of avuncular and grandfatherly figures. Where the father is absent through death, or from necessity for some period, his presence as an absent object may fulfil the necessary function in spirit while the actual psychological services are distributed among intrinsic or extrinsic male figures. But often the community is looked to for this function and these services. This is particularly true of the matriarchal family which has been constructed around the strength and anti-masculine aspects of the mothering person. It is this configuration in particular which most easily slips into the BA Dependent relation to the community, not in a hostile parasitic way but taking for granted the benevolence and generosity of the community, particularly of male figures in authority. Bank managers, social workers, ministers, doctors and solicitors are naturally looked to for services and are preferably brought into some degree of avuncular intimacy with the family group. The education of the children and their health supplies the motivation and justification for any degree of financial, moral or intellectual support, and since the mothering person often, in her vitality and optimism, makes an attractive figure, this support is readily proffered. The possibility of sexual entanglements is never far off but is generally avoided unless marriage seems feasible, even if unlikely.

The atmosphere in the home tends to rest upon discipline through guilt, and the standards are different from those of the growth-indicators of the couple family. In the matriarchal family the standards are more likely to be moralistic, aiming at adaptation to the supposed standards of the community. "What will the neighbours think?" is therefore more important in a persecutory way, as if the moral status of the mother were in question for unaccountable reasons. This is most pressing where the mother is divorced or the children are illegitimate.

Unlike the outcome one would expect in the couple family, serious maladjustment of an antisocial, psychotic or defective sort cannot easily be contained by a matriarchal family structure. Children who come into these categories tend more easily to be farmed out to childless relatives, grandparents, or placed in care in the community.

It is unusual for the matriarchal figure to be able to carry all four of the introjective functions of generating love, promoting hope, containing depression and thinking. One or more of these tends to be placed out, as it were. For instance a good baby may be treated as the generator of love; a particularly clever child may be the thinker; a cheerful one the generator of hope; or an obsessional one the reservoir of depressive feelings. Since these surrogates for parental part-functions are more able to represent than actually to perform the function, the basic instability of the situation declares itself whenever these functions are strained. The move into BA Dependence or regression to a more narcissistic pseudo-family organisation ensues.

The Patriarchal Family

A very different atmosphere is found where the paternal figure is very dominant, in particular if the mother has become incapacitated for psychological reasons, for example, alcoholic or depressed; or because of diagnosed physical illness, generally presumed to be post-partum in origin.

A soft type of paternalism may resemble the matriarchal family, and again where strong bisexuality in character exists may approximate to the couple family even when the mother is one of the dependent figures. But where the patriarchy is imposed by the father's aggressive and often somewhat grandiose character, and particularly where the mother has defected, a stern discipline rules both girls and boys, often supplemented by the father's unmarried sister or an aging mother. A bullying and punitively scathing type of tongue-lashing may follow upon the actual beating of younger children and the relics of religiosity are brought in to shore up the authority of the father.

A feudal system arises with economic control at its centre, from which the adolescents are quick to escape, being 'ungrateful' to their father. But girls may be held in masochistic-quasi-sexual submission well into their twenties, partly to protect younger children from the father's harshness and partly for unconscious erotic attachment to the father, characteristically followed by equally unsuitable marriages.

The relation of the patriarchal family to the community is one of proud independence and of unacknowledged dependence, for the father is unlikely to notice how much nurturing his children seek and get from neighbours, teachers, club leaders, etc. Denigration of the female is unmistakeable, tenderness is held to be soft or weak, and lying is the worst crime, for it threatens to plunge the family into a paranoid atmosphere. But the goodness of the father in terms of dependability, selflessness and unequivocal devotion to the children may save the atmosphere from dourness.

The father may be able to carry some of the introjective functions, particularly those of promoting hope, of containing depression or of thinking, if he is an educated man. But the more common pattern would seem to be that the generating of love becomes the grandparental function and binds the children very closely to these figures, the maternal ones in particular when the mother has died. The function of thinking may pass at an early age to the most forward child at school when the father is of low educational level. The containment of delinquent or even of psychotic or defective children is much better than in the matriarchal family, aid being sought from relatives or the community only when the best interests of the child seem to demand it.

The prospect of the father's remarrying, where this is a possibility, is held to be remote on the basis of his presumed 'seriousness', implying a desexualised state based on disillusionment. Only if the children are numerous and still very young does the figure of a housekeeper appear, gradually metamorphosing into wife in name, but not really in acknowledged function.

The patriarchal family is far more unstable in certain respects than the matriarchal one because of the ease with which the tyrannical aspect can escalate into gang-formation on the one hand, or the quasi-religious aspect slip into BA Dependent organisation of a particularly delicately balanced sort. Illness in the father can bring sudden disorganisation, at which point the unacknowledged dependence on the benevolence of the community becomes apparent. If the father's wage-earning capacity is thereby threatened, disintegration and dispersal may result, the children going to relatives or into care. Family reorganisation after such a breakdown is far more difficult than in a matriarchy because once the authority behind the discipline is broken it is difficult to reconstitute.

The Gang-Family, Amazonian and Titanic

Both matriarchy and patriarchy tend easily to slip into the more narcissistic state of gang-formation when the dominant person's character is precariously balanced between maturity and pseudo-maturity. But the more characteristic configuration arises when either one or both parental figures are strongly impelled by negative identifications. This is to be found in people who have established an early independence from parents whom they considered inadequate, bad or misguided in their methods of child-rearing. Since policies built upon the foundation of criticism of the grandparents have largely negative implications, positive policies tend to be constructed intellectually rather than on the basis of feeling for the children or understanding of and sensitivity to their feelings or anxieties. An underlying determination to be right, to demonstrate their superiority and thereby justify their earlier rebellion, promulgates a certain urgency to make the children conform to expectations, whether these be of 'goodness', or 'independence' or 'accomplishment'.

In this atmosphere the introjective functions tend to be simulated rather than performed, so that their titular roles and their dramatisation replace the genuine functions. Feelings of love are replaced by seductiveness, cuddling and indulgence. Hopefulness is simulated by manic cheerfulness, thereby denying the quantities of depressive feeling; thinking is replaced by slogans, cliché, dogma, catechism, often at a shallow level dealing with posture, dress, deportment, cleanliness, accent, the status of friends' families and other forms of snobbery.

Rebellion or failure to meet the requirements tends to bring sharp rejection and recourse to punishment or exclusion. Since the gang-family is matriarchal or patriarchal (Amazonian and Titanic might be better terms), it is not inclined to acknowledge its dependence on the community, but adopts a delinquent and scavenging attitude towards the facilities and services that are potentially available. Its tendency to metamorphose at a moment's notice into a BA Fight-flight group is forestalled by the excitement of the delinquent system. The evasion of feelings of guilt, by projecting all responsibility for exercising ethical judgment, places the gang in a field of high tension and attention. Bold and clever exploitation of the loopholes of either the benevolent social services or the potentially punitive legal system places a premium on the capacity to lie. Since this in turn depends on some considerable recognition of the truth, leadership of the family gang can easily pass from parental hands to those of the clever child who functions as prime minister to the ruling parent. Thus a high premium can be placed on gift-of-the-gab, especially in so far as it includes a facility for misrepresenting the truth, either in terms of historical facts or logical operations.

The aggressive attitude towards the community tends to find its most unassailable position in defence of debilitated members of the family, particularly if this is due to physical illness, accidental injury or mental deficiency. Righteous indignation in defence of the weak against the strong serves as a banner for endless raids on community resources.

The gang-family, by virtue of its ambiguous relation to the community, at once defiant and yet seeking acceptance, greedy and at the same time scornfully proud, imposes a confusing task on its members vis-à-vis the educational facilities available; its members are forestalled from forming a dependent and trusting relation to teachers and are yet expected to make sufficient progress to substantiate the ethos of the home environment and its avowed principles of child-rearing and social organisation.

Defiance of authority and scholastic accomplishment are unlikely partners until a firm foundation of learning skills has been established. This can seldom be expected before late adolescence because of lack of skill early on and lack of discipline later. Consequently low accomplishment or unbalanced school achievement seems to be the rule. Where it is possible to rationalise away the responsibility, the situation is then used as a further pretext for raids on the community's facilities for special schooling. The strong tendency to *folie-à-deux* relationships of parents and children predisposes to school refusal and school phobia.

The Reversed Family

A hostile caricature of family life may arise when one or both parental figures are either psychotic or are dominated by sexual perversity or criminal tendencies. The reversal of values sets the family group in defiant relationship to the community and its values in an isolating way which tends to be obscured by its mobility.

Since its members are seldom skilled, their economy is precarious with a clear tendency to be illegal. The relation to neighbours is therefore clearly predatory and provocative where it is not frankly collusive with similar families. It tends easily to accrue new members from migratory figures and gravitates towards gainful activities in the entertainment, second-hand goods, criminal, prostitute or corrupt political areas. Gambling, drinking, promiscuity, drug-taking, sexual perversions, incest and assault are part of the atmosphere of family life.

The introjective functions, and therefore thinking and planning, are almost absent. Consequently action tends to be unrestrained with the result that the mental pain (almost entirely persecutory) tends to circulate in the intra-familial pecking order and eventually to be evacuated into the community by predatory actions. The tyrannical order strongly promotes projective forms of identification with the stronger figures, although measure of strength is not always physical. It may reside in intelligence operating to promote confusion, aggravate rivalries, promulgate distrust or foster irrational persecutory anxieties.

In consequence the titular roles in the family tend to be a travesty while the functions migrate in a haphazard way. The tendency to chaos plays an important role in the reversed family's strong tendency to move into Basic Assumption Pairing, especially if the community reacts against its predatory or defiant attitude or actions. It can quickly tighten, become a kind of guerilla band and take to the road. This, added to its general peregrinating tendency, increases the likelihood of the children being maladjusted at school and unintegrated into any community or organisation of neighbourhood children.

Such a description may seem to suggest a class implication, and in a sociological sense this may be true, but ethnically it is not. The characteristics of speech, mannerisms, attitudes, interests and habits; the educational level of the parents; existence of private wealth and property: all these are extremely variable and might place such families in any class from decayed aristocracy to non-traditional gypsy.

We think it correct to say that bizarre beliefs, superstitions and delusions, along with a tendency to sexual perversity, arson and semi-accidental suicide are always close at hand. The flirtation with satanic religious sects and practices may be constant and can suddenly gel into a BA Group with religious pretensions, caricaturing hopefulness that relieves the atmosphere of general despair hidden behind paranoid anger.

The Basic Assumption Level of Family Organisation

There can be little doubt that a community, whether it be a nation, a business firm, a ship on the high seas, or a photographic club, has a wide-ranging capacity for organisation. Bion divided these manifold capabilities into two large categories: the Work Group and the Basic Assumption Group. While time, thought and communication in close cooperation is required to establish the former, the BA Group may spring up in a moment whenever two or more prople are present. It may have absent members who are just as important as those present, and its mode of functioning is by unconscious common consent in the myth which is its Basic Assumption.

Bion has described three of these Basic Assumptions: BA Fight-flight, BA Dependence, and BA Pairing. We will follow his lead here while placing upon these categories and their interaction with one another certain constructions of our own. For instance we will suggest that the three BA groups have a natural sequential relation to one another. This sequence could be described by the following narrative myth: in the beginning all the needs of the embattled group were fulfilled through the wisdom of its leaders (parents) so that the natural envy and enmity of the surrounding groups (tribes) was held in check. But as they grew older and more retiring, disagreement among the younger aspirants to the succession produced conflicting policies: some of flight, some of fight. The result was that on the death of the leaders the group broke into two, one sector remaining to fight and the other fleeing in search of more peaceful neighbours. While the former was gradually decimated or assimilated, the latter waited for the birth of a new leader (BA Pairing) and in due course one appeared who seemed to fulfil by his wisdom (BA Dependence) all the needs of the group, having first, by his fighting spirit, established and stabilised their relations with the new neighbours.

We will take this myth as paradigmatic of the circular movement (BA Pairing→BA Dependence→BA Fight-flight→BA Pairing) as the Basic Assumption level of organisation *vis-à-vis* the community of its neighbours and surrounding social and political structures. In other words we will presume that a family may at any moment shift from a level of organisation of individuals (family, gang, or reversed family) having multilateral relations, into a level of organisation dominated by a unanimously held, but unconscious, historic myth as to its origins. This is characterised by an ability to organise momentarily on the basis of a homogeneous, shared state of mind generated by mutual projective or adhesive identifications. Although the titular family roles may remain unchanged the distribution of functions undergoes a drastic alteration which has less resemblance to a family than to a primitive tribe. We will now examine them in more detail.

Basic Assumption Group: Dependence

Whether the leader is in the form of the combined parents, of one or other parent, or of a child, relative, lodger, neighbour or absent member, the function of leadership falls naturally into the hands of the most quietly grandiose member of the group. The function of the leader is to represent (not by any means to perform) the function of thought and therefore of planning and carrying of responsibility. While one would expect this to devolve upon the person with the highest verbal gifts, in fact golden silence more easily passes for wisdom.

The leader of the BA Dependent Group generates towards the surrounding community an attitude expectant of benevolence, generosity, peace and good will. Evil is not denied but is placed at some distance, say Russia or Mars. Where one of the two sexes is dominant this dominance is assumed to inhere in the benevolent community as well. The mythology of the group then includes indications of the historic inferiority, inadequacy and unreliability, though not necessarily viciousness, of the recessive sex. Family history plays a large role in the justification of policy and attitude. The non-conformist or scapegoat may be an important member and binding force.

Basic Assumption Group: Fight-flight

The leadership of this group tends to fall to the most violent, regardless of age or sex or titular family role. Violence, mistaken for strength and conviction, generates an attitude of ruthless greed towards the surrounding community, whether in the service of "seeing justice done" and "getting our rights", or for the purpose of scavenging supplies in preparation for flight to a new neighbourhood.

Time is felt to be pressing, too pressing to allow for thought. Action is the essential thing, for the world is too imponderable to be approached in any way and a general pessimism of the "can't beat City Hall" type urges flight, comforted by some degree of scorched earth policy. If the vitality for flight is inadequate or the community fails to respond with persecutory colouring, the fight may settle into a war of attrition: the cold war of parasitising and wasting the community's resources through litigious perseverance. But this leads to decimation of the group as the young slip away to more exciting possibilities.

Basic Assumption Group: Pairing

The world surrounding the BA Group becomes progressively more alien and persecuting when the ethos of the group (as represented in its conscious, or more often unconscious, mythology) moves from dependence through fight-flight to pairing. The Pairing Group is leaderless but lives in expectation of the arrival of the new leader, either in the form of an actual baby or of some facsimile or representation of a baby. This might be a new (old) idea, or a place, or an undertaking like a business, but whatever its galvanising focus it has the meaning of a nuptial chamber where the saviour is to be brought into existence. For this reason sex, or at least the atmosphere of sexual passion, pervades the thoughts and attitudes, with the love-making in a near manufacturing sense and with love as a vendable, or at least transmittable, commodity as its central activity. It may be highly represented, as in 'natural' farming, free of chemicals and the noise and odour of machinery ("the cut worm forgives the plough" – Blake, *The Marriage of Heaven and Hell*), or nudism, or a new Christian sect, or a family business – or just the procreation of a genius.

Having fled the Sodom and Gomorrah of so-called civilisation, the family feels every hand potentially against them so that geographic isolation as well as emotional isolation from the community is desired. They feel spied upon, resent laws which compel them to send their children to be corrupted in the ordinary schools, use money as little as possible except by way of business, aiming at self-sufficiency. Or rather they aim at preserving a delusion of self-sufficiency but not noticing the benefits of a technological civilisation of which they avail themselves, nor for that matter the absence of the genocidal tribal warfare that pervades stone-age cultures. Ignorance of history enables them to equate goodness with primitiveness, while ignorance of natural sciences allows for a similar equation of natural and kindly. No degree of isolation dispels the paranoid idea of being the centre of vast unfriendly curiosity.

In this group there is always a text with a Testamentary significance, occidental or oriental, scientific or mythical, which serves as the word of the prophet of the coming of the New Jerusalem. If the Messianic dream does not give adequate promise of imminent realisation, the children drift away unless held by tyranny, but they may be replaced by recruits from among the disaffected in search of a group. When thus amplified, the Pairing Group can become danger-ously antisocial in its sanctimony or in preparation for resuming the fight-flight stance in order to force its way back into, or even to take over, the community.

It is not possible to say much about the forces within a family which facilitate the shift to Basic Assumption Organisation. We would suggest that two factors must come into play at the same time: an impasse in some problem of family organisation, and the charismatic impact of a member whose vitality is matched by severe confusion between dream (myth), and external reality; someone to whom the past and future are far more alive and real than the present moment. Such an individual is able to galvanise a spirit of living *in* the past or *for* the future which caricatures selflessness, love and the overcoming of egocentricity. States of Basic Assumption Organisation in a family may be momentary or continuous. They are probably continuous but hang in abeyance when less primitive principles of organisation are dominant.

Bion has made the brilliant suggestion, which clinical experience strongly reinforces, that psycho-somatic disturbance has a closer relation to the Basic Assumption function when it is in abeyance rather than when it is put into action. This has a particular import for the BA Pairing Group with its religious atmosphere, since religion and curing tend to go hand in hand.

For this reason it seems understandable that, as the BA Fight-flight Group settles into a war of attrition and parasitism, in lieu of flight, its pressure on the community should become more and more focused on the health of its members. The responsibility of the community for curing them, which becomes indistinguishable from making them happy (since unhappiness makes them ill), heads the list of litigious clamourings.

On the other hand the BA Flight Group which has fled into isolation and is busy with its pairing mythology, defiantly and com-petitively declares its independence of the medical pretensions of the community and places its faith in more spiritual or magical means. These consist of essentially negative techniques for avoiding the sinfulness which ushers in these diseases, generally speaking seen as social ills. We do not wish to give the impression that BA functions are to be equated with madness, for this would be to confuse primitive and psychotic. However, it is true that the psychotic individual may far more easily achieve a position of leadership at the BA level because the capacity for reality testing loses its significance, being replaced as a guideline by the mythology of the Basic Assumption.

The Relation of Learning Types to Family Pattern

For simplicity it might be as well to draw up a list of this correlation before we go on to discuss its significance:

Family Pattern	Learning Type
The Couple Family	Introjective identification
The Doll's House Family	Projective identification and submission to persecutors
The Matriarchal Family	Obsessional collecting and submission to persecutors
The Patriarchal Family	Submission to persecutors and scavenging
The Gang-Family	Stealing and adhesive identification
The Reversed Family	Stealing and scavenging, also projective identification
Basic Assumption Families	Projective and adhesive identification

It must be stressed that this attempt at classification is part of model-making, based on clinical and life experience, intended for use as a guide for framing and evaluating research studies. One such study we have ourselves proposed. While it is all impressionistic it has the advantage of catching the problem in a cross-fire of multiple vertices or points of view. It also has the virtue of being highly dynamic, seeking only to afford a method of describing the momentary or cross-sectional state of individuals-in-the-family-in-the-community, recognising that these are highly unstable and at best can be taken as trends. It is also clear, therefore, that this system of classification, largely based as it is on the model of the mind derived from the extended metapsychology of the Freud-Klein-Bion development in psycho-analysis, is in no way exclusive of other systems drawn from sociology or anthropology. Rather it would be hoped that it would lend itself easily to combination with other approaches. Certainly it does not begin to be exhaustive, the variations in family patterns from these basic ones being as numerous as the flowers of the field.

The first thing of interest that can be said with confidence is that the order of classification given above corresponds precisely with the developmental fertility of the family milieu with respect to the growth of individuals comprising it, grown-ups and children alike. And in this sense the patterns are self-perpetuating with respect to cultural achievement of the individual children as the parents of the next generation. The exception to this dictum resides in the degree to which rebellion against the family pattern is stimulated in the children. It would seem to be greatest in the Patriarchal family, somewhat less in the Matriarchal, dormant in the Doll's House Family and virtually absent, because turned against the community, in the Gang, Reversed, and Basic Assumption families.

It is also of interest to note that the degree of harmonious relation to the benevolent aspects of the community diminishes as one goes down the list and reverses within the Patriarchal group. This also means that the children of these families will tend to be mobile upward or downward in their attitudes to skills, knowledge, economic and social status compared with their parents, in accord with this degree of harmony or conflict with the community, its resources and demands.

Similarly the type of psychiatric disturbance to be expected in the children of the family would slide from the neurotic symptomatology of the Doll's House children, through the character disorders of the Matriarch-Patriarch group becoming delinquent (Gang-Family), perverted (Reversed Family) and borderline or psychopathic in the Basic Assumption Families. These correlations have become more apparent in recent years in psycho-analytical work as we have been able to consider the patient's organisation, internal and external, with respect to groups. This extension of our awareness of phenomena has diminished the tendency to see the psycho-pathology of the child in a one-to-one relation to that of the parents (cf. the concept of the schizophrenogenic mother no longer seems useful).

In a sense the epidemiological significance of the classification depends not only on the self-perpetuating aspect of each of the family pattern types (in fact this quality is, gratefully, strongest of all in the Couple Family) but on the variable of the capacity of the family grouping to allow the individual child to enter into transference relations with other figures, present ones like teachers and therapists, or absent ones like cultural or historic heroes outside the family unit or extended family. This factor is the nemesis of the child guidance approach and lies behind the urgency with which a wide spectrum of therapeutic techniques and a precise method of assessment for their deployment is being sought.

Finally it is hoped that this model may serve to give form to studies of our educational system which may make it possible to get beyond the conflicts arising from philosophic and ideological bias in revising methods of pedagogy. When filled out with clinical evidence to correct and refine its crude impressionistic quality, such a model of the individual child in his family within the community could serve to frame a system at once flexible, workable and geared to the changing needs of the community as well as to the development of the individual.

XV

Concerning the Perception of One's Own Attributes and its Relation to Language Development

with
Mme Eve Cohen (Paris)

The differentiation in the clinical setting of psycho-analysis between the manifestations of delusions and the reporting of primitive perceptions would seem to be an area of observation and description opened up by Bion's Theory of Thinking. By offering us a model that enables us to conceive of such a differentiation he has made possible our monitoring the phenomena of our consulting room for their realisations. The theory of alpha-function and beta-elements has already proved itself fruitful for clinical observation in the area of communication of meaningful messages versus communication-like missiles of meaningless stuff. In work with psychotic children it has helped us to recognise their response to bombardment with emotional experiences for which they have no capacity either of containment or thought. It also gives us a basis for distinguishing between immaturity and psychosis.

A report presented by Mme Eve Cohen at a seminar held in Paris in April 1982 throws some valuable light on the problem. Mme Cohen's material concerned her patient, Henri, aged twenty-six, who had had a breakdown while abroad after six years of aimless wanderings following upon his mother's departure from the family home to live with a lover with whom she had had a secret liaison for over ten years. Among his complaints at the time of hospitalisation there was none of the usual delusional ideas nor was his demeanour and mode of communication bizarre or unfriendly or secretive. On the contrary he was very open in describing the many phenomena of perception of himself and the world which troubled him and prevented him from maintaining any settled mode of life.

Henri, clearly, was a highly intelligent and sensitive young man and he settled with interest and cooperativeness into psychoanalytical treatment, working out a plan of living alternate periods with mother and father while working in the father's food shop. The central complaint involved colours which he either saw or "sent out" during eating or while interacting with other people. These colour phenomena made it impossible for him to be "constant", which seemed to mean "being the same person", particularly before and after eating. This loss of constancy had become apparent to him when he had separated from his companion of long standing during his travels. At that time he became incapable of doing anything "automatically", in the sense that he could no longer remain unaware of the activities of his individual senses by focusing his attention on consensual objects. For instance the taste of the food he was eating could not distract his attention from what his eyes were seeing. The result seemed to be a bombardment of disparate sensa demanding to be meaningfully integrated and interpreted.

After fifteen months of therapy Henri began to complain of new phenomena which seemed to be closely related to the growing impact on him of experiences of separation in the transference. These new phenomena related to "things being added", "new attributes" which appeared as repetitive experiences during the course of certain activities. For instance, when he is cutting ham the number 69 appears on his back. In connection with some other activity a crown of feathers appears, or coloured lines across his forehead. These "attributes" are his personal experiences but are also felt to be apprehended, not necessarily visually or even consciously, by other people. It is not clear to him whether they are phenomena which affect his feelings and relationships, or only manifest what does in fact exist.

Henri would appear, from his history, to have lived his early years in a state of great obedience to his mother, having allowed her, in effect, to do his thinking for him. In a similar way, during his travels his companion had occupied the same position. In both cases the defection of the person performing these functions had apparently left him naked to the wind of perceptual phenomena, lacking the capability of thought necessary for containing and giving meaning to his experiences. In a certain sense he had had a breakdown, but in another sense it had been what Bion calls a "break through". As he appears in the analytical sessions there is a great effort to think and to elicit his therapist's assistance in thinking. It is a very different process from an analysis in that the phenomena of the transference cannot as yet be made the focus of attention. Rather, the therapist is placed in a position of supervisor of his own efforts, variously assisting his memory so that experiences can be better linked together and at other times offering ideas about mental functioning to help him to think about his experiences. The symbol formation which more ordinarily would take place in dreaming is performed laboriously in the waking state and this at times results in his using a very poetic and idiosyncratic language.

I approach this material from two different angles: first, from the

vantage point afforded by Henri's presenting us with conscious processes for forming the symbols which we are more accustomed to see
fully formed in dreams; second, from the point of view of the interaction of projection and introjection at the basic level of perception of
self and objects.

"These signs on the forehead probably have different meanings but
I do not know them. I was fine with the bar on my forehead, not too
strong. I did not feel, as I sometimes do, that I was crushing people. I
don't like that. I was in harmony with people; I did not feel impoverished by something; I did not feel superior to the people I was
waiting on (in the shop)."

"I think all the time that I always have something in my head,
illogical things which do not help me to be myself. If I let myself go a
little bit, even for a brief moment, it's a mess. For instance I have got
into the habit of not looking at what I drink, for if I let myself go and
cast a glance at what I am drinking, things go awry, there are colours
and such things."

"What isn't normal is the fact that I cannot look when I eat; other
people can do anything, at any time, but certainly not just anyhow,
although it looks to me as if they let themselves go, as if they abandon
themselves to the movement. I do not abandon myself to the drift but
fight with myself . . ."

"When they chew they don't pay attention; they can do anything. I
am not able to chew chewing gum because I think of the gum all the
time . . ."

I have taken these examples to show the way in which Henri is
observing and struggling to understand the mental phenomena which
interfere with his being "constant" and "like other people" who
appear to him to operate "automatically" and to be able to "do
anything" without having to notice and think about their actions.
When he is "thinking about the chewing gum", it is the same as when
he is thinking about whether he is "crushing people" or "sending out
colours" to them. In other words Henri seems to think that the
spontaneity and relaxation of other people is a consequence of their
being able to be unconcerned about the impact that their states of
mind and actions are having on people and things. He is unable to be
unconcerned in this way. He feels that there is an intimate connection
between his mental phenomena and those of others, animate or not,
although he recognises that the chewing gum does not have a state of
mind but must be representing something that does, a whole or a part
of a living thing. It seems strongly suggested that the "colours" are
representations of emotions as yet unconnected with symbolic representations which can be used for thinking. Later on he will refer to
them as "vibrations" when the colour phenomena have receded. But
by that time the colours have not disappeared but have begun to

integrate with other formal representations to form symbols or proto-symbols: the bars of colour on his forehead, the coloured feather head-dress, the number 69 on his back. All these phenomena he calls "attributes" and explains that they are new experiences in his life.

"I have the impression that my thoughts become material. True, it is I who think, but the attributes are external to me, anyway to the extent that I really have the impression that it is material."

We have as a starting point the obvious fact that all of Henri's preoccupations concerning constancy centre round eating and its impact on himself and other people. Working as he does in his father's food shop brings the daily activities of his life into close symbolic contact with eating, and with sexuality, which is held in a state of suspension in his mind as being far beyond his capabilities of thought, let alone action. Even the nocturnal emissions which vaguely trouble him seem to have no contact with his dream-life. In fact his dream-life is not available to him in any form different from his waking preoccupations: "I do not know whether I think while I sleep. I remember the last quarter of an hour before I wake and the first ten minutes before falling asleep, but I do not remember my dreams. Yet I must be full of thoughts at night too; I cannot be without thinking. Also apparently dreaming is necessary. I do not remember any dreams except for the famous one I already told you about." (Of this dream he said: "I was a kid; it was a long time ago. There was a well and I leaned forward and forward and saw myself as if I were double, at the same time above and below. I saw myself looking at myself and leaned so far forward that I fell. At the moment of impact I woke up in a sweat. It was a nightmare.")

The central problem seems to be a developmental one rather than one of delusion-formation based on omnipotence. It could be stated as a problem of differentiation of the external and the internal world, of phantasy from action, of thoughts from deeds, of self from objects. We shall assume, as the observations of mothers and babies suggest, that this is the normal state of the very young infant, to whom the behaviour of other people must seem nonchalant, even cavalierly unconcerned, to say the least. They must appear to behave as if they were either unaware or unconcerned about the enormous impact they were having simply by existing and thinking as well as by acting. But it is true that the organ of attention which can, in most people, be widened or narrowed, focused or unfocused, does operate to protect us from bombardment of the sort from which Henri 'suffers'. Or is it wrong to say that he suffers? Is it perhaps we who suffer from this narrowing, this scotomatisation of the world by the skilled employment of our organ of consciousness?

I would like to turn for a moment from Henri's material to a paper which Maria Rhode presented in May 1982 to the New Imago

Group, entitled 'The Parallel Structure of Words and Objects as a Stage in Language Development'. In this paper there were presented a series of observations of very young children between the ages of eighteen and thirty months. From the discussion about one child, whose transitions from 'private' language to conventional was exemplified, the question arose as to the nature of 'lalling'. Was it, as we had always assumed, a period of vocal experimentation to achieve mastery of the physical apparatus so that what was thought could be said to approximate to what emerged vocally? The 'private' period of speech in this child suggested another formulation, namely that lalling constituted play with sounds in the mouth, treating the sounds as objects of imaginative manipulation. This is not to imply a similarity to Piaget's formulation of "egocentric speech" but rather to be part of, an extension of, the small child's tendency to put objects in the mouth. Again we have always assumed that this was essentially a primitive form of reality testing where the differentiation of edible-inedible was the crucial problem.

In the observations of this child reported by Mrs Rhode the sound "bupf" seemed to be variously split and combined with other sounds to work out the concept covered by such words as two, both, together, double. His play in his mouth with the sounds seemed to parallel his play with objects, not merely as commentary on that play but as an alternative theatre of phantasy manipulation. The conceptual formulation which might be drawn – and this is the heart of this paper – would be as follows: lalling is to be seen as the vocal aspect of a more general phase in cognitive development in which the physical space of the oral cavity is utilised as the theatre of phantasy and play, a mid-point between external play and internal thought (dream-thought or phantasy). The placing of fingers and objects in the mouth is accompanied by the awareness of teeth, tongue, jaws, salivation and vocal capacity. In this theatre of phantasy the sounds can be manipulated as concrete objects devoid of fixed or determined meaning but rather driving their meaning from the immediate juxtaposition with other sounds and buccal objects. When the child moves on to accept the conventional meaning of the words in the discourse that he achieves through various forms of identification, this buccal theatre is moved outside the body because manual dexterity improves and play becomes less frustrating. But the tendency to employ the buccal theatre continues in the form of play with words based on homonymity, splitting and recombination of syllables, spoonerisms, puns, alliteration, ambiguity – in short all the devices of poetic diction.

If we now turn back to Henri's material we can formulate an hypothesis about his state of mental organisation which has an impressive cogency. May it be that we find this intelligent and sensitive young man, unaccustomed as he has been to think for himself, struggling with immature equipment to comprehend his new-found independent existence in relation to the world about him? Perhaps his equipment of thought is still somewhat fixed in this buccal stage so that the theatre of thought has not yet become located in his dream-life but is still in his mouth during waking hours. If this were so we might reasonably expect that what he does in his mouth would be poorly distinguished from actions in the inner world and thus in the outside world as well. Furthermore we might expect that his identification processes would be very volatile, since the state of objects would not be segregated into internal and external as a basis for stability of mood. Consequently any oral play or action which seemed not "in harmony", variously "crushing" or "sending out colours" for instance, would result in an immediate change in his objects of identification, namely changes characteristic of depressive illness. In fact Henri appears to be very depressive in his orientation rather than being persecuted by damaged objects.

Would this then not make sense of such complaints as his lack of "constancy", his inability to be "automatic" in his actions, his failure to be able to "let himself go"? If his buccal cavity is his theatre of thought, anything happening in his mouth might be expected to have the same impact on his view of self and world as we are accustomed for dreams to have. What sense can we then make of the new phenomenon of "attributes" such as the "69" on his back or the coloured head-dress? We would hardly notice the phenomenon if these attributes merely included such ordinary items as "looking well today", or "sexually attractive", or "my acne looks horrible". Their seemingly bizarre nature attracts our attention. Correspondingly we grow accustomed to see young people wearing sweatshirts with numbers or slogans on them, to multicoloured hair and mohican haircuts. In what way do Henri's attributes differ from these concrete items of decoration (or disfigurement, depending on one's point of view)? Does the concept of a buccal theatre of phantasy, with its attendant failure of differentiation of internal and external, supply an adequate form of description? We cannot be satisfied unless we account also for their being "new", apparently only having appeared after some eighteen months of analysis.

I would suggest that the answer may reside in the newness of another area of experience, namely of awareness of the absent object. He has become vaguely aware that the week-end breaks have some impact on him, that he can feel "superfluous", that these feelings are linked with his mother's defection and his travelling companion's departure which had precipitated his breakdown abroad. In other words I am suggesting that what is in fact "new" is an uneasy feeling that an object from which he has become separated can notice changes in him when they become reunited. This is such an absolutely common aspect of experience that, again, we would hardly notice it as a phenomenon unless it takes such a primitive form that it appears to be bizarre. But if an adolescent patient who ordinarily comes rather well-dressed were to appear at one session in a numbered sweatshirt we would surely assume that it expressed some transferential state of mind. The difference between Henri and our more sophisticated adolescent is that Henri would notice this change, feeling as if he had the number on his back, while it would be invisible as such to ourselves. We would notice the adolescent's sweatshirt and its implications while he would be unaware of its significance.

It is in exactly this way that Henri demonstrates as a pathological state of mind the peculiarly heightened sensitivity to self and world that characterises the artist and, in particular, the poet. While Henri has not learned to master and employ this heightened sensitivity most of us, on the other hand, have, in Wordsworth's words, "given our hearts away" for the sake of "constancy".

In order to bring this material and discussion into closer contact with problems encountered in work with children, I will review the material of Mme Cohen and Mrs Rhode from a more developmental point of view. In *Explorations in Autism* in the chapter on mutism, I outlined a psycho-analytical theory of speech development drawing heavily on ideas put forward by such people as Suzanne Langer, Wittgenstein, Cassirer, Chomsky, Russell and others. The central thesis was that language, in its genesis, is essentially two-tiered, having a primitive song-and-dance level (the most primitive form of symbol-formation) for the purpose of communication of emotional states of mind by means of the non-pathological use of the mechanism of projective identification, and that upon this foundation of deep grammar there is subsequently superimposed the lexical level of words for denoting objects, actions and qualities of the external world, that is, information. In connection with the outlining of the phenomenology of varying dimensionality in both disturbed and normal personality development, it was necessary to subscribe to a differentiation between meaningful and meaningless communications, in keeping with ideas already developed separately by Wilfrid Bion and Esther Bick.

More recently, in *Dream-Life*, I explored in some detail the concept of internal space as the 'Theatre for generating meaning' in connection with Bion's "empty" concept of alpha-function and the format of The Grid. The present paper can be seen to straddle the concepts of two- and three-dimensionality and to attempt to fill in some of the 'emptiness' of the concept of alpha-function by defining a developmental space that is neither internal nor external in its implications, the 'Buccal Theatre for Generating Meaning', tracing its implications both for speech development and for character. In order to carry out this task it is necessary first to discuss at some length both the concept of attention and some aspects of our ideas about symbol formation.

If we accept the idea that consciousness is best viewed, in Freud's words, as "an organ for the perception of psychic qualities", a Platonic view equating consciousness with attention, we tend to assume that we are considering an active function directed by interests derived from desires and anxieties. But that is, I suggest, only to take into account the penetrating type of attention which can be directed, narrowed or widened, focused for levels and perspectives, adjusted to levels of organisation or perhaps even of abstraction. Its object are, in a sense, already 'known'. But there is another type of attention which is far more passive, patient, receptive, awaiting the advent of the 'unknown'. Bion has spoken of it in connection with what he calls "thoughts seeking a thinker", awaiting the advent of the "new idea" which the "mystic" will retail to the group, or the mystic part of the personality will transmit to the internal group (see *Dawn of Oblivion*, Book III of *A Memoir of the Future*). It is this passive type of attention which apprehends the aesthetic. The aesthetic impact of the world on the baby has been largely neglected in psycho-analytical concepts of development. For psycho-analytical material and infant observation declare, as do the poets, that the 'aesthetic conflict' in the presence of the object is primary over the conflicts of separation, deprivation, and frustration to which so much thought has been devoted. The beauty of the world and its epitomisation in the figure of the mother, the breast, the face, envelops the baby but brings in its train the most acute pain of uncertainty in the three-dimensional area. To what degree does the beauty of the exterior of the object correspond to the goodness of its interior, its feelings, intentions, durability? In a word, is it a 'truthful' object? "Are you honest?" plagues Hamlet regarding Ophelia-Gertrude, great thinking baby that he is, not unlike our Henri.

This view, that differentiates active and passive attention, 'penetration of' from 'envelopment by' the object, also draws a sharp line between intrusive curiosity and thirst for knowledge. It rectifies a serious error in Melanie Klein's earlier work, drawn largely from experiences with psychotic children and only partly corrected in the *Narrative of a Child Analysis*, in which she took the view that the "epistemophilic instinct" was driven by sadism towards the contents of the mother's body. That intrusive curiosity which seeks the faults and defects of the object, stands in marked contrast to the awe and wonder at the beauty of the world which seeks to know and be known by the object. This distinction, which seems so often to separate science from art, holds more correctly for the difference between pornography and art on the one hand, and between Promethean and inspired science on the other.

The material from Henri gives strength to the formulation of a highly visual relationship between baby and mother, with eye-nipple penetrating the eye-mouth while the breast envelops the baby, and the mother and baby envelop one another in their eye-to-eye contact. The intrusive curiosity of the baby's eye-mouth counters that of the eye-nipple, which takes on the quality of the most primitive superego of the type mentioned by Freud in connection with delusions of reference. This contributes to the tendency to split nipple from breast, and for the former to take on qualities associated eventually with the father and his penis. On the other hand the mutual envelopment of the aesthetic experience between mother and baby (and it probably must be mutual to be long tolerable to either), with its passive, expectant and surrendering quality, brings the sense of mystery, of joyousness, but heavily freighted with the pain of the uncertainty of the aesthetic conflict for both. The hidden interior of the object, like the absent object, is a powerful stimulus to thought, perhaps the more powerful of the two, being in its nature far more passionate than anxious. While the anxieties engendered by the absence of the object tend to arouse violence in the service of domination and control of the object, the passion connected with the hidden interior of the aesthetic object promotes love-making, invites exploration.

Turning to the question of symbol formation before reapproaching the material from Mme Cohen and Henri, I must add an item to what has already been expressed at some length in *Dream-Life* about the nature of symbols. It is vital to understanding the way in which the "colours" have evolved into the "coloured head-dress" for instance. In the format of The Grid and his Theory of Thinking, Bion has placed alpha-function anterior to both dream-thoughts and myth, equating these two phenomena from the individual and the group. But I think this was a mistake based on the narrative form of the two which seems to me to be genuine narrative in the case of myth and contrived in the case of the dream. Myths seem to be stories, essentially true stories and therefore history. We probably do not encounter them in their original form either in folk-tale, religious literature or lay, but see them already subjected to some of the processes of condensation, ellipsis and hyperbole which will eventually boil them down, one might say, into a symbol. Think of the immense myth-content of the Cross, containing as it does both the New Testament and the Myth of the True Cross. Its power as symbol could never be comprehended without knowledge of what has been condensed within it; similarly, when symbols are brought into conjunction with one another and cross-fertilise, each being potentiated in its meaning by this conjugation. While dreams are composed of these conjugations, the narrative form they often take, which is hardly more than 'and then . . . and then' etc., is the product of what Freud called the Secondary Revision. It contributes neither to their meaning nor to their significance.

My point is that myth formation is anterior to alpha-function or, more likely, is one of the components of alpha-function as the mysterious process of symbol formation. Note that this step of filling the "empty" concept with some content detracts in no way from its mystery and probably hardly lessens its essential emptiness. But it does suggest that Bion may have been wrong in thinking that the function was essentially unobservable and therefore indescribable. It seems likely that in the prehistory of the race, the first leaps of imagination were of this myth-making variety, enacted in song-and-dance, with the decoration of the dancers representing the creatures and forces of awe, similar to Henri's coloured bars on the brow or coloured feather head-dress, leaving only a short step to their graphic or sculptural representation as gods and spirits. The psychoanalytical theory of thinking proposed by Bion would suggest that this artistic move in imagination must necessarily have been both prior to, and a precondition for, the technological imagination that could invent tools and weapons.

Returning to Henri's material with these two new considerations in mind, we can recognise that his mouth is not only an area, a space, of great emotional significance to him, but that it is the scene or theatre of dramas which are monitored minutely. In this respect we might think that his buccal equipment, especially teeth and tongue, are strongly linked to his visual imagination and stand in a strong identification with the eye-nipple in its super-ego function. But Henri's orientation to these events is a deeply depressive one; he cannot be unconcerned for the safety of the objects which enter his mouth, even when represented by something clearly recognised as inanimate like the chewing gum, because they are felt to be directly linked, though in mysterious ways, with external people. Early in the analysis when this concern presented as "sending out colours", it seemed delusional and perhaps hallucinatory. But as it evolved in the experience of the transference, taking on formal qualities to join the sensual ones, eventuating in the description of "attributes", this initial impression of psychotic processes gave way to the formulation of immaturity in his object relations. Throughout these first eighteen months of analysis Henri's distress was overwhelmingly depressive rather than persecutory, and when he later broke off therapy for a period to enter a mental hospital it was as a refuge from the bombardment of emotion impinging on him in the intimacy of the analysis and elsewhere as well.

When Henri compares himself with other people who seem to him to be "constant", to be able to act "automatically", to be "unconcerned", to be "able to do anything", or "to let themselves go", he seems to be describing a world of incredible nonchalance, of unthinking harmony and accommodation. And in a sense it is true: what Henri has to do with his immature, consciously controlled equipment for observation and thought, other people have long relegated to their unconscious and dream-life. But it is also true that this relegation has been accompanied by a degree, often severe, of denial of psychic reality in favour of acquiescence in custom, with a result of diminished sensibility, especially about their own impact on others. In this sense I would plead that Henri's concerns are quite realistic in their format if not necessarily in their sense of proportion. And his perception of his attributes, which is clearly not hallucinatory but imaginative, is likewise a realistic recognition of aspects of his character. The word 'character' is only surprising in this context because his character, like his mood, is as unstable as a baby's

In putting forward this formulation of the material I am depending rather heavily on the "famous" nightmare of the fall into the well. There I think we see precisely the story of his "illness" and why it may be seen more cogently as a "breakthrough" rather than a "breakdown", as Bion would say. It shows how the defection of his travelling companion, as a repetition of that of his mother, plunged him into contact (which he was, however, "leaning" towards already) with a split-off part of himself which has lived inside his object of dependence since babyhood, the part which was potentially a thinker, and perhaps a poet.

By linking Henri's material with the observations by Mrs Rhode I have framed a definitive hypothesis of a 'Buccal Theatre for the Generating of Meaning' as an early stage of internalisation and thought, and therefore of both internal discourse and external communication. In doing so I have perhaps added a certain definition and complexity to ideas put forward some years ago by Hanna Segal about a "third area" and by Donald Winnicott about the nature of "transitional objects". Perhaps it also has a link to the observations about "functional phenomena" in falling asleep and waking described by Silberer and rather recklessly attacked by Freud. The link also with the "envelopment by sleep" described by Schilder and recent work on REM sleep seems also suggested. But the most important implication for understanding child development probably lies in the implication that the evolution from the song-and-dance level of deep grammatical discourse of lalling and babbling, to the lexical level of social communication, is dependent on the move forward from a Buccal Theatre to a Dream Theatre for the generating of meaning.

This means that the differentiation of external and internal worlds is essential for understanding that if you want your thoughts to be communicated, you must vocalise them, a hard lessen for many to learn.

XVI

On Turbulence

If Bion's Theory of Thinking has some essential truth in it one must expect that new ideas, the ones which have an impact to produce catastrophic change, would appear first in dream form, only later to find some verbal and and abstract representation. This is no more than to say that symbolic representations of ideas are most likely to be generated by borrowing formal elements from the outside world to portray internal world phenomena. These formal elements may implicitly include abstractions which lend themselves to analogical use in dream-life. Thus do artists and poets operate to perform their social function of giving communicable form to the new ideas nascent in the culture. To succeed in this function they must disturb us, frame questions in order to set the audience in motion to seek the answers, answers which, of course, mainly take the form of new readiness for new questions.

Psycho-analysis has come some considerable distance in defining the spectrum of emotional nuances which hold the meaning of our mental experiences. It would be a cogent view of our so-called theories that they are merely descriptive devices for outlining the structure of the variety of internal and external experiences which manifest themselves within us as emotion. But I would suggest that one whole area of emotion has as yet found no place in our body of theory because it has been assumed to stand merely in a quantitative relation. I am speaking of passions. If we adopt Bion's basic formulation of L, H and K, these passions would be 'in love', 'in hate' and 'in awe', each with its negative counterpart, 'anti-in love', 'anti-in hate' and 'anti-in awe'. I think I am correct, certainly with regard to my own ideas, in stating that it has been assumed that passions were merely very intense emotions.

In this paper I wish to suggest another, and, I think, more interesting view, namely that passions represent states of turbulence arising from the paradoxical impact of one intense emotion on another, producing a turbulence by reason of the conflict with previously established ideas about the meaning of these emotions and their relevance to the organisation of our internal world, and therefore our view of the external world. To illustrate this thesis I will bring a piece of clinical material which, while it lies outside the context of an analysis proper, has nonetheless an analytical background.

A young woman in her early thirties, a professional musician and a person of charm and beauty, asked to see me some three years after the ending of her analysis. I knew from communications and occasional follow-up visits that she had had a long struggle after the termination of the analysis to achieve a state of joyousness in her work and social relations. This had its roots in an internal situation which produced severe self-criticism and elevation of extraordinary standards in her work and in her evaluation of her behaviour with friends, standards which sapped her pleasure in accomplishments. Its origins were essentially narcissistic, deriving from a relationship with an admired and loved elder brother whose outstanding professional achievements were not parallelled in his intimate relationships. A know-it-all internal figure operated by continually raising doubts about sincerity and motivation, caricaturing analytical work.

But I had heard that in recent months this problem had seemed to give way, opening up a new area of gaiety, feelings of freedom and trust in herself. The result seemed to be a greater adventurousness in work and social relationships, accompanied by a growing confidence that she would soon find a man to lavish her love upon, to marry and have the children she was longing for. But, as she told me, something very disturbing was happening, namely that she found herself intensely drawn to a man whom she did not like. It was not a matter of disapproval of his character, for he seemed a thoroughly decent chap. She just did not like him and kept noticing things about him, ordinary little things such as turns of speech or gestures or areas of interests that she felt antagonistic towards. Then two days previously he had left her a message breaking an arrangement for the week-end without any explanation, and she found herself feeling furious. It was not an act out of keeping with their degree of intimacy which, in fact, was still on formal terms. Nor did it seem to arouse distrust or jealousy. No, she just felt furiously frustrated at the delay in getting to know him better. She felt, in fact, that the unusual impatience had something to do with this paradoxical stage of her feelings, of feeling so strongly drawn to him yet disliking him in so many petty ways. That night she had two dreams which she found puzzling but thought interesting and wished to have my ideas about them. I too found them puzzling and interesting.

In the first dream *she was tuning a harpsichord for a woman, not in fact a professional musician but a former girlfriend of her brother, who was to give a concert. Indeed the time for the concert had already arrived and yet she had hardly begun the tuning. The trouble was that she was proceeding slowly because she was using the wrong method, namely of tuning each note to its proper pitch individually. Such a method she knew would take hours while the proper method of tuning middle C and then tuning every other note to it in fifths could be done quite quickly, simply by listening for the beats when each fifth was struck, rather than listening to the pitch.*

Actually she is a string instrumentalist and had only seen a harpsichord tuned once. There was no panic in the dream because the man running the concert was very gentle and patient with her about the delay. But she felt bad about keeping people waiting. The woman who was to play in the concert had never achieved a love relation with the brother for it had rather petered out, as had the patient's own last romance some years earlier.

In the second dream *she seemed to be standing on a high cliff overlooking a beach of silvery sand by the sea, thinking she ought to be down there sunbathing before the shadows of the cliff enveloped the beach.*

The two dreams taken together seem to make a more confident approach to meaning than either by itself. The first clear reference point is the sense of urgency in both dreams, clearly referable to her age and impatience to get to know her new friend. Sexuality is surely indicated by the sunbathing and the word 'concert'. Also the wrong method is an element in both: in the one by her method of tuning; in the other by her elevated distance from the silvery sands. But the most interesting element seems to be the two methods of tuning. It is these to which I wish to turn attention.

My impression from the follow-up material of the past three years is that this young woman has achieved a fairly considerable skill in using the self-analytic method. She is able to introspect quite deeply, to follow lines of association in a most useful way and easily to recognise new representations of configurations of feeling and conflict with which she had become acquainted in the course of her rather long analysis. Consequently she had made some genuine progress on her own, of which she felt proud. Also this had increased her confidence, independence and feelings of womanliness. But one problem in her character caused her great concern, namely that she continued to feel that her life was not, somehow, being devoted to the things for which she could develop a passionate interest and devotion. Of course it was probably a matter of lacking a love relationship and children, but also professionally there was the same uneasiness. She felt sure that her capability as a musician was not a measure of her talent, which must lie elsewhere, perhaps in some way to do with children.

In the past it had been assumed by both of us that this uneasiness was part of the phenomenology of the internal doubting of sincerity generated by the internal brother-figure. But now that seemed to have been mastered, and yet . . . Perhaps it was true that she felt more powerfully drawn to this new man than she ever had before, but it was hardly her idea of what falling in love ought to feel like. She could not say she was developing a passion for this man, but only that she felt terribly disturbed by him. Not that she had any grievances, even about the current cancellation. Her urgency to get to know him was somehow quite unpleasant, perhaps prompted by the desire to overcome being drawn to him rather than any hope of finding a love relationship with him.

I suggest that the wrong method of tuning the harpsichord may hold the secret of her mental state, namely that she is having a new experience with which she has no tried method of coping. She knows 'about' the right method but has in fact never used it. And furthermore it is a method with a completely different rationale, listening for the beats when the chord (fifth) is struck rather than the pitch of each individual note. Might we call it 'tuning her heart' rather than her harpsichord? Instead of paying attention to the individual emotions that she feels in the course of her experiences with her new friend, she is having to pay attention to the ways in which the various emotions harmonise or conflict with one another (the beats). Her preconception of passionate love is one of harmonious relation, of intense emotions to one another, a preconception drawn, perhaps, from the experience of splitting-and-idealisation in the management of her infantile feelings. That would dispose her to split off all the qualities of her friend which she dislikes and only relate to those which "draw" her to him.

In summary: I am suggesting that this young woman, newly arrived at adulthood, is being obliged to reckon with a new value system which dislocates all her previous values of precise emotional pitch and harmonious relations. It would be similar in her professional life were she, for instance, to find herself powerfully drawn to Indian music. A capacity for passion is perhaps entering into her life in this form, obliging her to notice and value the disturbance itself as the indicator of catastrophic change.

XVII

A Swiftean Diatribe

Although the magnitude of the threats that this planet and its population face seems to have escalated beyond anything previously known, it is perhaps not always useful to approach the problems facing mankind from this quantitative vertex. The difficulty lies in our limited capacity for thought and its foundation in adequate emotional responsiveness. It may seem, superficially, that cataclysm stirs us deeply but careful examination suggests something quite contrary. Such spectacles, descriptions, statistics and prophecies of doom excite rather than stir. That is, they excite in us the orientation of opposition to what is already known but do not stir us to discover the unknown. In that sense they activate perverse tendencies of mind, the negative links, minus L, minus H, minus K.

The 'end of the world' can be stated in megatons rather than, as by Laputa's astronomical mathematicians, in terms of the temperature of the tail of a comet – or, in the language of the Old Testament prophet, as God's wrath, but this does not make the concept any more stirring of emotion. For horror is a perverse state of excitement as is amply testified to by TV, film or pulp magazines and their addicted population. Individual mentality and the individual's participation in groups is somehow contaminated by the perverse appeal of modern warfare and its obvious kinship to magic.

It is of some interest to note that the term 'magic' has dropped out of the psycho-analytical vocabulary, probably since the forties. Its replacement, 'omnipotence', has very little punch owing to its vagueness, for it suggests in its etymology that this issue is an ability to do anything and everything. This misses the crux of the fascination of magic which lies in the ability to bring about certain ends without concern for the means. 'Wish fulfilment' also fails in impact, perhaps because the penumbra both of meaning and of music of the word 'wish' is fairly devoid of violence. 'Magic' covers these implications, implying all that 'wish' contains, plus the indication of action at a distance, plus disinterest in the means, plus a tinge of evil.

In our blasé relation to the technological apparatus of everyday life we fail to notice the appeal to a sense of magic with which the myriad devices of modern life abound. Turn the tap; press the switch; don't even touch the button of the lift, just bring your finger near to it; just approach the glass doors; change the channel without getting up from your armchair; don't add the numbers, press your calculator, and so on. Only when the gadget fails to work and we notice the infantile tantrum that rises within us, do we take pause for thought. Why the tantrum? We behave inwardly, and sometimes outwardly, like Rumpelstiltskin, with impotent rage. But why impotent? Whence comes the rage? Is it perhaps there all the time in the form of incipient irritability, that great pseudo-emotion that sends everyone scurrying for emotional cover, as when a dog comes out of the water. When the irritable person shakes himself everyone in the vicinity gets wet with impotence.

Hauling in our conceptual nets and finding this concept of irritability seems at first to produce a haul of flotsam rather than fish, for irritability is just the stick that is waved about in stick-and-carrot tyrannical organisations. It doesn't hit, it just rattles, or buzzes or growls. It 'shows the teeth' to the hierarchic inferior. The phraseology of irritability is interesting to note for its ambiguity, sophistication. Someone is suspected of being "tedious", or there isn't "time enough" to meet, or it "should have been thought of earlier". Things are "too expensive", "unsuitable", "controversial", "too original", "flamboyant" or "slightly vulgar". The smile is on the lips but the eyes are cool; the words are polite but the music is monotone; the spectacles have slipped down the nose as if the other person were four feet tall; the telephone is already being dialled while the conversation is brought to a close; one is assured that the problem must be looked into "some time".

It is indeed a somewhat mysterious thing that these manifestations of irritability have such a powerful effect in maintaining order within these hierarchical structures, of which all social institutions, to my knowledge, are examples. Perhaps the theory of signs will give us a better understanding of this important matter than will a theory of symbolism. For it is clear that these manifestations of irritability are entirely unspecific and cannot really be thought of as communication, but rather as actions which signal superiority of rank. This impression is strengthened by observations of the nearly universal method by which the inferior person in rank seems to counteract the noxious impression made on him, as dock weed is applied to nettle sting. The inferior invariably evinces what is called "dumb insolence". According to his intelligence and expertise, as it were, he is able to carry it off in a manner that can be undetectable to his superior. Or he may wish it to be detected, in which case its effectiveness resides in its being un-describeable, or at least un-documentable. But generally the inferior person does not wish it to be detected, for its function is primarily related to his personal economy, to rid himself of the unpleasant impact of the irritability of his superior.

It is true that persons of a like level in the hierarchy may also diminish their distress by confiding in one another their low opinion of their mutual superior or even of diverse superiors. This is an important phenomenon, for it is the basis of the inaction of the great silent majority. In fact hierarchic institutions, and therefore all institutions, contain a silent majority which could be said to embrace nearly its total personnel since every individual is in an inferior position to someone, including the person at the so-called 'top' who is in a state of terrified subjection to the incipient rebelliousness of the silent majority, i.e. the totality of his inferiors.

I put forward these banal observations which any thoughtful person can make, and most probably has already done so, because they may be the key to understanding the strange phenomenon among human beings (perhaps amongst animals as well) called collectively, 'politics'. I certainly think that Bion's formulation of Basic Assumption Groups and Group Mentality is an important and correct thrust into this area and that the delineation of projective identification as its means of communication is likewise precise. I am intent on examining a different aspect, namely the meaning of the content of such groupings. Again I would agree that from the point of view of thought these groups are mindlessly programmed and derive their action indications by logical or illogical derivation of the Basic Assumption. But while that describes the mechanism it does not catch the meaning in the life economy of each of the individuals who participates in it.

Of course it goes without saying that the meaning to the individual must be utterly unique for each one, but it may be possible to derive some common factors, general principles. Our argument thus far suggests that each individual member of the hierarchic organisation has two distinct types of pleasure: the obvious one of tyrannising over his inferiors, and the more subtle one of deceiving his superiors, of whom he is fundamentally contemptuous, who believe that he is submissive and respectful. Now the question arises (and the crux of the matter may lie here), how does the person who holds his superior in secret contempt while pretending submission and respect, maintain his belief that his own inferiors are submissive and respectful to himself? For it is in this belief that his pleasure in tyrannising over them must reside.

Our answer to this question must reside in a single word, stupidity. But it is not immediately apparent what could be meant by this; certainly not a lack of intelligence. Our prime object of study for discovering truths in this area rests with the observations of the spontaneous group social behaviour of young children. One cannot begin to ascribe lack of intelligence to them, when they demonstrate such sparkling capacities in other areas. But in their behaviour towards younger or weaker children they exhibit a stupidity which accounts for their behaviour being so indistinguishable from that of animals such as horses, dogs, monkeys, etc. This lack may more accurately be described as a deficit of imagination; and specifically as lack of the imagination which grows out of identification processes. Whereas the individual in the hierarchic structure can so well identify with his superiors that he can contrive the exquisite processes of dumb insolence, that same capacity for identification seems to fail him in the case of his inferiors. It is as if there were two distinct and non-communicating states of mind of inferiority and superiority, the one reaching ever upwards to identify with superiors, the other ever rejecting the pull downwards into identification with inferiors. This same lack is demonstrated when a person wishes to behave with kindness, consideration or benevolence towards his inferiors. He invariably produces a ludicrous performance that unmistakeably has the scent of patronage, condescension, overbearing insensitivity.

This argument only recapitulates something that we know well from the psycho-analytical study of the perversions, namely that they are reversible sado-masochistic games in which the sadist is the stupid one and the masochist calls the tune. Yet this seems an altogether paradoxical view when applied to politics, to the structure of hierarchic organisations. But if we carefully examine the means by which people rise in status in these organisations it is quite clear that they do so by the intelligent, imaginative, if cynical, manipulation of their superiors. It also reminds us that we should not be surprised if a politician or boss behaves in a stupid and unimaginative way with the tasks in hand when we remember that these faculties are being so lavishly expended on the management, each in turn, of his superiors in rank. The processes may appear hilarious when broached in an entertainment like 'Yes, Minister', but the ring of truth is there.

These considerations throw a light on the phenomena which we have, perhaps carelessly, classified as 'obedience'. We see that closer scrutiny reveals a far more complicated event than the word, with its overtones of reflex conditioning, suggests. A little thought about our experience as parents will tell us the same; the moment we exact obedience with an authority which love has not delegated we set in train a most complex process of passive resistance, outcroppings of insincerity and pent up resentment which will soon be vented on younger children, pets or furniture.

Perhaps it is necessary at this point, having touched on family life, and by implication its perilous tendency to degenerate into hierarchic structure, to affirm the existence of what Bion calls the Work Group. It does seem possible for human beings, under very particular conditions, to work together in joyous cooperation and mutual respect. The conditions can be spelled out with some precision, as Bion has done. There must be a task; there must be the knowledge and tools and materials necessary to carry out the task; there must be a table of organisation in which parts of the task are matched to the individual's capacities; and finally there must be explicit (perhaps implicit) rules of procedure and lines of communication, with a language apposite and adequate to the task.

It is useful to have made the conditions for Work Group Organisation explicit because they emphasise, almost without the need for emphasis, the conditions which favour Basic Assumption Mentality and the evolution of hierarchic structure. Something else is also implied which we have as yet not made clear, namely that hierarchic structures are structures of rank in which role and function are not necessarily matched. And the reason they are not necessarily matched is because the conditions for Work Group Organisation are either not met or only so tenuously met that they may momentarily be lost from sight. Of these conditions enumerated above, the one that is most frequently lacking is a task. This is not always apparent because real tasks and delusional tasks are not easily distinguished. The great example of this would, of course, be the church. It is of interest that in examining the psychology of groups Freud should have chosen as his examples the church and the army. One would not immediately grasp that the army had no clear cut task, as one, being an unbeliever, can say of the church. But is not the concept 'enemy' at least as delusional as that of 'the true God'. The 'true' enemy takes decades, perhaps centuries, to fashion by means of provocation, propaganda, double-dealing and secret alliances. Well, the Old Testament was not written in a day either.

This factor, the absence of a valid task or its replacement by a delusional one, certainly invests the area of government, although perhaps it would be more just to say that the task is misconceived. The word 'government' itself, with its roots in the Greek meaning 'to steer', betrays the misconception, for it clearly implies not only adequate control of the ship of state but a known goal, or at least direction, navigational instruments, etc. If statesmen were to believe themselves able, in this sense, to govern we would then say they were bent on a delusional task. But I suppose this has not been a widespread delusion since the lapse of the "divine right of kings". Perhaps the more obviously insane leaders have held it and communicated it to their followers. Although Hitler boasted that he would determine history for a thousand years, yet even he did not claim to know the direction of this determination. He was satisfied to be tying the tiller.

Nevertheless, so great is the human desire to be relieved of the necessity for thought, to be a passenger, that the professional politician is forced, in presenting himself, to assume the posture of superior knowledge of social, economic, diplomatic, military, pedagogical, technological, psychological and ecological matters. But the posture also determines the role he is to play, with the result that the antics of election campaigning carry over into the performance of duties – half in jest, one hopes. Yet the subtle schism between role and function begins to appear the moment a named rank is created, in all its mindless vanity and touchiness. The mace of irritability appears in a man's hand as if by magic be he ever so mild a creature previously.

It may seem a bias to lay such emphasis on language, as if to burden it with some root-of-all-evil stigma, but truly the names we give to things, and the very fact that we give a name which implies that such-and-such exists as a thing, plays a momentous role in the stifling of thought, ever eager as it seems to be to suffer such stifling. If instead of titles such as colonel, bishop, prime minister, janitor, dustman, etc. we were to speak only in terms of job-descriptions the matter would be altered, although the cumbersomeness of the method seems daunting. But you can see the inertia that would be encountered. The job-description would soon be shortened, then abbreviated, then acros-tic-ed, and a neologised title of rank would pop up, dewy and promis-ing of novelty where none fundamentally exists. I do not mean to voice French cynicism about change but only to remind of the subtle action of the inertia which has its roots in the aversion to thought and of course thereby, to responsibility.

I mention that type of cynicism, and disavow it, because it has its foundation in a poor opinion of human nature which, in many ways, psycho-analysis has tended to reinforce. Both Freud's death instinct and Melanie Klein's suspicion – I will not call it conviction – that destructiveness lay at the roots of the thirst for knowledge, tend towards a dour view. Certainly if one's knowledge of the world were to be derived from the newspapers and history books this view would be the only tenable one. But a stroll through the park on a bright Sunday tells another story, as does a tour of the factory floor when no indus-trial dispute is in progress. Given a task and the means for its realisation then men and women, even children, do joyously cooper-ate in harmony with the beauty of the world and wonder at it.

It is certainly true that this constitutes a return to a Socratic view of the just man who minds his own business, but it comes some distance from a merely forlorn formulation. It is well on the way to a definition of the meaning of 'task' and the requirements for participation in it. 'Minding one's own business' ceases to be a territorial concept with implications of isolation, and assumes dynamic qualities which can be made precise. A man's business is with the task in hand, with the functions within this task for which his skills and knowledge qualify him, and with the modes of communication with his fellow workers that the table of organisation has by agreement and convention laid down. Whether he is at the moment the father of the family, the captain of the ship, attending a film or waiting in a doctor's surgery, a task is present and his role has its functions implicit. Yes, it may be his role to function as a supervisor over others performing their functions in their roles, but that neither imposes nor bestows rank upon him.

Pedestrian as it may seem to focus on such items as rank, role, status and the postures thereof, these are indeed the flimsy members of the structure of an hierarchic organisation over which is draped a tenuous tissue of precedent and ceremony to give it a cathedral-like appearance of strength and stability. In fact it is nothing but the scaffolding of privilege hung about the more solid but obscure work-group organisation beneath, where adequate performance is only grudgingly acknowledged by the dubious granting of seniority. The aesthetic of factory and farm building design is far more subtle than that for temples and palaces. The fundamental lies that embody the type of historical accounts upon which the dazzle of ceremony is based would not have such serious consequences if their central function of entertainment were to be acknowledged. But when taken seriously as the basis for generating the negative links on which national pride, or any organisational pride, is founded, the subtle perversion of these emotions which bind human beings in sympathy with the wonders of nature, erodes our capacity for tears and joy, or rather tears of joy. As psycho-analysis again discovers, in the study of perversions and addictions, the damage that they do to the integrity of the personality is not only to be measured in the drift towards insanity but in the constant drain of vitality. So too with groups of any sort, the we-did-our-bit-club or the nation. War may be its ultimate extrapolation, as murder is with the perverse game, but it is not its great economic burden. The prototype may be found in the standing army. Once unthinkable except for a handful of despised 'soldiers of fortune', it is now a gigantic economic and social fact. Madness! A predatory clergy of Satan, respected and admired in proportion to the titre of paranoia in the community. One need not really look far for the 'enemy'.

I do not say that the serious study of history is unimportant, but if its function is to create understanding it must do so by revealing not the idiocy of our forbears, their primitive cruelty and stupidity, but our own shame for perpetuating the structures of privilege and tyranny they have erected. What we grant of tolerance and patience to the developing child we should not allow to the adult world. And yet the chambers of government, stripped of their sophistication, terrifyingly resemble the school playground.

Ruper Brooke's reminder of the "great lie" must be coupled with the recognition that it is compounded of all the little lies on which status and rank are based and sustained. Indeed the great lie is only the expression of the great delusion that a group is an organism. Human beings are not bees or ants or termites, no matter what the

King of Brobdingnag may think of us. All our actions can be the product of emotional thought, judgment and decision – and thereby of responsibility if it could be remembered that the corporate 'we' is a delusion. It is our great misfortune that this delusion, like any delusion, can be so precisely dramatised that the badge of reality hangs gracefully upon it.

Thus far, starting with a plea for the revival of the concept of magic as a dynamic force in human mentality and relationships, I have tried to trace its unnoticed role in the structure of hierarchic organisations. I reminded you that the separation of roles and functions which typify these groupings ensures that Bion's Basic Assumption Group and attendant mentality will prevail. I went on to cull out the basic interaction by which rank and status are maintained, stressing that the subtlety and sophistication of the techniques of irritability and dumb insolence drive their power to coerce and manipulate through being un-describable, and therefore unavailable for documentation in formal charges. All of this, perhaps more by implication than by specification, I have contrasted with the operation of the Work Group, in connection with which I have revived Socrates' concept of the just man, but have included more specifically a statement of the 'business' he is to 'mind'.

It is necessary, therefore, to stress that the hierarchic structure of roles, status and privilege depends for its viability on the Work Group structure hidden beneath this fabric of rank. The individual official or committee can operate 'magically' by making decisions, the means of whose realisation they need not consider. The magic wand in these ritual processes is generally money. By manipulation of the budget the appearance of life and death control over the Work Group is created and maintained. One would never guess that money was merely a notational system which, if honestly handled, would be simple arithmetic. But usury distorts all this simplicity, regardless of the rate of interest. It is the lending at any rate that is usury and converts money from a notational system to a commodity system. Nor is it any use to try to standardise money by relating it to a commodity like gold when one country can mine it and another not. The gold in Fort Knox does not make the dollar the most stable currency in the world and the closest we have to a monetary standard. It is the fortuitous fact of America's sustained economic productivity which does this, and this could change at any moment. No, were it not for the borrowing, the whole mad system for stabilising the unstabilisable would not exist. Thus buying a share on the stock market is different from buying a bond. Sharing the risk, acquiring a say in the conduct of an enterprise, having a portion of its profits and risking participation in its losses is part of human cooperation. Bonds, on the other hand, are usury.

The futile attempts to stabilise currency against some mythic standard, or against some one currency which is taken as the rock upon which all others rest, would be totally unnecessary in a purely arithmetic system where each country need only make public the amount of its currency in circulation for others to position themselves on the open market of buying and selling one another's currency for use, not for speculation. Similarly the motive of gambling could be eliminated with the abolition of marginal buying, selling of futures, etc. People who want to gamble have many opportunities without confusing the economic system. Again, as before, we come back to the prosaic fact that it is not money that is the root of all economic evil but usury, the magic of making money without having to perform the work of transformation or even of trans-portation.

The other tool of magic power is that of monopoly of the promotion-in-rank system. This cleavage in power is to be found everywhere and at every time in history. Aristocrats and peasants, gentlemen and scholars, officers and enlisted men, management and labour, administration and field workers, qualified and unqualified students, Adam and Eve. The power to elevate members from the ranks of the Work Group into the hierarchy of privilege ensures that the selection will take place on the basis of obedience, and where the euphemism of 'initiative' means simply the capacity to anticipate the wishes of your superiors. Obedience being in its essence unthinking docility, it demonstrates the individual worker's readiness to participate in the system whose function is, above all, conservative. It resists the constant pressure for change coming from the impact of new ideas and the implicit problem of their implementation.

It is not a matter of wonder, of course, that this system of monopoly of power resisted the fundamental alteration threatened by the concept of labour unions. Today we see the apocalypse they envisaged coming to pass, of the united Work Group members, from dustmen to university teachers, paralysing the hierarchic system. The method of elevating the more militant workers into the ranks of the obedient, thus splitting the union into radical and conservative factions, has only slowed the process. The split between leadership and shop floor simply recapitulates the basic cleavage of power. The magic of giving orders is beginning to fail as the Work Group develops techniques for sabotaging the structure of power and privilege.

The realisation that man is only potentially a thinking animal, that he is capable of levels of adaptation in no fundamental way different from the communal techniques of other animals, is a revelation that cuts both ways. It fractures the religious view of divine order disrupted by human wickedness just as it obviates the naturalistic view that man is a superintelligent animal manipulating sense data on his supercomputer. Whether the satanic element be attributed to evil or to aggressive and destructive drives, the necessity for a system of rewards and punishments for obedience and disobedience (where it is difficult to tell at times which is the more rewarded and the more punished) is equally implicit. Psycho-analysis, along with other psychologies and philosophies, has done little to alter this fundamental view of the human condition. But Bion's recognition of a more fundamental cleavage between thinking and un-thinking behaviour, along with his distinction between positive and negative emotional links, introduces a new key in the sense of a new entrée, and a new key in the sense of a new tonal system for the atmosphere of human relations, in the mass as in the home.

The key resides in the realisation that symbolic function, that natural urge to symbol formation as a peculiarly human activity, is set in motion by the complexity of the emotional experience of the beauty of the world, the aesthetic level. It calls for a total revision of our ideas about the nature of mental pain, shifting it from its epicentre of the experience of the absence of the object of gratification, to a new focus on the incipient disappearance of the object of admiration and awe. Every aesthetic experience is ravaged by this incipiency, as Shelley's Ozymandias reminds us. Permanence is absolutely not in the nature of the world, neither in stone, nor printed paper, nor children, nor organisations. All praise to the Tree of Knowledge of Good and Evil and to Eve's folly and Satan's guile. The picture of their ultimately frantic and unsuccessful pruning and tying in the attempt to keep the Garden unchanging is at least as daunting as that of Pandemonium.

This new but yet old idea (for the caves of Lascaux declare it quite unmistakeably) will be resisted fiercely because it requires just the kind of catastrophic change that Bion outlined. All our ideas and ways of implementing them need revision. But I think it is clear where it must start, namely in the methods by which we rear and teach our children, as "a parable of confusing times" has declared.

To explore the concept of privilege, rather than going to the dictionary as a point of departure, I prefer to set down, more or less randomly and off-the-cuff, a number of phrases in which the word privilege or its derivatives appear: "That is not a right, it is a privilege"; "It is a privilege to meet you"; "a member of the privileged classes"; "bar privileges"; "franking privilege"; "a privileged communication". What have these diverse usages in common that leaves the word unambiguous in its import? I would say that in each there is the implication 'singled out'. There is no implication that the singling-out has been earned or deserved – on the contrary it comes as a grace.

This word 'grace' is particularly apposite because of its religious overtones, and because it implies that a donor of the grace exists. Furthermore the religious vertex brings into strong relief a hidden aspect, namely that the reasons of the donor are inscrutable. In the religious realm, to question the justice of divine grace is heresy. In the social realm it carries an equally serious import, that of questioning not the donor, but the system that has invested him with his power of patronage. It is intrinsic to his rank. In Chapter IV I have recounted a cancer patient's dream about a headmistress who put in a teacher for an OBE, but then decided that he should be retrained instead – and this retraining consisted, eventually, in his brains being beaten out and his moustache being cut off. I suggested that in this dream all three methods of singling out – OBE, brain-bashing, and moustache-cutting – involved the granting and cancelling of privilege.

While we may rejoice that over the past two hundred years mankind has made progress in that the area of privilege has gradually been curtailed in favour of the concept of rights and social justice, there still remains another aspect of privilege that may concern us, namely privilege as a personality function, more particularly as it is seen to operate in family life and in the rearing of children. In this context it is no use curtailing parental privilege in favour of respect for children's rights because the atmosphere of patronage and grace cannot be dispelled by the granting of rights since the granting itself comes as a grace. Rights have to be wrested, they cannot be granted (viz. the impossibility of a benevolent despotism).

One great difficulty that faces us in discussing the problem of privilege in any particular way is that people tend to be strongly aware of the privileged position of others but not of the areas of privilege within which they themselves function. Their own are called, and felt as, rights; they are taken for granted as soon as won, and designated as earned or deserved without scrutiny of the basis on which this judgment rests. The great example I would cite here is parenthood. It calls for little thought to recognise that bearing a child comes as a grace at best, as an unwanted burden at worst (now largely eliminated in the West by contraception and abortion). But the question of deserving and earning is a retrospective judgment that must be postponed for many years, say, conventionally, twenty-one, although we know too well that even this is far too short a time for assessing the consequences of ill-advised methods of child rearing.

I cite this paradigm because it is the most indisputable case for the general proposition that any instance of just deserts is a retrospective judgment that must follow upon the history of the use that is made of any particular grace or opportunity. To my mind every opportunity that the environment affords the individual for the pursuit of his heart's desire comes as a grace of the infinite complexity of the historical process which started, say, in the caves. The essence of the historical inevitability of socialism rests just there, in the demand for equality of opportunity. Its realisation is dependent upon a revolution in our thinking that must depart from the wresting of rights and consequent curtailing of privilege, because these can only be made socially visible in material terms. This wresting and curtailing do not touch the essence of the elitism upon which the hierarchical, and therefore political, aspects of our culture, whether of the family or of the community, repose. Egalitarianism is a blind alley which can only eventually polarise, as it always has done and is doing at present, on a global scale.

So, being a devout believer in "who'd 'scape whipping", while I rejoice in the progress that has been made by the wresting of rights from the roster of privilege, I see it as reaching its asymptote, requiring a 'leap in the dark' as a next step towards social justice. This leap resides in the concepts of grace and opportunity which, like turning the other cheek, must include forgiveness and the giving of further chances. In the field of family life the grace of children must be earned by this type of dispensing of grace and forgiveness, if it is possible, and their corollary – the eschewing of demands for obedience and the inflicting of both punishments and of rewards. Such a leap to be made at the social level would require the kind of revolution in our concepts of human nature that is just beginning to take shape at the child-rearing level.

XVIII

Dénouement

This sort of book, which is the residue of clinical and teaching experiences rather than of any systematic research, seems a kind of compost heap. It is primarily intended to increase the fertility of the next developmental steps of others, to help them to bring to life their nascent creativity. But one also tends to hope that something alive of one's own may be found, unexpectedly, to be growing on the heap, a clump of mushrooms or a surprise of daffodils. Does the book add up to anything other than what it claims: a series of studies illustrating the use that Bion's ideas have found in my consulting room?

Bion himself was very opposed to a distinct 'school' growing up around his ideas, perhaps partly because the adjective 'Bionic' had such comic overtones of science fiction, gardening, electronics and quackery. But chiefly he felt, and I feel perhaps even more strongly, that the formation of 'schools' is a miscarriage of science. It is naïve to suppose that deep and significant differences exist. It is political to exploit them within the organisations of psycho-analysis. It fails to understand the impossible task of rendering in language the ineffable phenomena of the mind. And finally it shows little comprehension of the history of art and science. In so far as the metaphor of progress as forward movement is permissible, the development of art and science, or, in the case of psycho-analysis, art-science, moves forward in spiral fashion in some respects, or like a caterpillar in others. Those in the vanguard of development think they are miles ahead of the rear-guard when they reckon linearly, but they need only look sideways to see they are only inches in advance. Furthermore it is necessary for them to pause, and teach, and help the others to catch up before they can go on. If they fail to do this, their language, and soon their thought, becomes so idiosyncratic that they find they have departed from the social field and must find their way back. In a way this happened to Bion with *Transformations* and had to be rectified by altering his metaphors in *Attention and Interpretation*.

This process of catching up tends to be misunderstood in the context of school-formation and politics as if it were some sort of clandestine plagiarism, stealing ideas and couching them in different terminology. An example of this can be seen in the development of "self-psychology" around the work of Heinz Kohut with its strong reverberation of Kleinian notions. But closer examination shows that two other processes are at work: one of these is the refinement of the language of the vanguard to fasten it more firmly to its historic roots; the other is a watering-down of the concepts to achieve a greater respectability. Both of these have their value for the social structure of the psycho-analytical movement and its relation to the surrounding intellectual and scientific community. Neither of them inhibit further forward movement in the next wave of advance.

In viewing my own work as 'exploration', I like to think that some attempt should be made to trace in a more personal way what I see as the impact of Bion's ideas on my mode of life and view of the world (model of the mind, structure of history, evolution of political organisations, the role of the artist in the community, the nature of psychoanalysis as a thing, etc.).

In terms of Bion's concept of "catastrophic change" and the impact of the 'new idea' there is no difficulty in establishing what this idea was and the revolution it has wrought in my ways of thinking and working . . . and also acting in general. The 'new idea' was clearly something like 'in the beginning was the aesthetic object, and the aesthetic object was the breast and the breast was the world'. Of course I am using the word 'breast' as a technical term with only an implication of description, rather than the other way round. On the one hand it seems surprising to me that this idea did not reach me through Adrian Stokes to whom it was ever vivid; on the other hand it is difficult to say whence in Bion's work it derives. It is not in the Grid; it is only hinted at in *Transformations*; it tags along in a secondary position in *Attention and Interpretation*. Only in *A Memoir of the Future* does it find its place unambiguously. But it had reached me through Bion before that publication had crept into my thought and certainly into my consulting room. Not only had I become aware that the psycho-analytical method had taken on an aesthetic quality in my eyes but I had begun to see, mainly through dreams, that it had done so for some of my patients as well.

In retrospect I think the work on autism with its elaboration of the concept of dimensionality played an important role; the fine aesthetic sensibility of many of these children was so unmistakeable that one could not avoid wondering if their developmental failure had not been founded on processes for warding off the impact of the beauty of the world. Dismantling of the senses and two-dimensionality seemed exquisitely delicate methods for doing so without violence to the object, either externally or internally. The process of dismantling of the senses was too massive, too much like soul-murder, however, to illuminate the problem. But two-dimensionality held fascinating questions in its grip. At first it seemed that this shallowing of the world of meaning was self-explanatory, as if the dilution of meaning naturally resulted in an impoverishment of affects. Bion's ideas suggested the reverse, that a method of curtailing the intensity of affects resulted in the pallor of meaning. If this was the case, then the two-dimensional orientation to the world would be a defence against the impact of objects stirring emotions. But how? Melanie Klein's idea had been that interest in the inside of the mother, and thereby the epistemophilic instinct in general, had its origins in the intense emotionality of the mother-baby relationship. Did two-dimensionality then result from a denial of the psychic reality of the object rather than a regression to a prior stage in cognitive development?

Similarly old assumptions, tied up with Melanie Klein's delineation of paranoid-schizoid and depressive positions, were called into question. Esther Bick had revealed the identificatory processes connected with two-dimensionality (adhesive identification) so that it was feasible to think that an organisation of mentality prior to the paranoid-schizoid position might exist which would strengthen the assumption of a genetic sequence with a strong internal logic, placing the depressive position at a more sophisticated level of experience. But somehow Melanie Klein's formulation of the factors operating to set the epistemophilic instinct in motion did not seem to be satisfactory. Her failure to differentiate between intrusive curiosity and thirst for knowledge as factors in the little child's interest in the inside of the mother's body, weakened the conceptual fabric. Findings with autistic children suggested strongly that sadism and splitting processes were not intensely operative in their illness but only developed in force in the process of recovery and advance in development.

Dissatisfaction of this sort with the mind-model which operated in the consulting room must gradually have influenced a shift away from thinking in terms of genetic phases of development towards a field conception. The implicit complexity seemed to demand it. I remembered Melanie Klein saying in response to critics at a meeting that it was not she who made things complicated, they just were so. Of course the human mind must be the most complicated thing in the universe within our ken. And there must be a limit to the degree to which the mind, studying itself, can penetrate its mysteries. Perhaps mystery itself is an important aspect of its essence.

Bion's emphasis on consciousness, not as a system but as an organ of the mind, the organ of attention, had already been strongly recommended by the experiences with autistic children. Their diffusion of attention with its resulting dismantling of what Bion had, half-jokingly, called "common sense" (Sullivan's "consensuality") seemed at once a powerful and yet delicately sparing way of evading the impact of life both around and within themselves. The therapeutic indication of the importance of seizing and holding their attention with interesting talk based on acute observations, had demonstrated its efficacy, if also its tendency to exhaust the therapist.

The 'field' orientation which accepts multiple levels of simultaneous and more-or-less integrated functioning seems to allow the question 'how' and not only 'when' is the mental level called into operation to superimpose itself on the purely neurophysiological? Bion's approach to the problem, by assuming that the first operation is the creation of thoughts which then require an apparatus to think (manipulate, use) them, seems to be the crucial break with the traditional implication that thinking is prior as a function and generates thoughts. It enabled him to create the Grid and then to move on to examine the "transformations" by which thinking implements its utilisation of thoughts. More than that, it provided a framework for considering false thoughts, lies, misunderstandings, un-truth, misconceptions, propaganda, cynicism. When this is compounded with the great step of opposing emotion to anti-emotion (positive and negative L, H and K) a new abacus lies to hand for thinking about thinking.

To be able to think of the mental as 'level' and of its being 'called into play' by the focusing of attention on the emotionality being aroused by an experience, delivers a new freedom to our consideration of the problem. And it is not merely the semantic clarification that freshens the atmosphere, for it also sweeps away the traditional primary preoccupation with logic and thereby mathematics and linguistics as our supreme source of information, from the Greeks to the *Tractatus*. The "empty" concept of alpha-function is our new key. But the lock that it fits has also shifted; this is the crucial matter. We have been misled by confusing the creation of aesthetic objects as the work of rare and evolved genius with the perception of the beauty-of-the-world which Wordsworth asserted was inherent in the "clouds of glory" embodied in the mentality of children and their availability to the "splendour in the grass". Had he pursued the problem of the loss of this sensibility rather than accepting the facile explanation, essentially sociological, that "getting and spending we lay waste our powers", he would have recognised more clearly the nature of the pain that these sensibilities bring in their train.

Similarly Melanie Klein's loyalty to Freud's formulation of the duality of instinct caused her simply to by-pass the problem and explain away the evident ambivalence implicit in the epistemophilic instinct on the basis of frustration. This attitude is a bit surprising, considering that she knew very well that a certain optimal level of mental pain (frustration, persecution, envy, etc.) is necessary since development is driven by tolerable conflict. My own first glimpse of the problem was recorded in a paper called 'The Apprehension of

Beauty', where I also failed to grasp what I had glimpsed, as I think had Hannah Segal in her famous paper on aesthetics.

And so they came together: the key of alpha-function and the lock of two-dimensionality; and an apposite metaphor it seemed. The problem area that the key of symbol formation was called into play to open, was the enigma of the inside and the outside of the aesthetic object. Its power to evoke emotionality was only equalled by its ability to generate anxiety, doubt, distrust. While the sensual qualities of the aesthetic object could be apprehended with some degree of confidence, its internal qualities, being infra- or supra-sensual, carried no such comfort. Here observation needed to be coupled with thought and judgment, and judgment depended greatly for its firmness on experience. For it was in the matching or disparity of this outside and inside of the object of awe and wonder that its value for good or evil must surely reside. But the baby's experience of the world is almost nil. How is it to exercise such judgment? It cannot; it can only wait to see what will happen next.

This then would be the context in which absence of the object makes its crucial impact and tests the mettle. Bion has defined this problem of the absent object as "the absent object as a present persecutor" with respect to the "space where the object used to be", perhaps also by implication including Berkeley's "ghosts of departed quantities". These "times that try men's souls"[1] and find out the "summer soldier" in the depths must be infinitely more stressful for the baby when we remember their impact on Othello and Leontes, and 'La Belle Dame sans Merci'. Trust would then be a compound quality of mind, like foot-pounds as a definition of work: hope-hours, or minutes or days or years. In the very young it can at times seem more to be hope-seconds as the baby's face crumples when mother turns the corner out of sight.

By defining the fundamental problem of aesthetic relations in this way and by asserting the aesthetic relationship to the world and the primal stimulus to thought, we have adopted a position compatible with a field theory that is also inherently genetic. What it does, that the differentiation of paranoid-schizoid and depressive positions fails to do in their adherence to a Life and Death Instinct foundation, is to allow for a purely mental approach to values unencumbered by biological speculation. While the issue of mental pain and tolerance thereof loses none of its clinical vibrance as an arbiter of ego strength, a new factor is introduced to the dynamism of conflict. Trust, in units of hope-time, schematically speaking, would seem to have qualitative roots in the richness of the aesthetic experience to which separation is the sequel. And this richness is surely to be found in the element of mutuality of apprehension of beauty. For the baby must be held as an

[1]Tom Paine, *Common Sense.*

aesthetic object by the mother for the experience of their love-making to reverberate and escalate in intensity.

Such a basis which allows us to conceive the 'how' of the calling into action of the capacity for symbolic thought, the product of the mysterious alpha-function, more or less releases us from any great concern with the 'when' of the matter. Pre-natal or post-natal, it must occur. And if this conjunction of mutuality is its essential ingredient, its inception may be widely variable in time. But, sadly, we must recognise that it may not occur at all, as in the children who do not seem to make the post-natal adjustment or whose neurophysiological apparatus is not of sufficient complexity to achieve the aesthetic level of response. The autist and the non-developer may taste it and rebel against its dominance.

But more important for clinical practice is the corollary, that the defensive operations which psycho-analysis is specially fashioned to follow may mostly, perhaps entirely, be seen as moves against the impact of the aesthetic object, although this is not apparent in the early days of an analysis. It comes, in my view, at the threshold of the depressive position, after confusions have been sorted out. How then does this view essentially differ from Melanie Klein's formulations, and what precisely are the alterations in the consulting room which are generated by it?

Undoubtedly the first and most important alteration is a diminished emphasis on the 'correctness' of interpretation, perhaps a lessening of the urgency to interpret altogether. Instead the focus moves forwards, as it were, into the interaction, the relationship from which interpretive ideas emerge. The model of container-contained places a new value on receptiveness and the holding of the dynamic situation of transference-countertransference in the mind. But perhaps to state this as if the analyst were the container misses the point that it is the fitting together of the analyst's attention and attitudes to the cooperativeness of the patient that forms and seals the container, lending it the degree of flexibility and resilience required from moment to moment.

Interpretation therefore loses its explanatory function, partly from the altered nature of the situation but also because the analyst has lost his causal orientation to mental events. The field of mental states will not allow the language of linearity to assert itself, falling away in favour of attempts at description, hopelessly inadequate in a sense, as a painting would be useless as a basis for botanical research. Instead the metaphor of illumination replaces explanation. I well remember visiting a cave in the Dordogne, Combarelles I think, full of engravings of ice-age animals. As the guide moved his lamp about from one angle to another different superimposed images sprang from the wall.

This image of the analyst's verbal task, to shine a light of understanding from one vertex after another, modifies the atmosphere of communication to an extraordinary degree, diminishing the authoritarian expectations of the patient and sharing the responsibility between the members of the Work Group of two. It also allows an interpretive line gradually to form. Certain dreams – the dreams and not their interpretations – establish the landmarks for both members. The function of understanding, with all its uncertainty and readiness to yield its place, by divesting the analyst of the expectation of knowing, allows him far greater freedom of speculation. Intuitions for which the evidence is not as yet obtrusive can freely be given, the degree of uncertainty being indicated by the music of the voice. Since the mystification of seeming omniscience is thus stripped from the relationship, the patient becomes more interested in the method and welcomes explanation of the rationale of the analyst's behaviour. All this, including the improved definition of the shape which the psycho-analytical process seems to be assuming, tends to erect the concept of the science, the process, the method – taken together perhaps with its personal and institutional history – as a thing-in-itself that can, eventually, be apprehended as an aesthetic object.

This has far-reaching implications for the transference and countertransference for it establishes an object upon which are not imposed, in Freud's terms, the limitations inherent in the "particularities" of the analyst – his age, sex, appearance, known facts about his life situation, his values, politics, etc. In fact it allows for the formation of an object which the therapist and patient can examine together from a certain distance, in the same way that one steps back from most paintings to allow the composition to impinge, and then steps forward to appreciate the brush strokes and craftsmanship.

Psycho-analysis as a thing-in-itself, and its particular manifestation in the patient's own experience of analysis, comes to form a link to the internal part object, the maternal thinking-breast as combined object, breast and nipple. The functions that the analyst is felt to perform within the analytical process assume definitive shape, greatly clarifying the nature of the felt dependence. Acting out in search of substitutes during the separations stands out clearly both for the adequacy or the inadequacy of these facsimiles. The analyst is therefore in a better position to help the patient to appraise the usefulness of these alternative relationships and not merely to oppose them on the assumption that they must necessarily impoverish the transference.

It is in this connection that the externalisation of the patient's narcissistic organisation with the individuals and groups comes under a new and more precise scrutiny, for the basis of judgment need not rest on value alone. It is true that shifting the basis of value judgment from moral or even ethical criteria to developmental ones (which often means suspension of judgment) softens the harshness of the analyst's interventions with regard to narcissistic-based relationships, since his attitude is bound to lack a basis in demonstrable evidence, except for dreams. But when the modes of thought and avenues of communication can also be brought under scrutiny it is often possible to demonstrate the deficits in quality of thought. This is most clear when a Basic Assumption Group involvement is at issue, but even in the ganging with one or more acquaintances the "misjoyning" functions of the Negative Grid (Milton's "mimic fansie") can often be demonstrated.

This avenue of enquiry into group communication processes is surely a Bionic addition to our equipment for investigating the workings of narcissism. Nowhere is it more clear than with perverse areas of the personality which so quietly drain the vitality of object relations. And here Bion's formulation of positive and negative emotional links sheds a brilliant light. "But am I not a part of this man's emotional life?" the perverse area seems to say, claiming a certain respectability and rightful share in the world of human intimacy. A dualistic theory, of Life and Death, of Creative and Destructive drives, gives no definitive answer except a grudging, "Yes, but you must be subservient, integrated for good and creative ends", something the perverse aspect will smilingly accept, secretly triumphant. But when the perverse trends are recognised as anti-emotions, minus L, H and K, no ground need be yielded to them in compromise.

The concept of a Negative Grid and the recognition by Bion that knowledge of the truth is necessary for the construction of effective lies (lies to oneself as well as to others), has delivered a powerful tool into our hands for scrutinising the content and operations of cynical attacks on the truth. While I have never found the Grid useful for analytic contemplation, as Bion originally suggested[1], its format is wonderfully revealing of shifts of levels of abstraction and accompanying paradoxical statements. This leads on to greater skill in examining the defensive and evasive functions of ambiguous language usage as well as defects in logical operations, pseudo-quantifications, false equations and spurious similes.

Taken together these tools for minute scrutiny of processes of thought and communication place the analyst in a far stronger position than ever before in the struggle to wrest infantile structures from the domination or influence of destructive parts of the personality which organise the narcissistic or Basic Assumption groupings internally or in the outside world.

Finally we must examine the important matter of our private and corporate definition of psycho-analysis and its implications for our methods of work in the consulting room. I do not mean to refer to the

[1]See *Bion in New York and São Paulo*, p. 56, for his later thoughts on the subject.

political aspects of the problem, such as defining psycho-analysis as what members of The Psycho-Analytical Society do, or five-times-per-week by definition, or extra-institutional and so forth. These local definitions are fitted to local political problems and are not of scientific interest. The important problems are ones of private definition and public presentation to one's colleagues.

Essentially our private definition must rest on two piers, the method and the process that it engenders. Almost everyone in the field would agree that the essence of the method is the scrutiny and description of the transference by way of internal examination of the countertransference. There is far less agreement, or need of agreement, about the nature of the therapeutic process generated by these operations. It is not unlikely that the process varies from analyst to analyst, perhaps from patient to patient, in essential ways. But all would agree that each analyst needs, eventually, to have formulated his own conception of the type or range of processes that he considers useful in an analysis that is progressing. It is clear that he cannot use therapeutic criteria, either observed or reported. There is after all no need for analysts to claim any monopoly of therapeutic potency.

Having formed such a conception of type or range of process, the analyst should be in a position to be more flexible in meeting the demands of his patients with regard to frequency, duration of sessions, spacing, missing of sessions or periods of therapy, methods of payment, use of the couch, bringing or sending of written or graphic materials, interviews with relatives. Caution can replace rigidity of style and method when basic personal concepts of method and process have been established from experience with the particular patient and practice in general. Modifications in style and method introduced by the analyst should still be viewed with the greatest suspicion and avoided, probably, except for bona fide organised research. But a flexible response to a patient's requests, based on experience and firmness of concept, backed by careful scrutiny of the previous and ensuing material, can have a beneficial, humanising and encouraging effect. The consequences for the analyst are, however, far more important. Such an orientation obliges him to engage in continual careful scrutiny of the rationale of his procedures and thus to promote his own learning from experience.

Appendix to Chapter XVI

This chapter, which had its stimulus from the GERPEN seminar in Paris in 1982 and 1983 and drew its main material from the work of Mme Eve Cohen, supplemented later by some observations by Mrs Maria Rhode, had a second flush in the summer of 1985 when it was presented to the Rome-London Conference of Tavistock Child Psychotherapists. In that form it went to the printer in September 1985, but in the following month, at the 11th Stage of the "Harris-Meltzer" Seminars at the Instituto di Neuropsichiatria Infantile in Calambrone di Pisa organized by Professor Pietro Pfanner, this vital growth shot yet another leader into the air. On the Friday afternoon I had read the Tavistock version of the chapter, which was received with interest and complaint. It was too complicated, too dense, too convoluted. I agreed but felt unable to do anything to remedy its defects.

The following morning Dr Alba Greco, who had translated for us since the beginning of the series, presented a case from her practice in Pistoia. The material was so stunningly illustrative of the chapter that, with Dr Greco's permission, I determined to add her material and a summary of the discussion to the chapter. However, when I phoned the printer on the Monday, I learned that the book was already in page proof, hence the Appendix. I will present first Dr Greco's own translation of her material.

Andrea, age eight and a half, was sent by a colleague from the Local Health Service, but it was the mother who made the contact by telephone, asking for an appointment immediately, but on the condition that Dr Greco would be able to take him into treatment at once. A series of agitated phone calls from the mother, who had each time to consult with her husband, were required before an actual appointment could be agreed upon.

At the initial interview the contrast between the two parents was striking, the father practical, contractual and cool, the mother urgent and exclusively focused on problems supposedly consequent to the child's premature calcification of skull sutures and fontanelles in infancy. When this condition was recognised at about age two, it was felt to be already too late for surgical intervention. However, surgery for some cardiac defect at age three, a move of dubious necessity, was followed by other therapies related to his retardation in speech and motor activity. Nothing of this supposed retardation was presented as the immediate problem. Eventually it became clear that there was concern about his mentality, not so much in terms of intelligence as character. Andrea is seen as having "no sense of danger", as for instance in a recent accident on his bicycle. Also some academic failure seems threatening despite a good start in school. In the third year of primary school "he can't manage to concentrate, he refuses to think: he tries to give an answer at random even before he has finished reading the problem". In contrast to Andrea, his sister Barbara, five years his senior, is progressing well and affords her parents great satisfaction.

The first meeting with Andrea created an impression of great distress. He immediately settled to draw his house, but after rapidly doing a conventional outline, he spent most of the session colouring in one tiny area of the roof, one tiny line at a time, changing pencils for each line. But towards the end he began a pounding, distressed and unstoppable rigmarole of incongruous questions and answers: "Where are my mum and dad? They said they were going to drink a coffee and come back straightaway, so . . . in a little while they'll be here . . . they're coming back in 45 minutes . . . what are you saying, they'll be paying now, so in 4 seconds they'll be here, you'll see . . . how long are 45 minutes? Five hours? . . . they are only going to drink a coffee, so they'll be going into the bar now, won't they? . . . what's the time? Have three hours passed? Where can mum and dad have gone? etc., etc."

Attempts to make him aware of his state of anguish seemed to meet a hasty nod of agreement half-way before recommencing the rigmarole. Profound countertransference discomfort suggested that all the words were equivalent to plaintive weeping and mental retardation. But this suspicion was immediately dispelled when the therapist glanced at her watch and Andrea said, in a completely natural and calm voice, "Thirteen minutes from the end?" He had read the time upside down and calculated the remainder accurately. His glance on leaving suggested gratitude, perhaps for patient attention without attempts at reassurance.

A second observation session, almost identical to the first but including some interpretation of his anguish, resulted in his saying, "I'm almost about to cry". Regular therapy was proposed to him then and his response was to give immediate assent and to appropriate a large sheet of paper hanging on the wall to draw his flat for the therapist. Andrea drew first a room with a bed on which a figure was reclining, saying it was himself, and then an adjoining room with bed and the figure of his sister.

This introduction of Barbara into the material ushered in a period in which the initial verbal rigmarole was replaced by an equally repetitive, anguished, relentless behaviour. Each session began with a cursory attempt to colour the original house, followed by a process of progressive nudity and obsessive dramatisation. Initially he asked if the therapist wished to see his beautiful thighs and would she also show hers, unless she were too ashamed of them like the girls at school when he attempted to lift their skirts. He would draw his thighs, which he did on another huge sheet of paper laid on the table, having failed to pin it to the wall. However, in order to draw them, he declared he must look at them. So he stripped off trousers and underpants, sitting then to draw, eyes fixed on his thighs rather than on the paper, passing his finger tips lightly over the skin both in a caressing way and as if the finger tips had eyes. His look became torpid, vacant, just as when he had carried on the rigmarole about the parents having coffee. Interpretive comments seemed to pass him by as his excitement grew and gave way to actions, pirouetting naked about the room, penis in erection, chanting, "I am a ballerina". Then he lay on the couch, arms rigidly by his side, looking stuporously at his penis as if it were the centre of the universe.

This became the model for many subsequent sessions, introduced not by the desultory drawing but by such ritual questions as, "What shall we do? Let's say I have to go to work, so I must strip naked." On only one occasion, while in his reverie on the couch staring at his erect penis, did he give any verbal hint of its meaning, "I'm suckling, I'm suckling". (In Italian it is unequivocally transitive.) In a later session he moved off the couch to wrap himself in the large drawing of his thighs. It is of interest that the first time that Barbara actually appeared accompanying the father to bring Andrea to his session, the therapist was struck by the Botticellian beauty of this tall blonde girl. Since this impression was not confirmed on subsequent contact, it could be taken as countertransference evidence.

Discussion

That Andrea has suffered some degree of damage from premature closure of the skull sutures seems suggested by his slightly small and characteristically tented head shape, as well as slight evidence of damage on the TAC. But on the whole the problem may be approached as one of disturbed mental development in an unbalanced family setting, with a frantic mother, a cool and contractual father and a beautiful, idealised older sister. The central feature is retarded speech development, that is, late passage from lalling to employment of conventional words. Speech and psychomotor therapy may have hastened his emergence from this babyishness into a more clearly psycho-pathological process. The first five months of therapy suggest that separation difficulties are of a pregenital part-object nature, centring on the breast and nipple as an overpowering combined aesthetic object. This object is variously represented as his parents going for coffee (Mrs Klein's "breast that feeds itself"), his sister-with-a-penis in the adjoining room at night, or his own thighs and erection in bed or pirouetting about, examined and caressed by Andrea's eyes and fingertip-eyes. The ejaculation, "I'm suckling", makes clear the oral-visual attachment and the process of wrapping himself in the drawing shows the narcissistic (probably both projective and adhesive) nature of his identification as the "ballerina"-breat-and-nipple.

The striking similarity in near stuporous inwardness in both the naked activities and the verbal rigmarole suggests strongly that they may be equated. If we then take the rigmarole, which could suddenly be suspended to read and calculate the "thirteen minutes from the end", as a state in every respect identical to lalling-with-words, a totally internal commentary on phantasy processes, we can construct a concept of Andrea's retarded speech development. The "Botticellian" countertransference image of Barbara suggests a child ravished by the beauty of breast-and-nipple, uncompensated by the experience of being likewise viewed as an exquisite baby. What force will bring back such an object, lost in rapturous contemplation of one another's beauty, "drinking coffee" together, lying in bed together in an adjoining room? Separation made intolerable can perhaps best be obviated by narcissistic identification with the object, by wrapping oneself in it when present or in the theatre of one's phantasy, "I'm suckling, I'm suckling."

Index

absent object (Bion) 207
accretions of stimuli 23, 35
acting-in-the-transference 41
addiction 197
agoraphobia 50
Albergamo, Doctor Mariella
27–8
alpha-elements 103, 107, 116
alpha-function 10, 11, 14, 23, 24,
35, 36, 91, 93, 103, 116–21,
175, 181, 184
alpha-function in reverse 160
amnesia 83
analytical method limitations
80–81
anamnesic elements in dreams
96–7
Andrea (case study) 212–15
Antonio (case study) 50, 60–65,
67–8
The Apprehension of Beauty
(Meltzer and Meg Harris
Williams) 206–7
arrested development 12, 129

Attention and Interpretation
(Bion) 36, 39, 70, 102, 105,
116, 203, 204
autism 13, 15, 101, 122–5, 157,
181, 204
categories 123
Early Infantile Autism 123
mutism 181
speech development 181
see also infantile psychotic
disturbance
autobiography in development
92
autogenous meaning 92

BA *see* Basic Assumption
Basic Assumption function and
psycho-somatic disturbance
171
Basic Assumption Groups 11,
19, 35, 38–9, 48, 103, 105, 106,
136, 152, 159, 193, 198, 210
dependence 163, 164, 169
fight-flight 166, 169–71